On The Trail Of Liberation

Volume 4

A Recounting of Precious Moments with Amma

On the Trail of Liberation – Volume 4

A Recounting of Precious Moments with Amma

Edited by Karnaki Nolan

Published by:
Mata Amritanandamayi Center
P.O. Box 613
San Ramon, CA 94583-0613, USA

In India:
www.amritapuri.org
inform@amritapuri.org

In Europe:
www.amma-europe.org

In US:
www.amma.org

On The Trail Of Liberation

Volume 4

A Recounting of
Precious Moments with Amma

Edited by Karnaki Nolan

MA Center, San Ramon
California, USA

Contents

Ātma Kṛpa

A Message from Amma

Children, God is always showering his grace upon us. But to avail ourselves of it and let it benefit us, we need *ātma-kṛpa*, our own grace. There is no use closing the doors and windows to our room during the day and then lamenting over the lack of sunlight. Sunlight pervades the entire universe. To receive it, we just need to open our windows. Similarly, divine grace is ever flowing our way. To receive it, we must first open the closed doors of our heart. Hence, more than God's grace, we must first gain the grace of our own mind.

In India, students are given 'grace marks' to help them pass their examinations. However, to become eligible for those marks, the students must have a minimum score. One who has not studied at all will not receive any grace mark. Similarly, we need to put in some effort.

God is not just a judge who rewards good deeds and punishes evil ones. Above all, He is a treasure trove of compassion who forgives us for our mistakes and showers His grace upon us. However, he can save us only if we strive at least a little to become worthy of that grace. If we do not put in any effort, God's ever-flowing grace will not reach us. That is not His fault; He is an epitome of mercy. It is ours.

To avert the Mahābhārata War and the annihilation of the Kauravas, Lord Kṛṣṇa requested Duryōdhana to give the Pāṇḍavas at least a house. But because of his egoism and antagonism towards the Pāṇḍavas, Duryodhana repudiated that request. The result was total destruction. Duryōdhana lacked the ātma-kṛpa needed to receive the Lord's grace.

Newspapers regularly carry job advertisements. The advertisements will specify the educational qualifications, references and other prerequisites that the candidates ought to have. Even so, there will be candidates who meet all the requirements and who answer all the questions correctly during the job interview and yet do not get the job. The ones who get the job might not have answered all the questions correctly. The reason for this is that something about those candidates touched the employer's heart. That something is divine grace.

What makes us befitting of God's grace are good deeds. Therefore, even to gain the grace of God, we first need ātma-kṛpa.

1

32 Seconds

Vivek Kanematsu (Japan)

A few years ago, I had my first chance to drive Amma in Japan. It was just a short drive, half an hour from Tokyo *āśram* to the program. You can imagine how nervous I was. My heartbeat was running and jumping, but I was driving carefully because Amma was talking on the phone, and I didn't want to disturb her by driving fast.

Suddenly, Amma said urgently, "Viveka, late for the program...drive fast fast!" I almost had a heart attack. The next moment, I became a Formula 1 racer, driving full speed and covered in sweat. Like the car-race movie *Tokyo Drift*. At the hall, as Amma was getting down from the car, she said something in Malayalam to me. Then she walked away with a beautiful smile and open arms to the waiting Japanese devotees.

When I found out what Amma said, I was shocked and amazed. Amma said, "Vivek, 32 seconds late!" If someone said, five or ten minutes late, maybe even 30 seconds—okay. But 32 seconds?! *Two* seconds? Amma didn't have a made-in-Japan "G-Shock" watch. Even in the car there was no clock showing seconds. But Amma knows through transcendental awareness.

Amma has come to accomplish innumerable things in the world. She doesn't want to waste even *one* second.

Amma often says, "If we lose money, we can get it back. But if we lose time, we can never get it back." It felt like she was saying to me, "Time is precious. Don't waste even 32 seconds!!!" I know all time is precious; but the most precious time is our time in Amma's presence. Sitting next to Amma on a stage like this reminds me of some beautiful moments with Amma in Japan.

For the last seven years, I have been translating Amma's *satsaṅg* for the Japan program. This *satsaṅg* translation *sēvā* is the most rewarding *sēvā* I have ever had. And one of the scariest. It is quite funny how I got this *sēvā*. Seven years ago, I was in a difficult period, astrologically. It was *sade sati*—7 1/2 years Saturn return. I didn't have much energy. I felt lazy and didn't have any inspiration or enthusiasm to do anything. I was fed up with everything.

Amma knew it was a bad time. When I went for *darśan* that time, Amma looked into my eyes compassionately and said, "Oh, Vivek is getting depressed." Then, full of love and laughter, she put lots of sandal paste on my face, painting a big samurai moustache with it. And said, "*Dhīrata*!! (Be courageous!)" This "Be courageous!!" became my theme in life.

That was one month before Amma's Japan program. I planned to do some small *sēvā* during the program. I just wanted to spend time in nature, like in the mountains or at the beach. I just wanted to be alone. I was so tired of people. Five minutes after I had these thoughts, I got a phone call. It was Ramakrishnananda Swāmijī, who was in the car with Amma. "Oh, Viveka, Amma wants you to translate Amma's *satsaṅg* (spiritual talk) this year at the Japan program. OK?"

"Wowowahhh... oookkkeeii!" After that, I never thought about the beach or the mountains again. All I thought about was Amma's *satsaṅg*. I started spending more time reading Amma's books and became very tense with nonstop thoughts about Amma's *satsaṅg*. "Oh, no! I will sit next to Amma, on the stage. Oh my God...So scary!"

However, all my thoughts were centered on Amma. That was Amma's grace. Instead of all the negative thoughts I had been having, Amma helped me focus again and again, day and night, on her teachings and her *satsaṅgs* full of wisdom. With her transcendental awareness, Amma knows the right time to give the right *sēvā* to uplift us so we don't fall.

On the day of Amma's *satsaṅg*, I told Amma, "Amma, I am so nervous that my heart is almost coming out of my mouth. I feel like I am about to faint. I am not sure I can complete the translation." Amma looked at me. She was very calm and smiling beautifully. She looked straight into my eyes, and said, "Vivek, Amma has full confidence in you. Amma believes that you will do a good job. People will be so happy."

When I heard this, a silent transformation happened deep within me. "That's it! I will do it. And I *can* do it. I am ready," I thought. Amma always says, "Self-confidence is like a booster rocket. It helps us break free from the impurities and bondage of the mind and allows us to soar to the heights of spirituality. It is like fuel, giving us the power to forge ahead." Just one look and a few words from Amma gave me self-confidence. Amma knows us better than we know ourselves. Amma knows our hidden potential, and she knows how to bring it out.

The Japan program is like a silent retreat because Japanese people are very, very quiet. Silence represents respect, in

Japanese culture. In the US and Europe, people's responses are quite obvious. They express their joy and appreciation by applauding, and they laugh out loud at jokes. Japanese people are just the opposite. People listen very quietly. You can hear the sound of a pin drop. That quiet. Especially during Amma's *satsaṅg*.

I had a strong desire to make the Japanese people laugh or smile. Amma sensed it immediately and said, "Vivek, don't worry, even if nobody laughs. Amma tried for the last 20 years, and nobody has laughed." That made me even more determined to make people laugh—like a challenge. So, I put a lot of effort to make funny faces and strange noises, and even had some props to make the jokes more funny to the Japanese; and I practiced them a lot.

Amma says that some expectations are always hiding behind the love and dedication people show us. To illustrate the point, Amma tells a joke about an old couple that shared a pair of dentures. I actually borrowed French brother Tejas's dentures and pretended to put them into my mouth when I translated the joke! And, by Amma's grace, miraculously, people laughed.

Later, Amma said, "Oh Viveka's dream came true!" Dr. Priya, who helped me with the translation, told Amma, "Because Vivek practiced so hard and tried his best to make people laugh." Amma said "NO, NO, NO. Amma prayed very, very hard for Vivek that the people would laugh." And, Amma continued with a big smile, "Luckily people laughed."

This reminds me of Amma's teaching that, for success—regardless of the field—three factors are required: the proper timing, self-effort and God's grace. Amma gives the example of a man who had to travel a long distance for a job interview. The man put forth enough effort and reached the airport on time. But he didn't have grace, so his flight was cancelled, and he was unable to attend the interview.

Our selfless actions come back to us as God's grace. To get the Japanese people to laugh, when I put forth maximum effort at the right time, my heart opened up to receive Amma's grace. For the last seven years, the Japanese devotees have been laughing when hearing Amma's jokes. If Amma smiles, everyone will smile spontaneously. I would say, the whole universe smiles. I have witnessed how Japanese people spontaneously open up and heal in Amma's presence. Amma helped me to overcome my shyness and gave me self-confidence and courage. It is my experience that, when Amma gives you something, it is not just for you. She wants to give something to the world *through* you.

Another time, there was a huge crowd at one Kerala program. Amma was giving *darśan* at full speed beginning at 10pm. By 6am, Amma's white sari was stained dark brown on both shoulders with dirt and sweat from people's faces. The sun was rising, and the sky was getting brighter when Amma hugged the last person. Still, she didn't want to leave.

Finally, Amma stood up. Before she left, Amma gazed at the crowd and lovingly asked, "Did all my children get *darśan*?" Amma's unending energy, patience and compassion are amazing. Amma actually came to the stage at 7pm and gave the *satsaṅg*, followed by *bhajans* and meditation. And *then* she gave *darśan*. She had been sitting for 11 hours! Still, there wasn't even one iota of impatience or haste in her actions.

Many *brahmacārīs* and *brahmacāriṇīs* were waiting for Amma in front of her room. Amma looked fresh, even after such a long *darśan*. Amma's shining eyes made her smile even more beautiful. She stopped and spoke a few words with everyone. Then, suddenly, everyone's eyes were shinning brighter and wet with tears. I asked one *brahmacārī* what Amma had said. He said, "Amma wants to cook *uṇṇiyappam* for everyone! Not the small ones but the BIG ones!"

Then, with a big smile, she looked around at everyone and went inside her room. *Uṇṇiyappam* is a sweet ball that Kerala people like very much. Who can say such sweet words after sitting the whole night hugging people, without eating or drinking or sleeping? If I work overnight without sleep, I want to go straight to bed, without even looking at anyone; forget about talking. Everyone was blissed out. Then I realized that Amma had already fed everyone the *uṇṇiyappam* of her Love.

How long had Amma stood there, smiling at everyone, saying how she wanted to make *uṇṇiyappam* for everyone? Amma knows the value of 32 seconds. Standing there, gazing at all of us with motherly love and compassion, how happy Amma made all of us! For Amma, 32 seconds are precious. She knows how many people she can make blissful in that small amount of time.

Amma often says:

> In today's world, people experience two types of poverty. The poverty caused by lack of food, clothing and shelter; and the poverty caused by lack of love and compassion. Of these two, the second type needs to be considered first. Because, if we have love and compassion in our hearts, then we will wholeheartedly serve those who suffer from lack of food, clothing and shelter, thus solving the first type of poverty.

Amma always finds ways to make our hearts overflow with love.

32 Seconds

For many years, my main *sēvā* on Amma's foreign tours was selling Indian snacks like *bhaji*, *pakora*, *laḍḍu*, *dōśa*, *iḍḍly* and chai. The Toulon program in Europe is always one of the biggest. European devotees *love* Indian snacks and chai. They even enjoy just looking at them and asking about them. So, there is always a long queue all day and all night. That makes me smile.

One *Dēvī Bhāva* day was particularly intense because the crowd was even bigger than usual. After the morning program, people queued up outside to get their *Dēvī Bhāva darśan* tokens. Our team went outside to sell chai and snacks while the devotees waited in line. The crowd was so big that many people could not get inside the hall during Amma's *satsaṅg* and *pūjā*. So, instead of taking a break, our chai-chai team went outside again.

To be honest, I was exhausted after selling chai all day. But just seeing so many people's big smiles when they saw chai and Indian snacks was real joy for me. I wondered if I was serving them, or they were serving me by giving me the chance to make them happy. We were all so happy. Maybe Amma was sending extra love to those who could not enter inside the hall.

When *darśan* started, there was another big rush for Indian snacks. Hungry people rushed towards us like big ocean waves. It went on for hours and hours nonstop. By this time, I was *really* ready to collapse. When I finally got a break, I went up on the stage to see Amma. *Darśan* was going on at top speed and there was another long line for *mantra*.

I was looking at Amma from the far side of the stage. Then Amma called me. "Vivek, what happened? Amma is worried because you look so sad." I said, "Amma, I was serving Indian snacks with love and a smile in the beginning. Then, after so many hours, I was exhausted and just wanted to punch everyone who came!!!" Amma laughed and stressed the importance of patience, using the example of a pregnant woman who waits for nine months with so much care and love. Amma continued, "Oh, Amma can give you *prasād* anytime you want, and you can come for *darśan* anytime. But Amma wants you to be happy!"

Then Amma told a story. A boy used to pass by an orphanage on his way to school. At Christmas time, one day, he saw the sad faces of the orphans. He felt so sorry for them and longed for them to feel loved. When his parents gave him $50 to buy masks, toys and fire crackers to celebrate Christmas, he thought, "What will these poor children do for Christmas? Who will give them gifts and treats to celebrate?"

He discussed, with his friends, his idea of donating their Christmas gift money to help the poor orphans, but they were not interested. So, he bought some masks to sell at the bus stop to make some money for the orphans. He wore the masks and made funny gestures to attract the attention of people passing by. Many people started smiling and laughing.

The boy told them, "While you laugh like this, please remember there are some poor orphans who cannot smile and laugh like this. You can help them by buying some of these masks. At home, you can laugh with your children." Touched by the boy's innocent words, many people bought the masks. With that money, he bought presents for the orphans.

At the orphanage, all the orphans were sitting around with sad faces. When the boy took out his presents, the kids became excited and joyful. The boy passed around the gifts to everyone, and the orphans were so happy they began dancing and singing. The orphanage was transformed into a festival ground. The boy watched the happy faces of the orphans silently and became totally absorbed in their happiness. His heart was so full that tears of joy streamed from his eyes. Each little orphan enjoyed their Christmas filled with loving, caring and sharing.

Amma tells this story to show that we should always care for the needs and happiness of others, and find happiness in others' happiness. You can always derive strength and inspiration by looking at what Amma does every moment of the day. Her love and compassion for her children never diminishes.

Amma says,

> If we can fearlessly, courageously practice compassion, then everything else will follow. Compassion gives our decisions and actions special beauty, spontaneity and power. Human calculations may be wrong, but compassionate thoughts, decisions and actions can never be wrong, because compassion is the law of nature. When we quiet our thought, 'I am doing action,' we tune to the universal mind. Then we will not make mistakes, because, the universal power is acting, not us. Compassion tunes us with the universal energy. The spiritual path begins and ends with compassion.

After one US Tour, a friend offered me a job on a beautiful island near Japan doing gardening, landscaping and some carpentry work. I was plotting how to save maximum money for Amma's Europe tour, coming in three months. I never wanted to miss time with Amma and was ready to undergo any difficulty for that. Since the salary was fixed, I decided to spend money only for food, nothing else. Finally, I also reduced my food expenses. I decided to eat only once a day. Every day, for two months, I ate the same lunch—brown rice, dal, and quinoa, cooked together in a rice-cooker, topped with *acchār* (spicy pickles) and mayonnaise.

Many times, it was hard. I got bored always eating the same food. Sometimes I craved ice cream, pizza, *parippavaḍa*, *masāla dōśa* etc. But mostly, I was happy. We all know that, to get something, sometimes, you have to sacrifice something. And I knew I was going to get the most special thing—time with our beloved Amma. So, all the hard work and semi-fasting became enjoyable. But, I lost almost 16kg (35 pounds) and got very tanned working outside under the hot sun. (I thought I had become more handsome.)

When I joined the European tour, everyone noticed how I looked. Many devotees asked what happened to me? I told them I was on a health program at the beach for two months. One night, I had a line-shift *sēvā* right in front of Amma. Radhika *cēcci* told Amma that I was working very hard on the island, under the sun, eating only one meal a day, just to save the money for the tour. Amma was giving *darśan* and listening to Radhika *cēcci*. I was laughing shyly. Then, slowly, Amma looked up at me. I was shocked and froze. The smile on my face faded away. Amma's eyes were filled with tears of compassion that started rolling down her cheeks. *Dēvī* broke the silence. She said, "Amma never wants you to suffer like this. Amma cannot bear it." Amma continued in a strong voice, "Amma will definitely take care of your food the next time you go for work."

Then Amma started to calculate something, mumbling in a low voice. "Okay, 5kg of rice, dal and some vegetables, and so on and so forth..." Amma was planning a menu for me. My heart was so full, thinking of Amma's unconditional love and compassion.

Amma smiled beautifully and gently touched my chin. I will never forget this beautiful blessing from the Divine Mother.

Some senior swāmīs told me that Amma *frequently* mentioned me over the next few days. Another Swāmijī said, "Viveka, in this lifetime, you will never starve. You have Amma's *mahā-saṅkalpa*!!!!!!" It's true. Wherever I go, in Japan, US, Europe, South America, or any other place, I always get more food than I need. Sometimes I even *gain* weight! But, the real blessing is not only good food, but that now I feel that *all food* is Amma's *prasād*. I cannot waste anything. Amma says, "When you waste time, you will never get it back, so don't waste!" But Amma's *prasād* is as precious as time. Also, whenever I eat, I remember that beautiful moment with Amma, and time stops.

Success, for me, is not becoming rich, famous or powerful. It is how much I can remember Amma, because Amma is one with the Divine. To think about Amma's love and compassion is to think about God's love and compassion. To think about Amma's selflessness and patience is to think about God's selflessness and patience. The more we think about those divine qualities, the more our life aligns with them. That is my experience.

This is not the end of the story. A few years later, my friend offered me the same job again. So I went up and asked Amma if I could take this job. Amma asked me, "How long is the work? How many hours per day work? How much money do you get?" I answered everything. Then Amma said, "Okay, Amma will give you food for work."

I told Amma, "My heart is soooo full of your LOVE!! Please Amma, you don't need to give me anything more." Amma said strongly, "NO, NO, NO! Amma will give you food!! You must take it with you!!" I thought that even if today was the last day of my life, I had no regrets. Only pure happiness!!

The last day of the program, Amma gave a long list of grocery items to Radhika *cēcci* and asked her to get all the items from the kitchen. Later, Radhika *cēcci* returned to the stage with two big bags full of groceries. Amma checked all the items very carefully, and nicely put them back in the bags. Then she handed them to me with a big smile. I was simply blissed out feeling Amma's love and care.

And you know what happened after that? Our Amma's love is so big, my suitcase became overweight for my flight! In the end, only Amma's love was inside my suitcase. What else do we need? We are so fortunate to meet Amma in this lifetime. It is the most precious gift. Let us keep Amma in our heart every moment. And be grateful for all the love and compassion she showers on all of us.

Ammayil mānasam cērnnu
ende jīvitam dhanyamāy tīrnnu,
ende jīvitam dhanyamāy tīrnnu.

My mind is immersed in Mother.
Oh mother, my life has become fulfilled.

2

"Your Mind Should Never Waver"

Kamalaja Handler (United States)

Many years ago, when I had reached a point in my life where I couldn't see my way ahead, I went to Amma and cried in her lap. Seeing my desperate state, Amma lifted my head and said something that has been a guiding light ever since. She said, "Daughter, no matter what happens, even if the Himalayas come crashing down upon you, your mind should never waver." Amma wants us to remain unshakeable in any situation. Remembering this in difficult times gives me courage to take one small step forward.

Once, during Amma's 2006 program in Toulon, France, Lola told Punyavati and me that Amma wanted her Dēvī Bhāva garlands to be brought to the next city so we could use the petals from them in the next city. We enthusiastically agreed to help. Later, we got a shock when we saw eight, large, heavy garlands. Our flight tickets allowed us only one small bag each, and our bags were full.

At the airport, we begged other staff members to help, but everyone was in the same predicament. Suddenly, we had an idea: we would *wear* the garlands. Even though this felt inappropriate, we were determined to keep our word. Praying for Amma's forgiveness, we each put on four garlands. They covered our bodies, hanging all the way to our knees. Amma's fragrance and presence were so strong, it was like having darśan!

The people from our tour group looked on, embarrassed, and pretended not to know us. But we hardly noticed. As we passed through security, the police officers did not object to the garlands. In fact, their faces lit up upon seeing us!

In Ireland, the next stop, everyone was talking about what we had done, and it became a big joke. We were both happy that we could obey our Guru's words. When we told Amma about it, she rolled with laughter. She said she was pleased with us. Amma described how all the profits from our flower *sēvā* help poor people; and those who attend Amma's programs will see this and also be inspired. The donations of the people who offer garlands are often enough to fund a child's education. Only for this reason does Amma allow devotees to garland her.

Then, suddenly, Amma told me, "When you give a satsaṅg in Vallickavu, make sure you tell this story!" As I am terrified of speaking in public, I froze. "What does Amma mean? Why give a satsaṅg in Vallickavu?" I did not understand what Amma meant and even forgot her words over time. But 14 years later, Amma's words came true. This is not really a satsaṅg. I'm just sharing some beautiful experiences with Amma and the lessons I have learned from them.

Though Amma is the greatest spiritual master that has ever lived, she remains as humble as the earth. Amma always inspires us to practice self-sacrifice by setting the perfect example herself.

This reminds me of an incident during Amma's visit to Sri Lanka after the 2004 Asian tsunami. When we landed in Sri Lanka, there was not enough space in the bus for the relief supplies and our personal bags. We piled the luggage in the aisle and decided to figure out a plan later.

When we stopped for lunch at a temple, we stood surrounded by excess luggage. Actually, the luggage did fit inside the bus, but we weren't happy about a long, uncomfortable ride ahead with luggage piled high. Suddenly, Amma's car pulled into the temple compound. She asked what was happening and someone explained.

Without a moment's hesitation, Amma said, "Put it in my car." Our hearts sank. We pictured Amma travelling the with our luggage crammed into her vehicle just so that we could sit comfortably in our bus. She asked us to open the back door of her minivan. We tried dissuading her from taking the luggage, but she was adamant. She leaned over the last seat of the van and told us to pass her the bags.

Some handed bags to Amma as others began to sneak luggage back into our bus. Before we knew it, the work was done and we were on our way. Needless to say, during the rest of the journey, not one person complained about the luggage inside the bus. Witnessing Amma's self-sacrifice kindles a spark of the same spirit in us.

Amma, the perfect master, is a great ship carrying countless souls across the ocean of *samsāra* (cycle of births and deaths). By her grace, she has taken each one of us into the shelter of her ship, and she gathers more and more passengers from even the most unexpected places.

Once, in an airport in Europe, Amma was looking for a place to sit with us. One lady, who was not part of our group, was sitting in an empty row of chairs, reading a book. Amma chose the spot right next to her. When Amma sat down, the lady didn't even look up until we descended like a swarm of honeybees, all trying to get the spot closest to our Queen. We occupied every chair and the entire floor space around her.

Feeling the lady might be uncomfortable, someone suggested that she might want to sit somewhere else. She looked around and asked me, "Do I have to leave?"

I said, "No, of course not. You're welcome to stay." The lady nodded her head, looked at Amma, and continued reading her book. Amma began talking to our group.

After five minutes, the lady put her book down and sat very still. She leaned forward and whispered, "Who is she? I feel like crying and I don't know why." I told her about Amma's darśan and charitable activities. The lady listened carefully, and with eyes full of tears, she put her book aside and turned in her chair to see Amma better. Then she whispered, "Can I also have Amma's darśan? I want to visit her in India." The same lady, who, only a few minutes before, found her book more interesting than Amma, had been transformed by Amma's presence that now she wanted to come to Amritapuri, half-way across the world!

I explained everything to Amma, who gave her a beautiful darśan and her consent to visit the āśram. Truly, Amma is the most humble and compassionate Master. She gathers her children from every corner of the world, even from airports!

Amma's every look, word and touch are filled with her infinite transforming power. But transformation is not always easy. Once we have boarded the Guru's ship to cross the ocean of samsāra, the storms of our *prārabdha karmas* (karmic burdens), doubts and fears will rage and strike. We might feel pushed beyond our limits and even fear drowning in our own darkness. The Master will even create these storms so that we have to face our weaknesses and confusions. Thus, the Master exhausts our karmas, and shows us our negativities to eradicate them so that our true self can shine forth brightly.

I grew up in a small town in America. When my parents were in their 20s, they accepted a saint from India as their teacher and began to meditate every day. My sister and I did the same. Although the people from our town were kind, they did not understand any religion other than Christianity. If kids at school found out we meditated, they would call us crazy.

As a child, I wondered if God really existed. The meditation we did seemed dry and boring. I was searching for something deeper. I had many spiritual questions but couldn't find any satisfying answers. One day, I told my father that, if our family's teacher was in fact my Guru, then I should be able to meet him, ask him doubts, and even live with him. My father explained that nobody was allowed to meet him.

I insisted that I would go and sit outside his house until he let me in. Laughing, my father said, "Well, you better not do that, or the police will take you away!" I began to pray to God to please show me my Guru. The *Bhagavad Gītā* says, "Learn the Truth by approaching a spiritual master. Inquire from him with reverence and render service to him. Such an enlightened saint can impart knowledge to you because he has seen the Truth" (4.34). I was searching for such a Master.

I began to pray intensely to God to show me the way to my Guru. A few months later, I came across a book about Amma and wanted to meet her as soon as possible. On July 2, 2002, my family and I saw Amma for the first time in Chicago. I couldn't bear to leave Amma, so I continued alone on the tour. The last night of the tour was the turning point of my life. As I waited for darśan on Dēvī Bhāva, I felt a deep dispassion towards the world and a longing for Amma's love. I wanted to ask Amma if I could come to India. As I didn't know if I was allowed to speak to her, I didn't say anything; but, Amma lit the fire of longing inside me.

I wandered out of the hall into the warm, summer night, all alone in nature. Realizing the impermanence of life, I cried from the bottom of my heart for Amma to save me from samsāra. After a long time, I went back inside and sat at the back of the stage. I prayed, "Amma, please forgive me for testing you, but if you know my heart and I can leave everything now and come to India, please look at me."

Immediately, the crowd mysteriously parted. Like moving chess pieces on a board, Amma shifted the people so I had a clear view of her, and she looked straight at me for a long time. I felt as if lightning had struck me. "Amma is God! She knows my past, present and future." I was convinced by Amma's powerful glance and decided to leave everything and move to Amma's āśram in India.

On Guru Pūrṇimā 2019, Swāmijī spoke about the power of Amma's glance. He said,

> The closest translation of the Malayalam word '*kaḍākṣam*' is 'glance'. We cannot simply call it a 'look'. 'Glance' is something that God, the Guru alone, can do because it comes from a totally different level. It's a secret communication between Amma and a particular person. We have to be ready for it.

> To put it in Amma's own words, 'When the Guru glances at us, it is like a tremendous waterfall, like the Ganges falling from Lord Śiva's head onto you. You are completely washed away, and you will never be the same person again. You cannot be the same.'

It is the power of Amma's glance that has brought us all to her.

I have had health problems all my life. Two days after I was born, I almost died. My chances of survival were slim or none. In truth, I am alive today only by Amma's grace. In 2010, Amma told me I was going through a bad astrological time. Severe pain, vomiting, fevers and fainting were my state for years. Often, I couldn't eat anything, and I struggled to meet my own basic needs. I became exhausted and weak, and my state of mind sank as my health declined.

The more I suffered, the more afraid I became; not just afraid about my health, but afraid of not being able to stay near Amma. I was devastated. I had to go to bed early and miss the night darśan programs. I became focused only on what I was missing with Amma instead of on all that I was receiving from her.

I will forever be grateful to Amma for the love and guidance she has given regarding my health. Once, when I was about to faint in the airport, Amma gave me her own *tulasī* tea to help me recover. When I was not able to eat anything, Amma always saw to it that I got her *kañji* (rice gruel) and suggested remedies for my pain and nausea. In fact, it was Amma who first diagnosed the cause of my illness when no doctor could do so.

Despite my sickness, Amma has always encouraged me to travel with her. She told me, "Whether you stay back at the āśram or come on tour, you will be sick either way. If you travel with Amma, you can share your heart with her."

Once, before Amma's Europe tour, I was exhausted after her birthday celebrations. I decided that the next year, I would leave a week early to rest before the tour.

But the following day, on the way to Europe with Amma, that idea vanished. To change terminals between flights, we took a bus with Amma. When I got inside, Amma motioned for me to sit next to her. Feeling it might be inappropriate, I only moved near her. But Amma insisted; so, I sat down next to Amma, feeling like a child. Amma spoke to me the whole way to the terminal. Any ideas I had of leaving early before a tour disappeared. Being in Amma's divine presence is the *only* true rest and medicine for our heart and soul.

Amma only thinks of alleviating our pain, and never her own. In fact, Amma has no karma. She takes on the karmas of her children to relieve their suffering. Realizing this profound truth has helped me try to focus on Amma's health rather than my own. Seeing Amma's unending flow of love to each one of us, regardless of any physical pain she endures, gives me immense strength and motivation to keep moving forward and not wallow in my fears and self-pity.

Once, when we landed in Australia, I was standing by the baggage claim as Amma walked past. She stopped in front of me, and I asked Amma if she was tired from the long flight. Immediately, with sparkling eyes, she laughed and said, "I don't think. I simply don't think." I knew her words were the answer to all my problems. Suffering exists only at the level of the mind; but, for Amma, there is no mind. Her body may feel sick, but in her state, she never feels the burden of it.

At times, when my illness was acute, I was admitted to the hospital, and it became impossible to join Amma on her tours.

Sometimes Amma has ignored me externally, even when I thought I needed her attention the most. Then, the mix of physical pain and anguish in my heart from missing Amma's guidance and love felt like more than I could bear. But Amma knows our limitations better than we do ourselves.

When Amma's external guidance was seemingly missing, out of despair I used to pray, "You hold the entire creation in the palm of your hand. You create and destroy millions of universes just by opening and closing your eyes. Why won't you help this child?" Little did I know that Amma was giving me exactly the help I needed, just not the help I thought I needed.

I remembered Amma's words, "Even if the Himalayas come crashing down upon you, even then your mind should never waver." Although I knew I wasn't living up to this ideal, Amma's words gave me enough strength to take a small step forward. She slowly guided me to turn within and awakened a spark of self-confidence and strength inside of me. By 'ignoring' me, Amma achieved what would never have been possible through external love and affection. She often says that she doesn't want anyone to depend on her. Rather, she wants her children to become independent, established in the Self.

Mahātmās (spiritually illumed souls) like Amma transform even difficult times into blessings. It is for us to realize it. A story in the *Bhāgavatam* illustrates this. One day, Kṛṣṇa's children found a giant lizard in a dry well. Unable to rescue it, they called Kṛṣṇa, who came and lifted the lizard out with his hand. Immediately, it changed into a celestial being who had once been a righteous king. The king explained that he had once accidentally given away the same cow to two different brahmins. He begged their forgiveness and offered them *lakhs* of cows, but they angrily refused and walked away. Later, when the king died, Yama asked him which he wanted to experience first: his large amount of *puṇya* (merit) or the *pāpa* (sin) of that one mistake?

The king chose to experience the results of his sin first. Yama said, "Then fall." The next moment, he found himself to be a huge lizard fallen into a dry well. The king then told Kṛṣṇa, "Your merciful eyes have seen me, and your hands have touched me. I now think it was not a sin that pushed me into this well, but all my good actions put together; otherwise, how could I have the blessing of being rescued by you?"

By Amma's infinite compassion, she is lifting us up and saving each one of us, converting all our mistakes to good fortune. How many times has she embraced, touched, and blessed us with her divine glance. But do we reflect and make the most of these experiences with her? In the story, Kṛṣṇa touched the king only once. How can we begin to appreciate the immense fortune of our countless interactions with Amma? It's a mysterious and incomprehensible shower of divine grace.

The Amma inside us is ever waiting for us to tune ourselves to her and realize our oneness with her. One night, on a US tour, I dreamt that Amma was gazing at the crowd at the end of Dēvī Bhāva. Suddenly, she called me inside the tent after the curtains closed. Amma was still standing, and I knelt as she hugged me tightly. In the dream, I told Amma that I wanted to be like little Siddharth, who was always in her physical presence. Amma smiled and said, "That is good, but those times are over. Now, you have to go inside."

I woke up prostrate on the floor, my face wet with tears. I wanted to ask Amma about the dream. In the next city, I left my room early one morning to write my question to Amma. As

I closed the door behind me, I heard another door open. Amma walked out with only Siddharth, who skipped happily down the hallway and disappeared around the corner. I was all alone with Amma.

She allowed me to fix her sari for her as she spoke to me. After a few minutes, the Swāmīs also joined us. Amma took me with her down the elevator to the program hall. When the darśan started, I asked Amma about the dream. She said, "It's not that you can't be close to Amma physically, but inner tuning is needed." Amma gave the example of the radio tower transmitting waves. We can enjoy the music only if we tune our radio to the station. Then Amma said, "If inner tuning is there, that will surely manifest outwardly as well."

Amma reminds us that, even in the darkest times, she is always there protecting and guiding us. If we turn within, with patience and surrender, she will show us the way. She will never let go of our hands.

Once, I got a chance to hold a flashlight for Amma as she walked in the dark. Suddenly, Amma reached forward and grabbed my hand. She said, "Turn off the light. With that small light you can't see the bright light of the full moon."

I contemplated on the deep meaning of Amma's words. The flashlight is like our small self, our individuality. The moon, which reflects the light of the sun, is like Amma's eyes reflecting the light of the Self. As long as we try to light the way with the small light of our ego, we will never see the bright light of the *Atma*, which is always guiding us within.

By Amma's grace, may we overcome all obstacles and realize our oneness with Amma's divine effulgence, and, thereby, be able to shed her light to the whole world.

3

Love is the Best Medicine

Dr. Nibodhi Haas (United States)

In the *Tao Te Ching*, Lao Tzu says, "Those who know do not speak, and those who speak do not know." I am about to speak, so, I obviously do not know, except that I know nothing at all.

I don't understand much about *Vedantic* philosophy or the *Upaniṣads*. I don't even know Sanskrit well enough to chant my favorite verses from the *Bhagavad Gītā* without causing pain in your ears. I also don't know what I could have possibly done in this or any other life to deserve to sit here next to the Supreme Goddess of the Universe.

Amma has said that Ramakrishna Paramahamsa's devotees were already polished radiant gems. She often compares her devotees to lumps of coal that she is transforming into diamonds. In me, she got more than just a lump of coal. She got a whole coal mine! I pray that, through Amma's *prāṇa-śakti*, my words become her words and are of some benefit. Any mistakes are solely due to my own ignorance.

Hafiz wrote:

> The subject tonight is Love.
> And for tomorrow night as well.

> In fact, I know of no better subject for us to discuss until we all die.

Love is what and who we truly *are*. When unclouded by ego, only Love exists. Love, UNCONDITIONAL Love, is the rarest commodity in the *Kali Yuga*. Finding Unconditional Love is like winning the biggest jackpot in the universal lottery. We have all won! We have Amma, the supreme embodiment of Unconditional Love. Amma always tells us, "Love is our true nature. We are all beads strung on the same thread of love. Life is filled with God's light, but only through optimism will you experience that light. Children, fill your hearts with love and gratitude."

The first step to truly *being* Love, is to be grateful. Gratitude opens us to the light and love within. I want to express my eternal gratitude to everyone here in Amṛtapuri, and to Amma for her unfathomable, infinite Grace. You are all truly Amma's precious gems. Amma's family of immortal bliss is her army of divine warriors of love.

My journey with Amma (in this life) began almost 25 years ago. Until the covid pandemic, I had not been away from Amma's physical form for more than a few months at a time. Being physically away from her for so long has been deeply painful. My heart goes out to Amma's children all over the world in this same situation.

There were times, during this period, when I felt very alone. Your prayers, *satsaṅgs*, love and compassion are more precious than any words can describe. I don't think anyone who stayed here in the āśram during this covid time can comprehend what it means to the devotees who are not here in the āśram. So, to everyone here, I offer the deepest gratitude.

Hearing everyone's beautiful *satsaṅgs* helped transform the feeling of aloneness to the feeling of Oneness. It is only a very fine line between alone and all-one! Amma says, "We should learn to love everyone equally and express this love, because, in essence, we are all one, one *ātmā* (soul)."

While I was studying Naturopathic Medicine and Yōga, I realized the importance of a living *Guru* and was praying for this. One day, my yōga teacher showed us a book called *Daughters of The Goddess.* The page I opened to was Amma! Immediately tears came to my eyes. Instantly, I knew that she was my *Guru.* I felt such deep familiarity and more love than I had ever felt. I photocopied Amma's picture, put it on my altar, and started meditating on her.

Soon after, I met Amma in San Ramon. After those programs, I quit school and came to Amṛtapuri, intending to stay with Amma forever. I was quite happy sweeping and mopping the Kali temple, cleaning the toilets and doing sand and cement *sēvā.* I happily imagined doing that *sēvā* for the rest of my life. But, after a short time, Amma made it very clear that I must return to the US to finish school before moving to Amṛtapuri. For the next several years, while completing my studies, I returned to India whenever I could, and would always do Amma's summer and fall US tours.

By December 2002, I had completed Naturopathic and Yōga school and earned a degree in Ayurveda as well. Shortly after this, in early 2003, I met my wife, Gunavati. I knew that we were meant to spend our lives together serving Amma. Gunavati had the same idea, but she also had some serious doubts, as I was rather wild and uncontrollable at that time. That summer, in San Ramon, Gunavati asked Amma about our relationship, and

Amma said she had made a *saṅkalpa* for our relationship and we should move to the āśram after tour.

Amma is truly a *kalpavrikṣa* (wish-fulfilling tree). For many years before meeting Amma, it was my dream to live in a community and be of service to the world. By her grace, this has manifested far beyond anything I could have imagined. Since 2003, I have been blessed to live here in Amṛtapuri and do *sēvā* here and on the World Tours.

Every year we used to go to the US to work before summer tour. In 2020, shortly after arriving in America, the pandemic hit, and we went into full lockdown. We ended up spending almost one year away from Amma.

As with so many devotees who are physically away from Amma at this time, I experienced many emotions which led to deep reflection. I experienced that Amma is with us in our every thought, emotion and action, good or bad. Amma is always holding our hands and walking with us. Even when we feel alone, Amma is carrying us.

While I was in the US, people everywhere were filled with fear and anxiety. In addition to the pandemic, there was racial violence, social injustice and a general feeling of extreme heaviness. Such darkness can only be dispelled by tuning to the light within. The real challenge exists within myself. Wherever I go, my mind and ego follow. I wondered if it was because of my *karma* that I was far away? Or was this Amma's way to bring me closer to her? This was the daily turmoil in my mind. I often wondered if I had failed as a devotee.

It took months to surrender and trust that everything is a divine mystery, and ultimately, EVERYTHING is Amma's grace. These times provided so many priceless lessons. We could not collectively gather, but there were still many chances to do *sēvā*. We could also use the time to reflect and strengthen our inner connection to Amma. Being away from Amma led to some harsh realizations. One was how often I took Amma for granted. I pray that I can open enough to receive the experience of the Self that Amma is offering.

As a doctor, trying to understand the root causes and pathology of covid, I spent a lot of time studying Ayurvedic texts, doing research, listening to lectures and attending virtual conferences. This gave me the chance to hear opposing opinions, beliefs and religions, and different political and environmental views from different social and economic segments of society. I came to understand that it doesn't matter if I agree with others. Love must be there if we are to survive. Amma has always taught this. Love weaves the fabric of creation and spins the web of life. Love holds everything together.

We don't have to agree with everyone. We don't even have to *like* everyone, but we have to try to love everyone. Likes come from the ego. Love comes from Consciousness. We *are* One. We can disagree, but we should never shut anyone out of our hearts. Only unconditional love will save us.

We have heard many amazing stories about how Amma saved someone's life. She also saved my life, more than once. In 2004, I visited Varanasi on the way to the US to work before the tour. Shortly after arriving in the US, I developed a very high fever and was getting weaker and weaker. Gunavati took me to many doctors, but they all told me I just had the flu. My fever got worse over several weeks, and I would lose consciousness. I couldn't even hold my *arcana* book. All I could do was chant my *mantra*.

When it seemed I might die, a new doctor finally diagnosed me with typhoid fever. The friends we were staying with got scared and asked us to leave their house the day they heard my diagnosis. I was so weak I could barely walk. We had no place to stay and absolutely no idea what to do. We were in Hawaii and could not afford a hotel or even a ticket to fly to the mainland. We were at the end of our money.

It was local farmers market day, so Gunavati packed our few belongings, and we went there. I was resting under a tree while Gunavati went shopping for food. Both of us were praying desperately to Amma for some solution. Then a girl came up to me and said the Divine Mother told her inside her head that she should talk to me and help me. She was filled with compassion after I explained I was sick and that we had nowhere to stay. She invited us to stay at her home as long as we needed.

On the way there, we told her about Amma (whom she had never met). When we woke up the next morning, the house smelled exactly like Amma. Gunavati and I wondered if the girl was using some perfume. Just then, the girl then came in and said, "Amma appeared to me in a dream, surrounded in a Divine Light and said, 'Thank you for taking care of my children.'" The girl then asked us what perfume we were wearing. We told her that we had no perfume, but the fragrance was the exact scent of Amma.

Even a friend, who visited later in the day, noticed the scent and asked about it. The only explanation for the Divine Fragrance was that Amma was there with us. The girl let us stay with her while I healed. Then, she came to meet Amma, and now she and her mother are devotees.

Amma's ways are mysterious, unfathomable and mystical. Amma's love opened this girl's heart and provided us with a safe and nurturing place. I am grateful to Amma for saving me, and also for what I learned. I had never had any serious illness in my life before typhoid. Being so sick and close to death helped make me a better doctor. It gave me a deeper understanding of what sick people go through and their feelings of helplessness. It has also given me firm faith that Amma will always, in all ways, be with us.

Also, when I was too sick to do any *sādhana* but chant my *mantra*, I realized the power of the *mantra* Amma gives us. Amma says, "Chanting your *mantra* will protect you from all dangers, like an armour." My *mantra* was my lifeline and will always be so.

Amma's love and healing power is not limited to living beings. Her love and grace flow even to inanimate objects. That same summer, we did Amma's tour in a van my father had lent us. It was old, but in good working condition. After the last *Dēvī Bhāva* in the US, we were driving to Canada, with several friends, for Amma's first-ever Toronto program. Near the US-Canada border at Niagara Falls, just before sunset, we stopped to see the waterfall.

As we pulled into the parking lot, the "check engine" light came on. Smoke was pouring out of the engine. None of us was mechanically inclined, but it looked like a very serious problem. It was Saturday night, and all the mechanics were closed for the weekend. Even if we got the van towed, there was nowhere to take it for repair. We were heartbroken thinking we might miss Amma's first program in Canada.

Feeling sad and helpless, we went for a walk near the waterfall and prayed to Amma. When we returned to the van, we saw our *Dēvī Bhāva prasād* on the dashboard, and we decided to pour the *vibhuti* onto the engine. If it works for people, animals and plants, why not try it on the vehicle? Chanting some *mantras* and praying to Amma, I poured the *vibhuti* all over the engine.

We waited a little while, prayed some more, and then tried to start the engine. And guess what? YES!! It started! We reached Toronto in plenty of time. In fact, we drove all the way back to Southern California (more than 4000 kilometers) and returned the van to my parents without any further mechanical issues. My father, who is very good at fixing vehicles, looked at the engine and determined nothing was wrong with it. He continued to drive this van for many years with no further engine troubles.

This last story about how Amma saved me happened in Amṛtapuri! I had just entered into my *Sade Sati* astrological period. It was monsoon season, and the rains and wind were very strong. One day shortly before evening *bhajans*, Gunavati realized that in the afternoon storm, her only pair of shoes had blown away and had landed on the *bhajan*-hall rooftop.

The only way to the roof was through the *Brahmacārī* building; so, she couldn't get them herself. At that time, the roof was fiberglass. I asked around if the roof was sturdy, and several people assured me it was definitely safe. This was definitely poor advice, and I was certainly lacking discernment when I ventured onto the roof.

After only a few steps the roof broke! The next thing I knew I was clinging to a pole dangling from the rooftop. Only Amma's Grace saved me. Miraculously, I fell where there was a pole to grab onto. I think Amma grabbed the pole with my hands. I had no awareness of reaching to catch the pole.

My first thought was not my mantra, or even "Amma save me." It was, "OH NO! I broke the roof!" My next thought was, "OH NO! Amṛtātmānanda Swāmī is singing, and I just crashed through the roof!" My third thought was, "OH NO! Amma is coming soon, and I am hanging here!" Then I realized the severity of the situation. I was bleeding and dangling from the roof. My arms were so shaky I couldn't pull myself up. I have no idea how long I hung there before someone rescued me. If not for Amma's protection and unconditional Love, I am sure I would not be here today.

This reminds me of a story Amma tells. Reviewing his life, a man saw two sets of footprints in the sand. One was his and one was God's. At one point he saw only one set of footprints. He realized that the single set of footprints was during the lowest point in his life. He asked God why He abandoned him then. God replied, "Son, when you saw only one set of footprints, I was carrying you."

Nothing is separate from God. Amma says, "We must remember that everything is sentient. Everything is full of consciousness and life. Everything exists in God. There is no such thing as mere matter; consciousness alone exists."

In addition to my gratitude to Amma for saving me again and again, I am also grateful that Amma has allowed me to serve her doing something I love — Ayurveda and Naturopathy. While Ayurveda has very sophisticated healing and curative practices, its chief objective is to prevent disease, preserve health and restore consciousness. It describes the laws of nature, as well as the symbiotic and delicate relationship between humans and nature. When followed in a conscious way, we can create and sustain balance in the world.

Amma speaks often about the importance of living in harmony with nature. She says, "Living in harmony with nature will itself bring happiness and contentment. Nature is a textbook from which we must learn. Each and every object in nature teaches us something..." Amma also says, "Renunciation and selflessness are the greatest lessons that we can learn from nature. Nature is an indispensable part of life on earth. Without nature, no creature, not humans or anything else, can live. Therefore, it is the duty of human beings to serve and take care of nature, which, in turn, will supply us with the necessary things for life."

In this time of a global health pandemic, we can see that the climate catastrophe, and the financial/ social/political collapse, are entirely human-created hardships. Ayurveda understands that all of these "symptoms" are interrelated, and Ayurveda offers a remedy for these afflictions. It is the same remedy that Amma offers: LOVE. Amma says, "Love is the best medicine. Love is the only medicine that can heal the wounds of the world." When our hearts are filled with love and compassion, the solutions will come easily. Science and Consciousness must work hand in hand. We already have the technology to heal the planet if we act NOW.

Ayurveda understands that it is essential to identify causes in order to solve problems and heal from our past mistakes. Our disconnect from nature and our over-consumption and greed are the cause of the world's imbalances. These destructive tendencies will inevitably cause the breakdown of ecosystems and the extinction of species. It is no mystery how we got into this situation. The leading cause of death in the world is Heart

Disease. We are, literally, dying from a broken heart, a lack of love.

Ayurveda prescribes a very simple cure: *Sattva Vijaya.* This refers to the lifestyle that restores the connection between heart, mind and Self. *Sattva* is the qualities of purity, wholesomeness, and virtue. Of all *sattvic* qualities, pure love is the most fundamental. Now, I would like to share the healing properties of Ayurveda's best medicine: Love.

Love is an Adaptogen: As an adaptogen, love helps us adjust and adapt to every situation. Amma tells us, "We cannot change all situations in life, but we can change our attitude towards them."

Love is Anti-inflammatory: As an anti-inflammatory, love soothes the inflammation of desires and ego, and eventually eliminates them.

Love is Anti-bacterial/Anti-viral: As an anti-bacterial/viral, love stops the spread of the greed bacteria and the ego virus.

Love is Anti-cancer: Love cures the cancer of anger and hatred.

Love is a laxative: As a laxative, love purges the toxic waste of "I-ness" and "my-ness" from the system.

Love is a Neuro-regenerative: Love restores Consciousness to its natural state. Love protects and regenerates the brain. It restores balance to the heart-mind connection. Love especially balances *sādhaka-pitta*, *prāṇa-vāyu* and *tarpaka-kapha.* These control the flow of *prāṇa* between the Heart/Mind. This is what western medicine is now calling our "Psycho-Neuro-Endocrine-Immune System." Ayurveda calls it *prāṇa*, *tējas* and *ōjas*, which control our cellular and emotional intelligence as well as our innate immunity and longevity.

Love is a Probiotic: When we are in the state of love, we produce the most important neuro-hormones. GABA and dopamine (the contentment hormones), serotonin (the happiness hormone), oxytocin (the love hormone) and anandamide (the bliss hormone). More than 90% of the serotonin in the human body is in the G.I. tract. When serotonin is healthy, we have *sama-agni* (a balanced state) of digestion, and we easily digest, assimilate and transform our life experiences. All of these neuro-hormones are regulated by interaction with the approximately 38 trillion bacteria and more than 350 trillion viruses living in the gut that support *prāṇa*, *tējas* and ōjas. Without a healthy gut-brain connection, we cannot think or act with discrimination, and we will continually make wrong choices and disrupt the natural way of life.

Love is the only medicine that can heal every disease. It removes the root cause of the disease, the ego. If the medicine of love isn't working, the solution is to increase the dose. There is no risk of overdosing. You can take as much as you want until you are intoxicated. There is no risk of a hangover. And love is totally compatible with every other medication. The very best part is that love is absolutely free and in unlimited supply.

In addition to creating the universe, Amma has incarnated as the Divine Doctor. Her *darśan* is her medicine. Amma is the remedy for absolutely everything! We came into this world with nothing. We will leave with nothing. Amma has given us everything. She will continue to give us everything. We should offer everything back to Amma, the Source.

For me, the journey of love, back to the Self begins with gratitude. Being grateful for everything Amma has given us and making the best use of this precious human birth.
Ādi Śaṅkarācārya says:

> It is difficult to attain a human birth. To be born pure and with a desire for learning and spiritual attainment is even more rare and only comes after thousands of incarnations. Strive to find a genuine spiritual teacher, a *Guru*. And by practice of yōga, learn discrimination. Study the ancient spiritual writings, and, by tranquility and purification, try to gain knowledge of the ātmā. Among the means used for the search for liberation, the foremost is devotion.
>
> This is the means by which the *yogis* have crossed. The ancient writings have said that śraddhā (faith and attentive awareness), *bhakti* (love), *dhyāna* (meditation) and *yōga* (self-discipline) will bring the results you require. These will release you from the bondage of reincarnation."

But, beyond all the qualities mentioned by Śrī Śaṅkarācārya, we need Amma's grace. No matter how much effort we make or how much discrimination we have, it is nothing without her grace.

If Amma can make an entire coal mine like me useful, then I am certain that Amma can transform all human beings, and the world can change for the better. The most beautiful and fragrant rose grows out of compost mixed with excreta. Likewise, the most radiant lotus flower grows from the darkest, murkiest pond.

I pray to Amma to take the excreta of our minds and turn it into organic compost and grow a beautiful rose to offer at her Lotus feet. Also, please take our filthy, murky *vāsanas* and *samskāras* and grow a beautiful lotus that spreads the fragrance of your Love everywhere your wind blows. May we all eternally bathe in the River of Love that is our Amma.

4

From Despair to Hope

Karthika Flora (United States)

In 1987, I was teaching in a small, very isolated, Eskimo village in Alaska. There were no roads into the village, so you had to fly in to get there. Eskimos are tribal people who live near the North Pole. Like tribal people in many parts of the world, they are experiencing many problems with alcoholism and drug abuse, and all the social problems that go along with this. I was saddened by the stories of abuse and neglect of the children in the village. I lived and worked in this environment for three years. Finally, feeling overwhelmed by it all, I was planning to move to New Mexico in a few months.

One day, the principal of the school asked me to

let a 15-year-old Eskimo teenager live in my house. The principal didn't give much detail. He only said that her village was some distance away, and her home was not a good environment. It seemed urgent, so I agreed, and she moved into my house. (I'll call her Mary.) I didn't know anything about Mary, except what little the principal had told me.

Mary enrolled at the school where I taught. She had been staying in my house for a couple of weeks, when, one morning, the principal came to me, saying that Mary hadn't come to school, and I should check on her. So, I went home, saw Mary, and asked what the trouble was. She said she had swallowed a bottle of aspirin to commit suicide. I made her vomit immediately and called the principal. He arranged for me to take Mary to the nearest hospital, which was hours away by plane.

During the trip, I tried to remain composed for Mary's sake, but I was full of stress and anxiety. At the hospital, the doctors admitted Mary. They would keep watch overnight, and I should stay at the hospital as a bystander. The only available room was a white, padded cell where they normally keep mental patients. Finally, I fell into a restless sleep and had a vivid dream. I was on a boat, floating peacefully down a river in New Mexico. A woman in a white gown, with pale skin and long, flowing blonde hair was with me. She smiled lovingly and embraced me for a long time.

I woke up feeling completely enveloped in love. Before I slept, I had been extremely anxious; but now I was relaxed and comfortable. I was full of wonder at the change in my emotional state, and curious about the woman in the dream. I am now certain that my mysterious companion on the boat was Amma with blonde hair. At the time, I was very opposed to Indian *Gurus*. I had the wrong idea that all Indian *Gurus* were fake.

Mary recovered and we returned to the village. Some days later, two nuns from the local Catholic church visited my home. I thought they wanted to know about Mary, and they did; but mostly, the nuns wanted to know how *I* was doing. The nuns knew Mary and said that Mary had attempted suicide more than ten times before. The nuns wanted to reassure me that Mary's suicide attempt was not my fault. They were loving and concerned for my well-being and assured me that I was not to blame. In retrospect, I feel Amma sent the nuns to console me, even before I had met Amma.

I was very affected by my experience in Alaska. I couldn't see any solution for the Eskimo people whose habitat and lifestyle had been disrupted by the white men who had taken over their lands. There was government funding for social and medical services in the villages; it just wasn't enough to lift the people out of the devastating cycle of alcoholism and abuse. Witnessing the utter failure of social interventions, I felt deep sadness and despair at the plight of the Eskimo people.

I had no belief in God and was without a basic understanding of the nature of the world. Amma says, "All the calamities and problems that exist in the world come only from lack of faith and devotion, from a lack of love. Once we lose faith in a Supreme Controller or God, there cannot be any harmony or peace in society. People will act and live as they like. Morality and ethics will disappear from the face of the earth. People will be tempted to live like animals. Absence of faith, love, patience and forgiveness make life hellish." (*Awaken Children* 6, p.208)

To leave these painful experiences behind me, I moved to New Mexico. At first, I enjoyed the change from the village to the wide-open spaces of New Mexico; but something was missing.

I was longing for meaning in my life and the world around me. Amma says, "All things that we place our faith and hope in will one day prove useless and meaningless. That day will come sooner or later. Yet until then, we remain unfulfilled because of our lack of faith. We remain skeptical and rigid. But, one day, we will surely call out, 'O God, I am helpless. Come and save me. Help me! Protect me!' We will call out when we realize that all hopes end in hopelessness." (*Awaken Children* 6, p.81)

After living for some time in New Mexico, a friend introduced me to the Sathya Sai Baba Center of Albuquerque, New Mexico. After only a few weeks, I became completely attached to Sathya Sai, his form, his words, his wisdom, his charity. This is remarkable, because I had been cynical about organized religion and had no interest in spirituality. It just shows that Divine Grace puts this attraction into the devotee's mind at the perfect time. I became convinced that spirituality was the only solution to mankind's problems. I also appreciated the concept of *prārabdha karma* because it explained why people suffer in seemingly unfair situations.

About a year after joining the Sathya Sai Center of Albuquerque, I picked up a yōga magazine and opened to a page with a big photo of Amma, announcing that she would be visiting Santa Fe, New Mexico, which was only 45 minutes away. As soon as I saw the photo, I thought to myself, "Baba is the Father, Amma is the Mother." Again, due to God's Infinite Grace, I somehow knew immediately that Amma was Divine, that she knew everything about me, that she was omniscient and omnipresent. It is my good fortune that thus far, I have never doubted that Amma is God in human form. While I don't claim to be a good devotee, at least I know that Amma is God. I am sure that this has kept me on the path, despite my laziness and other negative traits.

So, I went to see Amma in Santa Fe. What an opportunity to meet God! I spent half of my time very nervous, because I knew Amma could see my mind and my soul. I spent the other half of my time crying. When I returned to my teaching job, some of the students asked me why I was so quiet, and why I was sitting up so straight!

Although I remained a Sai devotee for some years after meeting Amma, I continued to see Amma when she came to America. One time, I nervously joined the question line to ask Amma to tell me what my greatest faults were. I wanted to know my faults so I could correct them, and I knew Amma could help me. When Amma heard my question, she started talking. And she talked. And talked. On and on she talked. I was sure she was listing the mountain of my deficiencies. But no!

When the translation came, it turned out that Amma was saying what a huge effort it takes to get rid of negativities. Amma told several stories about this. She said I had to keep trying, just like when a toddler falls down and gets up again and again. All my fear dissolved into a feeling of self-acceptance. Self-acceptance is essential. Without it, we are too defensive and weak to witness the negativities in our mind. With self-love, we can learn to accept and sometimes even laugh at our weaknesses.

Which brings me to another question I asked Amma in those early years. At one Amma program in America, I had a good seat close to Amma. Then the person in front of me started rocking back and forth like the clock pendulum. I got really annoyed and irritated. Amma smiled mischievously and moved her head back and forth in a teasing way. I couldn't help thinking how weird the people acted around Amma. Still irritated, I later asked Amma about all the weird-acting people around her. "How can I cope with this," I asked? Amma answered, "Don't take yourself so seriously." What a perfect answer!

Lucky for me, over the years, I've had many opportunities to remember this precious advice. To quote Mark Twain, "Humor is mankind's greatest blessing," and so much funnier when the laugh is on us. It is also true, as Amma says, that "Just as you feel that the other person's ego is unbearable to you, your ego is just as unbearable to someone else."

At the November program in California one year, I did something foolish. It was embarrassing at the time, but later I laughed at myself. The snack shop was very busy; and, for some reason, I was not feeling any connection with Amma. I gave *prasād* during my short break and was very frustrated to be so close to Amma, but to feel no connection.

Then, the security man offered to let me open the car door for Amma. I was so excited. After receiving instructions, I thought to myself, "This can't be hard. Even an idiot can do this." Then, I proceeded secretly to practice opening the car door. I would find a private place, and then visualize the car in my mind, like a *mānasa pūjā*, and rehearse slowly opening the door for Amma. I practiced over and again, probably 50 times total.

Finally, it was time. Amma was to arrive. There I was, standing at the curb, nervously facing in the direction the car was coming. The car pulled over and stopped. Then I saw!! I was on the *wrong side of the door*! I had practiced the wrong way *50* times!! I quickly leaped to the other side of the door; but, to my horror, I saw Amma's hand on the door handle as she opened it herself. The security men had a good laugh. They were especially impressed by my leap.

Like a diamond, experiences with Amma have many facets. This simple task of opening a car door for Amma contained many lessons: Lesson one: Think and plan carefully before you act. Lesson two: See the humor in your mistakes. Yes, it is important to try to do things right; but when you mess up, try to let go of your ego and see the humor in the situation. Amma once said, "Seriousness is a disease." Lesson three: Amma is the doer, the opener of car doors, not me! Lesson four: If you don't feel connected to Amma, don't give up. Because, guess what? After the car-door experience, I suddenly felt very connected with Amma!

Over the years I have become more involved with Amma's organization. I have witnessed with wonder and gratitude all the projects that she has initiated. AIMS Hospital in Kochi has provided free medical care to more than three million patients. 45,000 homes for the homeless have been built throughout India. The Self-Reliant Village project has given tools to 101 villages for developing sustainability in areas such as health, education, and agriculture. The Empowering Women project provides vocational training and start-up capital to help 100,000 women start their own businesses.

When I go to AIMS for a checkup, I like to talk to the other patients. One time, I chatted with a young man whose father was getting a heart checkup. His father had undergone a major heart surgery at AIMS. The son warmly praised the heart surgeon, saying that the doctor was like a God to their family, because he was so full of love, meeting with the family often to ensure that everything was ok. Indeed, the doctor was a testimony to Amma's Love.

I am not directly involved with any of these projects. My *sēvā* here in Amṛtapuri allows me to be a small part of the much larger picture. When participating in Amma's activities, we are part of the whole, just one of Amma's thousands of children doing her service with Love. This is the path to Oneness, to Universal Love. It is our great good fortune that all of Amma's charities are designed and directed by Amma, herself, the Divine Embodiment of Compassion and Wisdom. When I remember my experiences in the Alaskan village, so many years ago, I am deeply grateful that Amma came into my life to save me and give me a glimpse of the power of Love. Where would any of us be without Amma?

In 1997, we were at the Chennai program. One evening, I thought, "I will come to Amma's *bhajans*, and then go to sleep." I knew that Amma likes people to stay up with her on these special program nights, but my sleep *vāsana* had overtaken my mind.

Then, a woman with a mental disorder was climbing over people and moving too close to Amma. I was invited to sit on the stage to prevent this woman from getting near Amma. I sat there thinking there was a wall behind me, and I leaned backwards. But *there was no wall*, only a curtain. As I tumbled backwards off the stage, I thought, "I am either dead or paralyzed." The back of the stage was at least 10 feet high. When I landed, it felt as if I landed on something very soft. I thought, "Oh, how lucky I am. I must have landed on a pile of cushions."

People came running to ask if I needed help, and was I alright? I was *so* embarrassed that I said, "Yes, I'm fine," and stood up on my own. I just wanted to hide somewhere. Others came running to me, saying, "Amma is looking for you! She wants you to come for *darśan*!" Feeling extremely embarrassed, I was escorted to Amma. She asked me, "Pain? Head ok?" I replied, "Yes, Amma, I'm fine," and that was really true. Except for a mild pain in the back of my neck, I really was fine. Amma gave me a beautiful hug, and then asked, "Stage sitting, or sleeping?" Amma was looking at me fiercely, which scared me. I knew that *she* knew I had planned to sleep right after *bhajans*. Feeling ashamed, I meekly replied, "Stage."

After I had made a spectacle of myself in front of 6,000 people, the last thing I wanted to do was sit on stage. So, I sat *near* the stage, relieved to be by myself. But somehow people found me. This time they escorted me to a seat right next to Amma, facing the crowd. Unfortunately, I did not enjoy this at all, because of my extreme embarrassment and shame.

The next day, I was talking to Janani, the āśram photographer. I told her how lucky that I had fallen on something soft and had only a slight pain in the back of my neck. Janani had seen my fall, and she showed me where I landed. I had fallen on a metal trunk, and my neck had hit the sharp edge of the trunk when I landed. When I saw the trunk and where my neck had hit the sharp edge, I realized Amma had saved me from serious injury or even death.

Amma says, "Children, only out of compassion does the *Guru* come down to walk with us. As we slowly walk behind him, we follow in the light of his grace. It is his grace which protects us and saves us from falling down. The *Guru's* grace helps us not to get lost in the darkness of narrow lanes and slip into dangerous pitfalls." (*Awaken Children*, 5 p.221)

Amma has rescued me many times. She has saved me from physical injury as well as mental and spiritual downfall. I struggle with my weaknesses, yet how can I possibly fathom the ways that Amma has lifted me out of my own darkness? How many lifetimes of accumulated mental dirt is Amma removing from me? I will never know, because it is beyond my comprehension. Only Amma knows.

Amma reduces our *prārabdha karma* when she can. When suffering is inevitable, we can turn to her for guidance and sustenance. It is essential for a spiritual aspirant to understand the principle of *karma*. In Amma's words, "Any action done with the right attitude, understanding and discrimination will take you closer to liberation. If, however, the same action is done without the right attitude, it will bind you. An action can either serve as a purifier, which will finally help you realize your godly nature, or it may add more and more to the already existing amount of negativity, which will eventually cause you tremendous suffering." (*Awaken Children* 8, p.74)

I am immensely grateful for all Amma does for us, for the planet and for all creatures. I feel especially blessed to give the *satsaṅg* today. Swāmī Jñānāmṛtānanda arranged this date not knowing it turns out that today (23 November), is the birthday of my first *Guru*, Sathya Sai Baba, who, I know, led me to Amma. It is also the birthday of my biological father, who taught me many good values. May Divine Love grow within us and may Amma bless us to keep her ever in our thoughts.

5

Both Compassion and Surrender

Dr. Kurunandan Jain (India)

Sanātana Dharma, (also called Hinduism), is unique. It may be the only religion that teaches the oneness of God and the universe (including man). God alone *is*. Pure consciousness, alone, is *all that is*. The ancient sages and the Hindu scriptures say God is *not* a separate entity, totally other and far away from us. God is our true nature, our inner Self.

Amma says, "God is not an individual who sits up above the clouds on a golden throne, judging—blessing only the good people and punishing everyone else. God is all-pervading consciousness, undivided and eternal presence. The good and bad we experience is due to our *karma*. It has nothing to do with God." My whole life and my being here today is thanks to Amma's infinite grace.

My journey with Amma began in 1989, *before* I was born. My father was experiencing a difficult time. On top of economic pressures, his relatives were pressuring him to have a son to lead the family in the future, even though they already had a daughter.

One day, my father's closest friend, Paul, told him about Amma, and they went to meet her. After his first *darśan*, my father felt his troubles melt away. He was sure he had reached the lap of the Divine. For the first time in years, he felt safe from the dangers of the world. Right in front of Amma, he told my sister, Revathi, "This is the Divine in a human form sitting here in front of you. Ask anything, and it shall be fulfilled."

Innocently, my sister said, "I want a baby brother." She could have asked for *mōkṣa*, but even adults ask Amma for trivial things, so we cannot blame a six-year-old child. Actually, most people are likely to waste their good fortune on indiscriminate desires. In *Bhagavad Gītā* 2:44, Lord Kṛṣṇa says, "There is no fixity of mind for those who cling to pleasure and power and whose discrimination is stolen away." After my sister announced she wanted a baby brother, Amma laughed, turned to my father, and said, "You want to have a son?" My father answered, "Yes."

My father did not tell Amma that the doctors had said it would be impossible for my mother to conceive another child, as there were too many complications with my sister's birth. We all know that Amma already knew this. Amma replied, "Don't worry my son, everything is possible in this life with sincere effort and grace."

My father returned home full of faith and good news. He knew Amma was sending him a son; so, immediately, he started buying boy's clothes and toys. My mother, after suffering alongside my father for so many years, was dubious. She said, "You are so gullible. You shouldn't buy into this prediction. If we are to have a child, it will be because of my prayers to *Mātā Durgā* and not because of Amma."

Lo and behold, within a few weeks, my mother was pregnant. The medical team in Ireland was in disbelief. Anyway, my mother gave birth to a healthy baby boy, which is me. Later that year, when Amma returned to the UK, my father, mother, sister, and I went to meet Amma.

Wanting my mother to form her own impression, my father left my mother and me alone waiting for Amma to arrive. When my mother first saw Amma, she was smitten, but could not understand why. Amma approached my mother and said, "My daughter, are you happy now that you have a son?"

Straight away my mother started crying with love for Amma. At that moment, she realised Amma was the divine mother, just as my father had already said many times. She had so much faith in Amma that, five years later, she didn't hesitate to ask Amma for another son. My parents visited Amma in Europe every year after that. One day, when I was five, my father and Paul took Amma's permission to cook food and snacks for everyone who came to the Europe tour programs. I travelled along with them.

We all know touring is not easy, but the early Europe tours were especially challenging. The whole kitchen was run by only a *handful* of people. Paul and my dad cut the vegetables, cooked the food, cleaned the pots, packed everything into a small van at the end of *Dēvī Bhāva darśan*, and then drove to the next destination! So many times, we had no place to sleep or even take a bath. More often than not, I travelled in a giant pot in the back of the van because some devotee was desperate for a ride to the next destination.

One program, in 1997, stands out because the only available accommodation was a barn. Without hesitating, my father and Paul slept there. I refused. I thought, "How can my dad and Paul expect me to sleep in a haystack? And no hot water for a bath the next morning?" And the horse stable next door stank! No thanks! I slept in the pot. Nobody forced my father and Paul to do their *sēvā* in such circumstances. Only their Punjabi culture and their love for Amma and *sēvā* motivated them.

The next day, my father and Paul unloaded the van. One by one, they took out every pan, utensil, and ingredient. Near the end, totally exhausted, they tried to lift an unusually heavy pot out of the van, and nearly dropped it. I had slept in that pot, convinced it would be more comfortable than sleeping on a haystack. My father and Paul really pushed themselves on those tours. Every day, without hesitation or complaint, they served Amma with complete surrender and faith. Every challenge created a new lesson, and they applied every lesson to improve the kitchen.

Things can get tough in the āśram and in the world. Sometimes, it is hard to find the will to persevere. At these times, I remember my parents and the countless other devotees who paved the way for us to be sitting with our Master today! I also remember that a difficult situation today can be a lesson for tomorrow. Remembering that I once slept in a pot means that I can sleep just about anywhere in the world. Except for a stinking horse stable.

When I was seven years old, I was shocked at the dedication of Amma's *sevites*. I said to Amma, "You always talk about the ultimate Truth, the ultimate goal. My father and his team do *sēvā* long hours every day, sometimes missing food and sleep. Is this the only way to achieve this goal?"

Amma laughed and said, "Son, Amma knows how hard they work, and Amma always tells them to delegate some tasks to others, but they are so enthusiastic that they do most of it themselves. Along with *sēvā*, however, you need to show compassion, *all the time*, no matter what. To do so, we need surrender to God. Then we can really say we are growing spiritually." These two qualities, compassion and acceptance (surrender) in every situation are the foundations of spiritual life. Amma often says, "The spiritual journey starts and ends with compassion."

When I first heard this answer, I thought, "This is easy. Amma is *Dēvī*, Amma is God. Why would I *not* surrender to God." But I really needed to work on compassion? Out of exhaustion, or lack of understanding, or even out of pure selfishness, how many times do we forget to show compassion to our brothers and sisters, or to our parents?

During my 10th standard, I was racially bullied by a peer for many months. Our school in the UK had only two Indians, out of roughly 1,000 kids. This made me a *minority*. At first, I thought, "Ok, he must be struggling with life too. Why else would he need to bully me? This is what Amma wants. There is a lesson here. I do not like this, but I cannot change him. I can only change *my* approach to the situation. I'll just take a longer route home. I'll stay back an extra hour after class. I'll start wearing headphones all the time to block out the chaos."

But, no matter what I did, this boy was always there, laughing in my face. I thought I only had two options:

1) I could fight back. But then what? What happens if *I* get hurt? Then I won't be able to write my exams. How would I explain that to Amma?

2) I could tell my teacher or the principal. But then I would be labelled a *snitch*. Then no one in school would trust me.

The solution wasn't obvious, but I would rather have one person hate me than the whole school, so I kept trying to push through. I prayed to Amma every day for strength to survive this, but the trauma was weighing on my mind.

My intuitive father knew something was wrong and asked me about it. I told him I was being bullied and I could no longer stand it. Within days, my dad had a restraining order put on this boy. At first, I was *so* happy. I would never see him again. However, I was still in pain. I forgot Amma's teachings of compassion. I wanted justice. Like Amma says, "Instead of forgetting the birds of the past, we allow them to build a nest and sit on top of our head."

Ironically, he came back into my life three years later. After the restraining order, his life took a terrible turn. Every store in our town banned him because he tried to steal groceries. He couldn't get a job and hadn't passed high school. Even though he was not allowed within 100 meters of my father's business, once he came into the shop anyway, begging my father to serve him. He pleaded, "I know I wronged your son, but help me. I cannot go anywhere. They say this is the only shop that will serve me."

My father was incredibly angry and even threatened to call the police. I was ecstatic! Finally, *karma* was coming back to him from all those months he bullied, teased, and beat me up. Heartlessly, I even thanked Amma for giving me justice. I felt like throwing him out into the cold rain. Then, I remembered Amma. I froze, stunned at my stupidity. I realised that by hurting him, I was perpetuating the cycle of violence and revenge. Throwing him into the street would not change the pain I had endured for months.

Amma gave me eyes of compassion. I was so disgusted with myself that I couldn't look in the mirror. Amma says, "We polish and beautify our body and the world outside, but our mind remains a mess. Do all this polishing and beautifying *inside*." Finally, I told my father to give him whatever he wanted, and not to charge him any money. After that, he regularly came to my father's business. In our community, people usually said, "I'm going to *Lavan's* shop." This boy always said with pride, "I'm going to *Kurunandan's* shop."

Amma says, "Anger cannot conquer anger; only love can conquer." As if to remind me of this, the moment I was about to get revenge, Amma "sent" me a message. She showed me the *asura* (demon) within and asked, "Son, is this the path you want to take? Revenge will not bring you happiness. Do you really want to continue this vicious cycle of suffering and bad *karma*?"

Remembering Amma brought me back to *dharma*. Amma says: "Earlier, the *dēvas* (gods) and *asuras* (demons) were in two different worlds. But, in the *trēta yuga*, they moved slightly closer to two different countries (in the *Rāmāyaṇa*). In *dwāpara yuga*, they came even closer. They were in the same family (in the *Mahābhārata*). Now, in *kali yuga*, they are both within each one of us.

Amma showed me two things in this situation. First, only by forgiving those who hurt me can I practice compassion and grow spiritually. Second, how easy it is to sacrifice my spiritual progress to my inner demons (negative tendencies). Amma is always trying to help us reach our full potential. In these situations, she shows us our demons. She holds up a mirror and gives us the opportunity to choose the right path. This is why we chant:

Ōm asatō mā sad-gamaya
tamasō mā jyōtir-gamaya
mṛtyōr mā amṛtam gamaya
Ōm śāntiḥ śāntiḥ śāntiḥ

Om lead us from untruth to truth,
From darkness to light,
From death to immortality.
Om peace peace peace.

We pray that our Master takes us from our demons (darkness) into light, so that we can walk the righteous path. I understood that the surrender that seemed so easy was actually fragile, and I needed to protect it vigilantly.

When I was 11 years old, I was sitting in the *darśan* line. From 20 meters (66 feet) away, Amma's eyes locked onto me. It was not the smile we all long for; it was the smile Amma shows when she is cooking up something. I instantly looked away and tried to hide behind my little brother and my elder sister.

When we reached Amma, she smiled and said, "Son, you have to study!" My jaw dropped, and my whole family started laughing along with other devotees near us. I was only 11 years old. What was there to study? All I wanted to study was TV shows and video games. I protested, "Amma I want to be a professional video gamer. What is the use of studies? I don't need to know geography or Roman history. I just need to know how to play video games."

Amma was not impressed. She looked stern and firm. Her eyes bored into mine, and she said, "No! You need to study. Nothing else!" I tried to barter with Amma and said, "How about 50-50?" Amma said, "Ok half and half." I tried, but my version of "half and half" was 99% video games and 1% studying. I did not value or obey Amma's instruction because I didn't appreciate the importance of studying.

Six years later, Amma's warning caught up with me when I performed so poorly in my 11th standard. It would not have mattered if I scored 100% in 12th standard, I was *not* getting into college. I had only two options.

1. Repeat 11th standard.
2. Study 11th and 12th standard at the same time.

I also had to apply for colleges. I realised that being a professional video gamer was a stupid idea. I should have studied the Romans because my empire was falling. I emailed Swāmī Rāmakṛṣṇānandajī to ask Amma what I should study in college. The next day I received a one-line response from Amma: "He didn't listen to me before, why will he listen to me now?"

Instantly, I knew what Amma meant—what was I *doing* the last six years? I dropped all my hobbies, switched off my mobile phone, and handed all my video game consoles to my parents and my little brother. (He had self-control).

I had to complete two years of content in one year. With hard work, lots of diet coke, and Amma's grace, I got college offers based just on my test results! Amma was right when she told my dad years earlier, "Anything is possible with sincere effort and divine grace!" I really enjoyed my bachelor's in mathematics, and even appreciated the benefits of studying.

By the end of my studies, I started thinking just like my peers: "I really need to get a job. I can't study anymore. I want to travel the world." I applied for jobs in banks in London, and actually got hired in a few of them. I decided to tell Amma I had a job. When I approached Amma's chair, before I could open my mouth,

Amma said, "Do a Masters." I had learnt the consequences of not listening to Amma, so I obeyed. The following year, she said, "Do a PhD!" I had only just started my masters, and now I had to apply for PhD!

By Amma's Grace, my bachelors and masters were straight forward. The PhD was not. I finally understood why everyone called a PhD "Permanent head Damage". Every research idea I had was blocked while my peers were moving forward. In those years, anytime I saw Amma I just wanted to cry, and quit my PhD. But Amma always gave me the most beautiful *darśan* and restored my vitality, and I would think, "Let's try again."

By the final year of my PhD, I had plenty of theoretical mathematic equations but no proofs. I was miserable. My parents never saw me smile, and I was so upset with Amma I didn't even want to see her. On the last night of the London program in 2015, my parents told Amma about my struggles, and Amma called me. She listened carefully, then took my hand and said, "Anyway, when you finish the PhD, you'll come to Amṛtapuri and teach at the university." Amma smiled reassuringly. I said, "Yes!" instantly. Later, I thought, "Wait! What did I just agree to? I never wanted to study, and now I am going to *teach* mathematics!?"

My parents were extremely excited for me and told everyone on the tour staff that I was moving to the āśram. Meanwhile, I kept thinking, "I am so far from finishing this PhD, I need Amma's grace now more than ever." When I told my parents my doubts, my father said, "But son, don`t you remember? Amma said '*When* you finish.' That means you *will* finish. Just stay strong and have faith."

These words and realizing that Amma was with me and wanted me to finish, must have triggered something. The very next day, while I was teaching, I worked through a theory and application of a particular concept. It just dawned on me, like when Archimedes sat in the bathtub—Eureka! I had the solution! After class, I ran to my office and implemented this simple idea which even undergraduate students know, but I had forgotten. In less than an hour, Amma solved everything I'd struggled with for three years.

After submitting the draft, I took a long overdue vacation with friends to Japan. I really wanted to thank Amma and get my dissertation blessed before submission; but I had spent all my money pre-booking this vacation, and Amma was going to be in the US. One day, my father called and said, "Tomorrow is *Guru Pūrṇimā* and *Amma is in Tokyo.* You should go and get her blessing for yourself and the family."

When I showed Amma my PhD, she smiled and blessed it and reminded me again to come to the āśram. Since that day, I never miss *Guru Pūrṇimā*. When I finally arrived in Amṛtapuri six months later, I felt a blessed shift in my energy. I had asked Amma 20 years before in Switzerland: "Amma, can I move to Amṛtapuri?" Then, Amma laughed and said: "Son there isn't enough food for you in the āśram. If you come there, the rest of my children will starve."

I had forgotten I asked this question, but Amma never did. She heard me and kept me waiting for *twenty years*! Through all those difficult situations, I began to learn the values of surrender, compassion, and discipline. All of which allow me to be sitting in front of you today.

Of course, that is not all she did. Amma adjusted my appetite, so there is still more than enough food to go around. And doing all of Amma's tours lets me travel the world, just as I always wanted. My video game *vāsana* remains; but thanks to Amma's grace, I can participate in virtual projects here in the āśram.

One of my earliest memories of Amma is of walking in the airport, holding my father's hand, and Amma grabbing my other hand. I tried to pull away from Amma, but her grip was so strong that I let go of my father's hand instead. Amma said, "Do you think you're stronger than me? I've got hold of you, and I am never letting you go." Despite my *vāsanas*, she has never let me go. Amma never lets any of us go. She tells us repeatedly that, no matter how long it takes, she will return to this world to ensure that we all cross the ocean of birth and death.

6

Fearless, Equanimous, Dear to the Lord

Meenamba Hass (United States)

When I was eight years old, I jumped out of a tree and bit my tongue. It bled a lot and hurt a lot. Despite that experience, I am not afraid of my teeth. Why is that? It is because my teeth are part of my own body. So, there is no reason to be afraid.

Amma experiences everything in creation as the ultimate Truth of her oneness with the *atman*. She sees nothing as separate from her own Self. Therefore, Amma is completely fearless. She explains this using the example of animal-shaped biscuits. She says,

> Will the rabbit-shaped biscuit be afraid that of the tiger-shaped biscuit? Will the tiger biscuit kill the rabbit biscuit and eat it up? Of course not, because, basically, there is no difference between them. The different shapes come from exactly the same ingredients. It is the same once you know that your true nature is the *atman*. (*Awaken Children 7* p.24).

I am so impressed with Amma's little children, both Indian and western. When they explain ślōkas from the *Gītā*, they speak so clearly, boldly and eloquently, using examples from their own lives and Amma's words. They show us that Śrī*mad Bhagavad Gītā* is a scripture that is truly accessible to all. They inspired me to choose a *Gītā* ślōka for this talk.

In the *Bhagavad Gītā* 12:15, Śrī Kṛṣṇa says the qualities of fearlessness, freedom from elation, and freedom from non-forbearance are the characteristics that make a devotee most dear to the Lord.

> *yasmān nōdvijate lōkō*
> *lōkān nōdvijatē ca yaḥ*
> *harṣāmarṣa-bhayōdvēgair*
> *muktō yaḥ sa ca mē priyaḥ*
>
> One whom the world does not fear,
> and one who does not fear the world.
> One who is equipoised in happiness and distress,
> fear and anxiety,
> that devotee of Mine is dear to Me.

The ideal devotee will not cause fear in others. If we are fearless, but we make other people feel afraid, their fear will come back to us through the law of *karma*. So, true freedom from fear means we have to be benevolent in our actions and not cause others to fear.

Before I joined the āśram, I thought I was a harmless person. However, after coming to Amṛtapuri, I discovered a "bully" within. Amma says that the *Guru* creates circumstances to reveal our hidden negative qualities and remove them. It's like when I went to the dentist as a child. The hygienist would give me a red tablet to chew to color the plaque patches on my teeth so she could easily see them and scrape them off. That's what Amma does with our weaknesses. When my weaknesses come out, if I openly admit my mistakes to Amma, she can redeem the whole situation.

My first *sēvā* in the āśram was in Ram's Bazaar (the second-hand shop). The first year and a half went smoothly. I worked very well with another *sevite* processing and pricing the donations. Then, in February 2006, with Amma's permission, I went to the U.S. to work for six months to pay back my student loans from graduate school.

When I returned to the āśram, I resumed my *sēvā* in Ram's Bazaar, but my trusted *sēvā* partner was gone. Nothing was where I thought it should be. Items were not priced the way I would have priced them. The items in the shop should have been in storage, and the items in storage should have been in the shop. *In my opinion*. And I was *very* vocal about my opinions.

The other *sevites* disagreed with me which triggered a power struggle. Looking back now, I could have practiced not causing fear. I could have compromised and brought harmony to the situation. Instead, I kept trying to force my agenda.

Tensions kept rising until, one day, a *sevite* got fed up with me and stepped in the middle of an argument between me another *sevite*. I told her to mind her own business. She said, "You listen to me!" and she grabbed my arms and backed me into the donation closet. Before I realized it, I pushed her off of me and, "Whack!" I hit her. Instantly, I felt terrible and regretted my action. By Amma's grace, she was not injured; but I knew what I did was wrong.

When Amma returned from her Europe tour, I immediately went for *darśan* and anxiously told Amma everything. Amma asked, "Who did you hit?" I said I didn't know her name. Amma asked her country. "Denmark," I answered. With a pensive look, Amma said, "Oh... Danish." Then Amma lovingly placed her hand on my cheek and said, "Don't worry!" I was so relieved.

Right after that, I saw the *sevite* I had hit. I hadn't seen her since that fateful day. I know that seeing her just then was Amma's blessing. This was my chance to seek forgiveness. "I'm so sorry, please forgive me," I said to her. She said, "I'm the one who should apologize. I never should have grabbed you like that." In that small exchange, all fear vanished, leaving only compassion and mutual understanding. Amma's grace redeemed the situation.

The weaknesses that we work on under Amma's guidance are often issues that will not resolve overnight. Just like plaque, once removed, builds up again, I have had to face my bullying tendency over and over again. But Amma, like a patient hygienist, keeps scraping away at it. I have started to take more precautions that greatly help me keep my inner bully in check.

The second point in the ślōka means that the ideal devotee of the Lord does not fear the world. The true devotee has taken refuge in the Lord and has full faith that the Lord will protect him and provide everything he needs. So, what is there to fear?

Amma says, "My children, once we take refuge in God, there is nothing to fear. God will look after everything." If, as spiritual aspirants, we are *not* free from fear, that indicates that *something* is keeping us from taking full refuge in God or *Guru*. Perhaps, unknowingly, we are still depending on objects, people and situations around us for support.

Amma tells a story. Śrī Kṛṣṇa and Arjuna were travelling in disguise. They stopped at a rich man's house for alms. The rich man refused to give them even a glass of water. After leaving the house, Śrī Kṛṣṇa uttered a blessing, saying, "May his wealth and prosperity increase."

They continued on and stopped at the humble cottage of a devotee of the Lord. He had only one valuable possession, a cow. The devotee received the weary travelers with kindness and fed them. After they left, Śrī Kṛṣṇa declared, "May my devotee's cow die," and, the cow fell down dead.

Arjuna was confused and asked Śrī Kṛṣṇa why he blessed the wicked man with wealth, and cursed the kind, sincere devotee by taking away his only source of livelihood. The Lord explained, "The rich man is not spiritually ripe. I blessed him with riches so that he will get more ensnared in *māya* and learn the lessons he has yet to learn. The devotee, however, had only one attachment left—his cow. Removing that, he has taken full refuge in Me."

> *(Here, Amma explained that householders should not be afraid that the Lord will take everything away from them. The story is a teaching in surrender for spiritual aspirants. The Lord gave so much to Sudāmā when he offered the Lord a handful of flattened rice. No one should misunderstand this story).*

Five years ago, when Amma was away on her Europe tour, I felt like *my* "cow" suddenly fell down dead. The āśram was snatched away from me quite unexpectedly. I was informed that my visa extension request had been denied, and I had seven days to leave India or risk deportation.

This was a total shock. Everyone who had applied for such an extension in the past had always been approved. The government policy had suddenly changed, so people from my country were no longer eligible to hold such visas. To make matters worse, I had almost no money because what I earned when I was working in the U.S. went to pay back my student loans. I had a credit card, but when I went to use it, I discovered that the account had been closed due to inactivity.

A month before, my parents had offered to buy me a plane ticket. I told them, "Thank you, but I'm not able to travel now because I am applying for a visa extension." When the extension was denied, I could have accepted their offer, but I didn't want to. They are loving towards me, and generous, but they did not support my spiritual life at all. In their opinion, by joining the āśram, I had thrown away a good education and a good job and was running away from my responsibilities. So, I felt that accepting their financial help would confirm their negative idea about me and spirituality.

That night, I had intense anxiety. When I finally did sleep, I had one nightmare that I was dying, another nightmare that I was sent to prison, and another nightmare that I was deported. With each nightmare, I woke up in a panic, my heart racing, until I realized I was still alive and still in the āśram. I resorted to pacing back and forth in the hallway and chanting my *mantra* until *arcana* time.

Clearly, unlike the devotee who is most dear to the Lord, I was *not* free from fear. I had counted on staying in the āśram for five more years. I had also counted on using my credit card. When this didn't happen, I panicked. The next night, a *brahmacāriṇī* sister started singing the *bhajan:*

pizhayentu ceytu nyan ammē
ezhayām nin makaḷ pizhayentu ceytu

Oh Mother, what error have I committed?
What error has Thy poor child committed?

Hearing these lyrics, I broke down sobbing. I felt so vulnerable, scared and abandoned, like I was free-falling without a parachute. I prayed to Amma with all my heart. "Amma please save me! Am I not your child? Whatever I did wrong, please forgive me. Don't abandon me, Amma! Don't abandon me now. I really need your help."

Slowly, my fear started subsiding, and I was able to see Amma's grace in the unfolding circumstances. I realized that it was not a coincidence that my parents had offered me a plane ticket a month before. I summoned my courage, phoned them, explained the situation, and asked them to pay for my ticket. Though they were quite surprised to hear from me, they readily agreed.

I also learned that Amma would be in Detroit, Michigan the day I was to arrive. One of my renunciate sisters gifted me the ticket for that flight without my asking, one of many acts of kindness showered on me by members of this community, both Indian and western, when they heard about my difficulties. I'm so grateful to Amma for this community.

I arrived in Michigan, just at the end of the morning program. By Amma's Grace, my renunciate sisters on the tour cleared the way so that I could go straight for *darśan*. In the *darśan*, I poured my heart out to Amma. Amma wiped my tears with her own hands. After *darśan*, Rasya, my childhood friend, introduced me to some devotees from the town where my parents live. They not only offered me a ride to my parent's house but offered me a job in one of their coffee shops. I accepted their offer.

When my parents saw me working hard to earn money and taking responsibility for my situation, their attitude toward me started changing. Just before I returned to the āśram, to my utter surprise, my father said to me, "It's a good thing you have Amma. She really helps people." This totally unexpected blessing would not have happened if I had not had to leave India. Amma proved through this experience that, once we take refuge in Amma, there is nothing to fear. Amma will take care of everything, and much more effectively than we could ever imagine.

The next point in the ślōka is that a true devotee of the Lord is free from "elation". It is easy to see how fear is a big obstacle to a spiritual seeker, but what is wrong with elation? Doesn't the Lord *want* us to be *happy*?

First of all, we need to understand what elation is, and how we come to experience it. In Swāmī Rāmakṛṣṇānanda Puri's book *Amritashtakam: A Vedantic Inquiry into Supreme Devotion*, Swāmī explains that *harṣā* is "extreme elation *upon the attainment of an object.*"

Desire for an object creates waves in the mind resulting in agitation. When we get the desired object, the waves in the mind subside, and the mind becomes still. In that stillness, the bliss of the Self appears, and we experience elation or euphoria. We mistakenly think this elation comes from the object attained. In reality, it is from the Bliss of the Self.

Amma gives the example of a dog chewing a bone: "When a dog gets a bone, he chews it and thinks the blood he tastes comes from the bone. He doesn't know he is tasting his *own* blood oozing from its *own* injured gums." (*For My Childr*en p.108) The elation doesn't last. Soon, another desire arises, and agitates the mind. Elation never satisfies us. It keeps promising happiness, but it never delivers. Elation is no substitute for the infinite Bliss of the Self we are really seeking. This makes me think of my sister.

My sister suffers from bipolar disorder, a chemical imbalance in the brain. We didn't know this until she was in her mid-30's. Starting at the age of 15, she constantly struggled with alcohol and drug abuse. We assumed *that* was her problem.

My family now realizes, that, all along, my sister was bipolar, and was using drugs and alcohol as a substitute for proper psychiatric medication. Once she got the correct diagnosis and medication for her illness, her addiction to alcohol and drugs fell away. She had the right medicine, so she didn't need the substitute.

Amma is the doctor who can give us the real medicine—the uninterrupted Bliss of the Self. We have settled for the substitute for so long, seeking elation (happiness) from external objects. Amma is ready to make the diagnosis and give us the proper prescription; but we must admit we have a problem and go for Amma's treatment. We must do *sādhana* according to Amma's instructions and make efforts to overcome our ego and negativities. Only then will Amma's grace flow, and the cure be complete.

Shortly after I brought my sister's photo to Amma and explained that she was homeless due to mental illness, she finally received the proper diagnosis and treatment. And incredibly, later, my sister told me her social worker has Amma's photo as his screen saver. I couldn't believe it...the social worker at the homeless shelter is Amma's devotee!

The final point of the ślōka is freedom from lack of forbearance. Lack of forbearance gets triggered when a situation is uncomfortable for us physically, mentally or emotionally. It's a kind of restlessness, or desperation that makes us feel, "I can't take this anymore." Śrī Kṛṣṇa says that a devotee, who is most dear to the Lord, will not give in to that impulse, but rather patiently endure the situation.

In extreme cases, lack of forbearance in difficult situations can even lead to suicide. Amma has been talking so much lately about never giving in to despair. Amma says, "Children, realize that suicide is not a solution. Even if you *feel* suicidal, turn away from it." (*The Stream of Eternity* p.75) I can say, from my own personal experience, that suicide is not the answer.

When I was 16 years old, I felt so lost and confused and sad that I decided I didn't want to live any more. I took a bottle of my mother's prescription backpain medication and swallowed all the pills. Then I went to bed thinking I would die in my sleep.

I didn't know Amma then, but I know that what happened was Amma's Divine intervention. My mother was angry at me and came knocking on my door, insisting that I take a shower. (She was very strict about us taking a shower every night before we went to sleep.) When I didn't answer, she burst into my room, dragged me out of bed, and led me to the bathroom.

And as soon as the water hit me, I thought, "What have I done? I don't want to die!" I quickly vomited up as much of the medication as I could. By Amma's Grace, I survived, and am sitting here in front of you, today, in Amma's divine presence.

Later, I saw an interview with a man who had tried to commit suicide by jumping off the Golden Gate Bridge. He fell 67 meters into the San Francisco Bay, and miraculously survived. Once he jumped off the bridge and was in the air, he realized, just like me, that he did not want to die. Hearing him tell his story openly, to the public, inspired me to share my story with others as well, and hopefully help people avoid choosing suicide.

In one of my room *darśans*, I told Amma about my suicide attempt, and some other difficult events from my youth. Amma told me to be grateful for all the experiences of my life. I wasn't expecting that. If it had come from anyone else, I would have said, "Yeah right, easy for *you* to say..." But since Amma said it, I started trying to be grateful for those painful events.

Soon, I realized that, because I have suffered, I have compassion for those who suffer. Also, I must have exhausted a lot of *karma* through those experiences. Lastly, I think, if I hadn't gone through that, I might never have looked for Amma. That pain brought me to Amma, and I am grateful beyond words.

It was shortly after I took those pills that I first saw Amma's photo on the wall of my friend Rasya's room, and I asked who that was. In the photo, Amma was standing somewhere here in the āśram, with her white sari draped over her head. The photo was black and white, and so I thought it was very old. I was surprised when Rasya told me that Amma was a saint from India, and that she had even come to her house. *A living Saint*—that was a completely new concept.

In July 1990, Rasya's mother brought me to Amma's Chicago program. We went to greet Amma at O'Hare airport. In those days, people could gather at the gate to meet the passengers coming off the plane. All of the other passengers came out first. Then, suddenly, an intense smell of roses pervaded the air, just before Amma appeared physically.

Right away, I knew Amma was very special—the way she moved and glanced at us. The way she was completely at ease, approaching each and every person and hugging them. It was so unique, and yet strangely familiar. When Amma came to hug me, I felt awkward at first, because I towered over her. Amma just pulled me down to her shoulder without any hesitation, and my awkwardness melted away.

It's difficult to talk about my relationship with Amma. Where my heart connects with Amma is beyond my comprehension. I only know that it is the truest and most constant element in my life, and it has never not existed.

For the first 12 years after meeting Amma I only saw her twice a year, at most. Imagine my surprise then, when, during my first *Vedic* astrology reading, the astrologer said, "Don't be surprised if you become disillusioned with the world and go to stay long-term in Amma's āśram." I didn't believe him. I completed my education as a Science and Biology teacher, then I taught in an alternative public high school in New York City.

On the second morning of my fourth year of teaching, some students rushed into the classroom and reported that a plane had hit the World Trade Center. The date was September 11, 2001. My school was less than a kilometer away from the Trade Towers, and I watched what was happening from the window of one of the classrooms.

Witnessing an event that snuffed out the lives of 2,606 people changed me forever. I reorganized my priorities and started putting God/*Guru* first. I stopped socializing with non-devotee friends and spent my free time attending Amma's various *satsaṅg* groups in New York. I also became more serious about my *sādhana*. Facing death is useful for a spiritual aspirant. It makes you stop wasting time.

Soon, I booked a trip to Amṛtapuri. I stayed only three weeks, but it marked the beginning of a process which led to my joining the āśram in August 2004. Thus, the astrologer's prediction nine years before came true. I would like to end this talk with a few lines of a song I wrote:

> Amma, you are here with me, always here with me.
> Across all time and space, in every circumstance,
> You are my saving Grace, always holding my hand.
> You are the only one who never ever leaves my side

7

Abundance of Grace

Gautam Harvey (United States)

It was a fine, summer day in 1998 the first time I ever wore all white. Almost everyone around me was also dressed in white. Many were chanting or praying. Suddenly, a hush fell. A single rocket was fired into the sky, and everyone took off running. I and a few other first-timers didn't know why everyone was running. A few moments later, a second rocket went off, and then the ground began to tremble and shake. We saw why everyone had run.

No. Rockets hadn't signaled the start of *darśan*-token distribution. Nor was Amma's car arriving in front of the San Ramon *darśan* hall. I was staring down a narrow, cobblestone street at a herd of very big bulls stampeding towards me. Terrified, I ran for my life. A few minutes later, after dodging a few bull horns, I was safe. It was San Fermín in Pamplona, Spain—the world-famous Running of the Bulls.

Buzzing with adrenaline and thankful to be alive, all I wanted was to call my Mom. A herd of charging bulls can erase a fool's bravado. Like a small child, I knew that Mother meant safety.

Little did I know then that the Divine Mother would soon answer my call.

Growing up in the West, I had everything material, including a great education, but I was a spiritual illiterate. Like the bulls, I chased wildly after the objects of the world. Even though I didn't know what a spiritual teacher was, or that I needed one, the greatest one in all history found me.

Not long after the bulls, I received a postcard from my best friend. He told me he had just received a hug from an Indian mystic named "Amma." That was an odd thing to write to me about, so, I called him. He told me Amma was soon coming to a small town (Estella) just half an hour from Pamplona, and I could get a hug too. My running with the bulls had actually been just a detour on the ancient pilgrimage route called El Camino de Santiago that crosses the entire north of Spain. I was just a hiker having fun, not a pilgrim.

I arrived in Estella a few days before Amma. Posters advertising her visit hung around town. I even went to see the small hall where Amma would have her program. But did I really want to hang around this tiny, boring village just for a hug? *Vēṇḍa*! I was after excitement. I wasn't ready to be a pilgrim. I needed more time with *Mahiṣāsura* before I met *Mahiṣāsura-mardinī*! I decided to skip the hug. Fortunately, though, four months later, I met Amma in San Ramon, in November 1998. *Then* I became a pilgrim.

Before meeting Amma, I was an elementary-school teacher. It's a beautiful, incredibly rewarding profession. You spend several hours a day with your young, impressionable students. You are their role model and their source of information. It can be great fun, but it is incredibly challenging, and a big responsibility. You have to know each individual student. For some, learning will be easy, for some impossible, and everything in between. Some students learn better by hearing a lesson; some by seeing it demonstrated; and others have to try it for themselves.

Now, imagine your class is *millions* of students, all different ages, all speaking different languages. Some are kindergarteners, some are PhD's; but *ALL* of them have special needs! Impossible job, right?

This is our Amma. We are blessed to sit in her classroom. She has an individual lesson plan for each of us, and patiently listens to all our silly problems. She teaches us every imaginable subject. She is the classroom teacher, the physical trainer, the coach, the janitor (cleaner), the social worker, the psychologist, the nurse, the cafeteria manager, and, of course, the principal. She even built the school, converting a remote coastal village into an international pilgrimage center, the holiest place on earth. Her school has classrooms all over the world. If you are watching this live online, you know she also teaches via remote learning.

As a teacher, I realized that anyone can teach 1+2 or the alphabet; but, a REAL teacher, like Amma, inspires us to find knowledge and power within, and gives us the self-confidence for that knowledge to blossom. When we sign up for her class, she guarantees an education perfectly tailored to our needs. And Amma promises that we will all definitely graduate. 100% of us will get *moksha* (liberation). An ordinary spiritual teacher may be like a small canoe that can take a few people across the ocean of *samsāra*; but Amma is like an ocean-liner that ferries countless numbers of people across. Her energy and inspiration are infinite.

One of my favorite parts of teaching was class fieldtrips. It was always a bit scary taking the kids out of the safety and familiarity of the classroom. But there are important lessons you can only learn outside the classroom. Amma also loves fieldtrips! She has spent much of the last 40 years on fieldtrips around the world, just to reach and teach her children. I have been blessed to accompany Amma for the last 20+ years. Her visit to South America remains the most memorable for me.

One year, I travelled to Chile, before Amma, to help the local devotees prepare. It was Amma's first trip to South America, and only a handful of the local people had even met Amma. The volunteers innocently asked, "What is *darśan*?" "What is *prasād*?" Most of them had seen the videos but had never received *darśan*.

The programs in South America followed the two-month North American tour. After *Dēvī Bhāva*, Amma flew 12 hours from Toronto to Santiago, Chile. She went directly from the airport to meet the President of Chile. Then she began the *darśan* marathon.

Even before Amma arrived on the first morning, thousands of people were queued around the parking lot. For the next three days, Amma gave almost nonstop *darśan* from 10:00am to 6:00pm, and from 6:30pm to 6:00am the following morning, with only a 45-minute break. The hotel staff watched Amma come and soon return to the program. They were sure there had to be *two* Ammas — one for the daytime and one for the evening. They simply could not believe there was only *one* Amma. The programs in Chile shattered all turn-out records for a program outside of India.

After Chile, Amma flew to Brazil for three more days. After those programs, Amma had a few hours in her hotel room before the flight from Brazil back to India. She met the local coordinators to tell them how much she appreciated their efforts. When everyone was leaving to the airport, I turned back and saw Amma, on her hands and knees, *scrubbing* a spot on the hotel's carpet. Swāminī Śrī Lakṣmi Prāṇā and I tried to convince Amma it wasn't necessary, and that the stain was likely already there before Amma came to the room. But our Amma insisted. She explained that we should leave the room *cleaner* than we found it and try to make the cleaners' job easier.

Amma had just finished two months of foreign tours and *must* have been physically exhausted. Still, she compassionately helped the cleaners who wouldn't even know she had done it. *This* is *selfless* service. Amma was teaching us how to put others before ourselves. Just imagine if we all practiced this lesson — putting others' needs before our own, in practical, hidden ways, leaving things better than we found them. How often do we miss such opportunities?

Despite our constant failures to practice the lessons she teaches us, Amma waits for us patiently. She repeats the same lessons, over and over, until we get them. I can share an example of Amma waiting patiently for 20 years for me to learn a single lesson. And then she waited another 15+ years before she tested me on my progress.

When I was three years old, my sister was born with cerebral palsy. She was dependent on others for everything, even her most basic needs like bathing and dressing herself. She was always childlike, but I never saw the beauty of that. For me, she was just a burden. I had been the spoiled only son. My sister's complicated condition disrupted that, and I resented her for that and for making my family sad. I was always embarrassed, ashamed, and angry that I had to endure her in my life. She was extremely innocent and loving, but I never accepted her and was incapable of loving her.

When I first met Amma, I sat for hours in awe at how loving she was with everyone. And I paid special attention to how Amma showered *extra* love and attention on people like my sister, who had disabilities. How was Amma able to love them and shower so much affection on strangers when I couldn't do that with my own flesh-and-blood sister? Like everything Amma does, the contrast was a mirror. How could I watch and admire Amma giving such love, and not try to emulate that in my own life.

Still, I couldn't just flip a switch and change how I had acted for 20 years. The second time I met Amma, I decided to ask her a question: "What role does my sister play in my life?" Amma replied, "You were also like that in a past life. Now you should try to see the world through her eyes."

That one sentence completely changed my perspective. I began to see my sister with new eyes. I imagined living in her skin and experiencing the world as she did. I was amazed how much my attitude changed, and how I could understand her and relate to her in a totally new way. With just a few words, Amma radically transformed this most difficult and painful relationship in a way I never thought possible.

When Amma said, "You were also like that," was she really saying that I had cerebral palsy in a past life? It's possible. But more importantly, Amma was reminding me of the essential oneness of all beings. How, if we want to be true human beings, we have to recognize, that the *Being* inside all of us is one and the same. We have to strive to see others' pain as our own pain, to see others' happiness as our own happiness. I had asked Amma what my *sister's* role was in *my* life. Amma reminded me what *my* role is in *all* people's lives: I should love and serve them, seeing them as my own self.

As Amma says:

> If the left hand is injured, does the right hand say, 'Oh, that's the left hand; it has nothing to do with me?' No, the right hand immediately presses and soothes the left hand and applies medicine if needed. This is because it does not see the left hand as different from itself. If we have true spiritual understanding, this is how we will respond to the suffering of all beings.

That was part one of Amma's lesson. Fast forward 15 years. Every year, I go to the US early to prepare for the tour and spend time with my family. While not devotees, my parents and sister had all been for Amma's *darśan*, but it had been quite a while since they last saw Amma. Usually, when I visit them, Amma is not discussed much; but this year my sister was constantly telling me she wanted to see Amma again. This quite surprised me.

When I flew to Seattle to begin the tour, I told this to Amma. She seemed more excited than I was. She said I should definitely bring my sister to the program. A few weeks later, I brought my sister to see Amma in Los Angeles. Most of my friends here in the āśram and on tour knew I had a sister but had never met her. So, when I brought her to see Amma, she had semi-celebrity status, and everyone wanted to talk to her.

My sister was probably the most open and friendly person I have ever known. She was thrilled at all the attention. When it was almost her turn for *darśan*, I became a bit nervous that Amma might scrutinize my heart to see how much I had changed towards her over all the years. I had had 15 years to prepare for this test.

When they saw each other, they were both so excited that no introduction was needed. After a long *darśan*, Amma asked my sister to sit beside her. Then they proceeded to "chat" for the next 45 minutes! Amma asked my sister if she liked to sing. My sister loved music and was always singing, but no one had ever told that to Amma. I assumed this was just a general question, but Amma actually saw my sister's innocence and asked her to sing a few songs right then and there.

So, with no shame in her game, my sister told Amma she would be happy to sing. Amma asked Swāmī Amṛtātmānanda to pause his *bhajan* session. Then, my sister sang three songs standing next to Amma. First, a Broadway showtune: "Memories" from the musical, *Cats.* Second, a Christmas carol, "Silent night," and one more, similar to those two, that I can't remember. Everyone in the hall stopped what they were doing to listen. I felt as if all eyes were on me, as if Amma turned a blazing spotlight of love on me to burn away any last traces of shame or embarrassment I still had.

After my sister finished her mini concert, to a huge applause from everyone, things quieted down on stage. My sister looked around and saw everyone meditating and said, "This is a quiet place, isn't it?" To which I replied "Yes." She then asked me if she should be quiet. I replied, "Yes." Amma looked at me and asked me what my sister had said and what I told my sister. When

Amma heard that I had asked her to be quiet, she turned to my sister and said, "No, no, please keep talking."

I was confused, but immediately Amma turned to me and said, "Whenever someone with so much innocence speaks, every word that comes out of their mouth is like a *mantra*." Those words sank deep into my heart. In a flash, I remembered all the times over the years when I had lost my patience with my sister and had asked her to be quiet.

Suddenly, Amma asked my sister if she wanted to come to Amṛtapuri. Because of her condition, I had never imagined my sister coming to the āśram. In fact, I had always been afraid about what would happen after our parents were no more. Would I have to leave the āśram to take care of her? I had never expressed this to anyone. After my sister said she would love to come visit Amṛtapuri, Amma turned to me and said, "Don't worry. In the future I can bring her to the āśram, and there will be so many people ready to lovingly take care of her."

Every teacher knows a pop quiz is one of the best methods to test where your students are. They won't know it's coming or have time to prepare, so their performance will genuinely reflect how much they have absorbed their lessons. Amma *loves* pop quizzes. All of Amma's lessons prepare us for the final exam that no one escapes—the day when we die. Will we be ready to take that exam with a smile?

On January 1, 2013, I thought I was preparing for another North India Tour. But Amma gave me a pop quiz that showed me how unprepared I was for my future final exam. The night before departure, I was finalizing preparations for several hundred people from all over the world who would be accompanying

Amma. I was hanging passenger lists inside the front windshield of the 13 buses so people could find their seats.

It was pretty easy since all the buses seemed to be parked just outside the café gate. We had a good system. I climbed up to reach into the drivers' side window and press the button to unlock the door on the passenger side of the bus. Then my fellow coordinator would go inside and hang the list.

The last bus was parked out on the Beach Road next to the āśram. To not block traffic, the bus was parked almost flush with the cement wall of the Ayurveda building. I was ready to be finished and hopefully run to my room for a few hours' sleep before embarking on the next day's long bus ride. My pop quiz was about to start.

Since the bus was parked so close to the wall, I had to squeeze between the wall and the bus to reach the driver's window to press the button to open the door. It was dark, so, I was trying to find the door button from memory. Unfortunately, this was a different model bus. It had been parked with the keys turned *on* in the ignition, the gear in reverse, and the front wheels turned all the way to the left. The button I thought would open the door was actually the button *to start the engine.*

The second I hit that button, the engine roared to life, and the bus started moving backwards. I was wedged between the wall and the bus as it lifted me off the ground and dragged me backwards, crushing me. I felt my ribs, hips, sternum all bending to the breaking point. My breath was being pushed out of my chest for the last time. I was being extinguished. This was IT. Was I ready? Was I smiling? No! I was terrified. I was completely and utterly helpless. For a brilliant moment, Amma showed me the fleetingness of everything and my powerlessness in the face of death.

Amma always says our next breath is not in our hands. That day she gave me the *experience*. I had breathed my *last* breath. But my *next* breath was in HER hands. I firmly believe the only the reason I sit here today is that my last thought before I lost consciousness was of Amma, and she couldn't let me go yet. Not like that. Just after that thought, the bus stalled, and I blacked out. Many people came to my rescue and pushed the bus away from the wall. I crumpled to the road, limp and lifeless.

After a few moments, I shocked everyone who'd just witnessed me turning into a human chapatti. I stood up, put on my glasses and stubbornly headed back to my room. But my friends forced me to stop at the āśram hospital. After several X-rays, no one could believe I was only a bit scuffed up. News of the accident had spread around the āśram, and Valiya Swāmijī, my neighbor at that time, was astonished to see me. I told him I intended to go on the tour. He protested and called Amma and handed the phone to me.

Until that moment, I had been in shock. Only when I heard Amma's voice did I realize what had happened. Amma told me only grace had saved me. All those years before, when I had outrun the charging bulls, I ran to call my mother. Now, calling out to my Amma saved me from being crushed by a bus.

Amma made me stay back in the āśram for a few days to make sure I was really ok. She called me every day to ask how I was. Stubbornly, all I said to her was, "When can I join you." For some time, I could clearly recall that feeling of helplessness. The preciousness of life and the miracle of each breath was so clear. Now, sadly, not so much.

In our Amma, we have the greatest teacher ever. No matter how many times we fail, no matter how slow we are to imbibe her lessons, Amma's patience never wanes. Amma has said that many people have already passed their final exam with Amma's name on their lips as they breathed their last. Amma says this is an even greater miracle than Kṛṣṇa lifting Gōvardhana Mountain. This is Amma's biggest miracle, her greatest gift for all of us.

8

Limitless

Puneet McCorrison (United States)

As many of you know, I have been managing the Amṛtapuri swimming pool for 10 years or so. Once, while Amma was away, the pool was closed for maintenance. One day, I was working by the water, feeling dejected and missing Amma. Suddenly, an eagle landed not far from me at the edge of the pool. Around this time, Amma was using the example of various animals and their babies to describe the attitude a disciple should have towards the Master. Kittens are blind and helpless, and cry to draw the mother cat to them. The mother picks them up and moves them, as needed. Baby monkeys cling to their mother as she jumps through the trees. But baby eagles sit alone in the nest while the mother searches for food. Though the mother is far away, she never forgets her chicks.

As I watched the eagle, I thought, "Amma? Is that you!?" Right then, a second eagle landed near te first one. I thought, "Wow! Is Amma checking on me!?" One eagle around the pool is not so rare; but I had seen two eagles there only a few times, and never more than two. Then, my doubting mind started. I thought, "Amma, is that REALLY you!?" Instantly, a third eagle flew over me, hit the back of my head with its wing as it passed, and landed near the other eagles. With three eagles staring at me, I overcame my doubts and simply said, "Thank you, Amma."

Amma is always watching over us, wherever we are. Amma is one with everything. She pervades everything and is always with us as the Inner Essence of everything. Through such experiences of her Divinity, Grace and Love, Amma reassures us that she is always with us. She gives tangible proof of the transcendental Reality, and points to our limitless true Self, which runs like a luminous thread through the entire creation. The doubting nature of the mind may rise up again and again; but, Amma patiently tries to bring our attention to that ever-present, Pure Reality. Sometimes, she mhay even give a playful slap on the back of our head to drive home the point.

In *Bhagavad Gītā* 13:29, Śrī Kṛṣṇa says:

> *samaṁ paśyan hi sarvatra / samavasthitam īśvaram*
> *na hinasti ātmanātmānaṁ / tatō yāti parāṁ gatim*

> Those who see God as the Supreme Self equally present everywhere and in all living beings, do not degrade themselves by their mind. Thereby, they reach the Supreme Goal.

Every day, after *arcana* and *bhajans*, we chant the *śānti mantra*,

> *asatōmā sadgamaya - tamasōmā jyōtirgamaya –*
> *Mṛtyōrmā amṛtam gamaya.*

> Lord, lead us from the unreal to the Real, darkness to Light and death to Immortality.

This is a call for Grace, and just chanting it purifies our mind. It can also guide our day, if we contemplate the inner meaning. When we complain, argue, slip into self-pity, or get lazy in our *sādhana*, do we choose the illusory, finite, ever-changing appearance of the material world, or the Pure Being that reveals it? Do we choose the darkness of ignorance, believing we are the limited mind and body; or do we choose the Pure Light of Consciousness in which everything shines? Do we choose, as the *Upaniṣads* say, to go from death to death; or do we align ourselves with our immortal, limitless True Self? Every interaction, every desire or aversion, everything we experience presents these choices.

We can invert Kṛṣṇa's statement to read, "Those who identify with the ever-changing mind and senses take the world as real and miss their changeless True Nature. Thus, they miss God, the Supreme Self, who is present everywhere and in all beings." We miss the Truth, though it is everywhere, staring right at us. Maybe in the form of three eagles. Do we choose to look through the names and forms to the Pure Existence in which they arise? Do we choose the Infinite or the finite, the Limitless Sky of Pure Awareness or the limited person?

Amma came to this world smiling. She has always known her True Nature. For her, there is no choice because everything simply *Is*. The Creator and creation are not two, but One; and, if all is One reality, what is there to choose between? For Amma, all are embodiments of divine Love and Supreme Consciousness; but, for us, who are identified with our illusory individuality, it is a struggle. In fact, the word person comes from the Latin root *personae* (mask). In ancient Greek theater, all the actors held large masks in front of themselves to identify the character they were portraying.

Amma often reminds us that an actor plays various roles but never forgets his real identity. Our problem is that we have forgotten that we are just playing a role. As *Guru,* Amma wants to shake us out of our mistaken identification as "this person," to the Reality shining through the mask we mistake ourselves to be. Amma patiently tries to untie our many knots of negativity and misconception to reveal to us our true identity as the Self. We have to *allow* the pain, and let her, the Divine surgeon, operate.

Not long after I joined the āśram, I began doing *sēvā* in the video department. Eventually, I was put in charge of filming and editing the ceremonies: the *pada pūjās*, baby feedings and weddings. One night, I was called to film an engagement ring exchange. This was before the Amrita TV channel began. In those days, Amma could be very unpredictable with the cameramen. Compared to now, it felt a bit like the wild west.

Back then, it felt like no one wanted you around; and you never knew when Amma might scold you, send you away, or give one of those looks that make you want to bury yourself. You also might catch a beating if you wandered over to the *brahmacāriṇī's* side to get a better angle. Because of all this, I was always nervous standing near Amma with a camera.

There I was, in front of Amma, waiting for the ceremony to begin. Suddenly, Amma looked at me mischievously. Her eyes got bigger and BIGGER. Suddenly, Amma said, "BOO!!" I jumped. Amma roared with laughter as she joked with all the people around her. Everyone was laughing and staring at me. I asked people around what Amma was saying, but no one would tell me.

I became angry, thinking, "I came up here to serve you, Amma, and now you make fun of me and embarrass me in front of all these people!" I wanted to escape, and looked for a way out.

After the ceremony, Amma got up to walk back to her room. I was still angry, so instead of following Amma to film, I looked for someone to tell me what she had said. A little boy had fallen asleep on Amma's stairs waiting for her, and a beautiful scene played out. Amma was tickling him with a piece of straw, trying to wake him up, but he kept falling back asleep. Finally, he woke up and was really cute and embarrassed at the huge crowd. Amma was calling for the "video boy," but I was off playing indignant and missed my chance to serve Amma and film the beautiful scene.

Finally, someone told me that Amma had said she liked the way my eyebrows danced; and that all the video boys were afraid of her, except for the 'little one' [meaning Sashvat]. When I heard that, my anger dissolved and I thought, "That's not so bad. What's wrong with being Amma's court jester?"

Who or what gets embarrassed anyway? These situations that Amma creates are our test papers. Have we assimilated the Truth that we are the limitless, all-pervading Self, or do we still identify as the mask, the personality in a body, which can be teased and insulted? This incident tested my ego and surrender, and like most of Amma's tests, I failed. But I still have that humorous experience to cherish.

Our identification as the body-mind, has built up over lifetimes. Even after hearing the Truth of the limitless Self, and maybe even understanding it somewhat, our ego and conditioning keeps pulling us along. It's hard to change. Amma's tells a story of the cat who wanted a new job. The cat was tired of chasing mice, and decided to get an education and improve himself. He got some books and a desk and started studying. But, then, the cat jumped for the first mouse that ran by, knocking over his desk and forgetting all about improvement.

Amma has said again and again, during lockdown, that the most important thing is to stop identifying as the mind. We are like clay pots filled with water, floating in the ocean. We feel we are this individual person, one of millions, billions of little, individual pots of water. But it's the same water filling and surrounding all the pots. The separateness is an illusion.

The Sanskrit word *anantam* means infinite or limitless. It implies freedom from the limits of space, time and object. It means all-pervading, eternal and non-dual. Amma (*Brahman*) is infinite, limitless, everywhere, all the time, not separate from anything. Amma says this is *our* true nature as well. She sums this up, in her deceptively simple way, when she says, "The Creator and creation are not two, but One." This reveals an inherent defect in our perception. We see difference, boundaries and separation. Amma sees only unity—boundless, undivided Divinity. "Creator and creation are not two, but One," means that everything we perceive as "the world," *including ourselves*, is nothing but God. We just don't recognize it.

I asked Amma, "If God alone exists and is everywhere all the time, what can I do to make this a living reality?" Amma said,

> The key is to see everyone as yourself, not as separate entities. An actor sometimes plays many roles, but he always remembers that, underneath, he is the same. We need to see that it is God alone who has become the world and is acting through all its inhabitants. The heater is hot, the fridge is cold, and the fan gives wind,

> but the power behind them is the same. In this way, the One Consciousness is behind everything. The electric current does not differentiate between appliances. It simply flows. Likewise, we shouldn't make distinctions between people, but instead, focus on That which gives Existence to everyone. This is the way to see everyone as God.

To experience the Truth that the Supreme alone exists everywhere, all the time, we need to stop identifying as the individual mind, and see that it's the one ā*tmā* in all these forms.

I began trying to practice this teaching during *bhajans*. I would focus on that divine Ātmā in everyone as they meditated or swayed side-to-side. This produced flashes of bliss, unity and peace; but it was hard to maintain throughout the day. It's nice to try to see everyone as Ātmā, but most of the time I am still identified as this individual. I finally remembered the Golden Rule we all learn as children: Treat everyone as you wish to be treated. Swāmī Nikhilānanda, a direct disciple of Śrī Rāmakṛṣṇna Paramahamsa, said,

> The perception that Pure Consciousness is the Essence and Reality of all is the foundation of the Golden Rule. One who is firmly established in the perfect equality of the Ātmā has overcome all repulsion, secretiveness, shrinking, dislike, fear, hatred and other perverse traits, which arise from the feeling of separation...He feels love and compassion for all and works for the welfare of all.

Isn't this a lovely description of our Amma?

Forgiveness, compassion and love spontaneously arise when we practice patience and humility; and resistance to the present moment also decreases. With humility and patience, we forgive other's mistakes as we wish them to forgive our mistakes. In this way, we become more compassionate and accepting of other people and situations. This acceptance reduces the volume of our mind's constant commentary. We are more relaxed and in the flow of life. Then we can allow that ever-present, all-pervading Pure Being to simply exist without judging its manifestations.

Mahātmās like Amma are living embodiments of the *mahāvākyas* (great statements) from the *Upaniṣads*, like, "*Satyam jñānam anantam brahmā*" *Brahman* is Limitless Pure Existence-Awareness, ever available and not separate from anything. If we were to ask a *Mahātmā*, "Where will I find God?" they might laugh and say, "Where will you *not* find God!"

During one US tour, someone told Amma something that wasn't true, making me look bad. And Amma seemed to support them. I felt wounded. I didn't want Amma to think badly of me. I forgot that we are an open book in front of Amma. She wants to lead us from the burden of relative truth to the freedom of ultimate Truth, and she creates all the circumstances for this.

In protest, I told Amma, "I don't feel like being here right now." Amma just laughed. Then she looked at me and said, "Where can you go?" From the sparkle in her eyes, I understood that Amma was saying, "Where can you go that I am not?" I knew it was my injured ego that wanted to run away, defeated. I replied through tears, "There's nowhere to go." Amma beamed and nodded her approval. I think I've never seen Amma more pleased with me than she seemed in that moment. The sparkle in Amma's eyes kept expanding until it seemed the whole universe was shining in her eyes. I sat mesmerized, feeling timeless. But the feeling of being an individual person descended again.

Amma talks with us, laughs with us, cries with us, sings and dances with us. Sometimes, we may forget and behave as if Amma is one of us—a very wise person but still just human. We should guard against superimposing our limitations upon her. Amma is *anantam*—all-pervading, eternal, not separate from anything. There is nowhere that Amma is not. We must willingly confront our doubts, weaknesses and negative tendencies as Amma's presence stirs them up. As long as we identify with the individual person, our negativities will follow us like a bag of rotten garbage. In the end, our limited efforts will produce only limited results. The *Guru* is the incarnation of limitless Knowledge. Ultimately, to reach the goal, we need Amma's Grace to complete our effort.

In the 18 months before I met Amma, I had some lessons on the limitations of my efforts. All my plans for my future and career crumbled. Serious health conditions forced me to drop out of music school, and I moved six times. Finally, I broke my ankle and was laid up for a month. This forced me to face myself and my life.

I clearly saw the limitations of my efforts to produce the results I wanted. I was exhausted. I had never prayed, but I considered myself spiritual and believed in some sort of cosmic intelligence. The idea of God was hazy. I didn't know who or what I was praying to, but, in my heart, I said, "If there's another plan for me, then I'm done fighting it. I'm tired. Please guide me." This was the turning point. I know now that I was praying to Amma; and, from that moment, Amma's love and grace came rushing in.

When my ankle healed, I began yōga classes to overcome my various ailments. There I met the yōga teacher who was my bridge to Amma. The wisdom, peace and contentment around her was so rare. I would stay after class and ask questions about yōga and life. About a month later, she invited me for a night of chanting at a new yōga retreat center. I knew nothing about Sanskrit chants, but was curious.

When I arrived, someone gave me *vibhūti* from Sai Baba, and some holy water from Amma, and then put an Amma doll in my arms. Hours later, she said, "Um, can I have my doll back?" I had forgotten I was holding it. During the night, a Hindu couple from Sri Lanka chanted the *Lalitā Sahasranāma*. Then we chanted *Lōkāḥ Samastāḥ Sukhinō Bhavantu* for a long time. There were pictures of Amma, Sai Baba and Paramahamsa Yōgānanda around the room.

I got a strong feeling that one of these Masters was my *Guru*. I knew Yōgānanda had left his body, and I really liked Sai Baba's hair. That night, however, I understood that the decision wasn't mine. While I slept, I received Amma's *darśan* in a dream. She pulled me in and cradled me, then looked into my eyes, before pulling me back. I had never seen Amma give *darśan*, but my dream was exactly the way it happens—kneeling in line, Amma letting me up only to pull me back again.

The next morning, I was ecstatic. This was no normal dream. I was in bliss for days. When I next saw my yōga teacher, she asked, "What happened to you?" I knew my heart had been longing for Amma. I learned Amma would be near San Francisco in just one month. Coincidentally, I had a plane ticket to visit my parents during the same dates, in nearby San Diego, and quickly changed my flight.

The first morning in San Ramon, I was one of the first people to receive *darśan*. Afterwards, I sat for hours watching Amma, talking with her inside, telling her all my problems. It seemed so natural. I experienced stillness. Real peace. Some clarity. When I arrived the next morning, they said that, since I had *darśan* the day before, I couldn't go again. This was fine with me. But as the morning progressed, I felt more and more confused and heavy. Then, someone came and said, "Amma is calling you for *darśan*." Amma was calling for anyone who was sad.

Before I knew it, I was in Amma's arms again. As I got up, I felt like a baby deer taking its first steps. As I walked away, a feeling that had been building rose to the surface. I ran up to the balcony and cried like I'd never cried in my life. Strangely, it wasn't bad. My confused anguish gave way to peace and bliss. When I opened my eyes, Amma was gone, and the hall was mostly empty. I knew then that there was way more going on here than I understood. I stayed for the remaining five days, got a *mantra* from Amma and felt peace and love I never knew existed.

Through the following months, the desire for that peace grew until it was the most important thing in my life. When Amma returned a few months later, I joined the tour and have never looked back. In the ensuing 18 years, the only times I have spent away from Amṛtapuri or Amma's physical presence were to earn money to return.

During one of those times away, while staying at Amma's San Ramon āśram, I developed a very painful infection around my ear, which spread rapidly until half my face was red and swollen like a football. In the ICU, the doctors were very concerned because it was so close to my ears and eyes and might spread to my brain and kill me. That day was my birthday. I was pumped full of antibiotics and kept overnight for observation. The nurses checked on me every hour to make sure I wasn't comatose or dead. When the pain became intense, I would repeat, "All is your Grace, Amma...all is your will..." This focused my mind and was surprisingly effective in reducing the pain.

The next day, to the doctor's surprise, the infection seemed gone, but the doctor sent me to an eye specialist to make sure there was no damage. In the waiting room, an āśram resident called me with a wonderful story. The night before, a friend had informed the office in Amṛtapuri of my condition, and the video department took a photo of me to Amma's room. As Amma looked at the photo, tears began to roll down her cheeks. She cradled the picture like an infant and kissed it repeatedly, asking again and again what my condition was. They said it was like witnessing a hundred *darśans*. It was so intense that some people wondered if I was going to die.

Amma said, "He's such a sweet boy, and he only went there to earn the money to be near Amma." When the call ended, the background picture of Amma flashed on the screen of my phone, smiling, looking right at me, as if to say, "I'm with you, I'm always with you. There is nowhere you can go where I am not." The thought of Amma shedding tears over me as she cradled me like an infant was more than I could bear. Feeling the depth of Amma's love and compassion, I broke down sobbing.

Amma is a great mystery. Even when we are physically far from her, space is no limitation for she is Limitless. For Amma, everything is Divine Love and the Supreme Consciousness. She says, "Where there is love, there is no distance." Amma is the Mind of minds, ever present and always available. Amma is not separate from anything and pervades all forms. She is always with us as the inner Essence of everything. Amma is the Divine Mother Eagle, always watching and waiting for us to abandon the nest of our ego, discover our True Nature and take flight to join her in the vast limitless sky of Pure Awareness.

9

From Darkness to Light

Kumuda Kamm (Germany)

English is not my native language, and I have never spoken like this before. So, if you understand me today, we will all know it is Amma's Grace.

Let me begin with a story.

> When God wanted to create fish, he spoke to the sea. When God wanted to create trees, he spoke to the earth. But when God wanted to create man, he turned to himself. Then God said, "I shall make man in my image." If you take a fish out of water, it will die. If you remove a tree from the soil, it will also die. Likewise, when man is disconnected from God, he dies. God is our natural environment. We are created to live in his presence. We have to be connected to God, because, only in God does life exist. Water without fish is still water. But a fish without water is nothing. Soil without a tree is still soil. But a tree is nothing without soil. God without man is still God. But a man without God is nothing.

When I heard this, I remembered how I felt before meeting Amma. Without God in my life, I felt empty but didn't know why. Amma lifts us from sorrow to happiness. Amma lifts us from darkness to the light. Amma lifts us from unreal to real. One of my favorite descriptions of Amma is in the *ārati*: "Thy aim is to lift the fallen ones." This exactly describes what Amma has done for me. Today, I would like to share some stories of how Amma, out of her endless compassion, has saved my life and uplifted me.

I was raised in a Christian family, and from a young age, my grandmother took me on her lap and told me stories about Jesus. I liked this a lot and wanted to hear them again and again. We went to church almost every week. But, when I was a teenager, I started spending every Saturday night out with friends. So, on Sunday morning, I wanted to sleep late. But my mother would start vacuum cleaning right in front of my bedroom to wake me up for church. She was very strict and never allowed me to sleep late like most of my friends.

In my village, everyone drank beer, wine and liquor. So, did my family, and, from a young age, maybe 10 or 12 years old, I also started drinking. The culture was only about fulfilling desires. We enjoyed nice food and stylish clothes, and talked about our cars, our houses, our jobs and positions. We thought only about ourselves and gossiped a lot. And our minds were narrow.

I started working when I was 17 years old. My goal in life was the same as everyone I knew. Get married, have children, live in a nice house and be comfortable. We knew there could be obstacles and difficulties, but we had no other goal in life. My family worked hard all day and watched TV every evening. I always chose to do handicrafts instead. Something was always missing. I kept wondering, "Is this all there is?" So, I started searching for a life that fit me.

I left my village and my family and moved to the city. I got a good job and worked hard to learn the skills. For a while, things went well. But I still felt empty. Something was missing and I felt I needed help, so I started therapy. I also found a small meditation group. There, a new life began.

In this meditation group, we would chant *Om* 108 times, and then the *gāyatrī-mantra* 108 times. Often, I had tears in my eyes. A subtle power was nourishing me after such a long period of emptiness. We practiced various meditations, and people spoke about spiritual matters. It was all new, and I was opening up to something unknown. I had a lot of treatments to heal myself and unload my burdens. Due to God's grace, many good people guided me. One spiritual teacher taught us to replace every negative thought with good thoughts.

Several people told me about Amma "who was an Indian spiritual healer," and my wish to see Amma grew. Finally, one lady agreed to call me when Amma was coming to Germany. When she called to say that Amma was coming, I took a few days off from work and went to Munich. This was in 1994.

At the hall, we stood waiting for Amma to arrive. Everyone formed a line and chanted, "*ōm amṛtēśvaryai namaḥ.*" It was like a stream of light full of peace and love was coming. I had never experienced anything like that in my life. When I saw Amma for the first time, I thought, "Oh my God! She is *tiny*!" We all sat down, and Amma guided us in meditation. It was very full and touching. Amma says, "Meditation is like the breast milk of a Mother." When I went for *darśan*, I felt that something was healing inside. Afterwards, when I closed my eyes, I felt full of love. Rose-colored light and energy were around me and inside my body. I enjoyed Amma's presence and her *darśans* for three full days.

Then I did something I had never done in my entire life. I almost never missed a day of work, even when I was a sick. But when Amma's program finished, I picked up the phone and called a friend who was a doctor. I asked him to write a note saying that I was sick. Then I called my company and told them, "I'm so sorry, I can't come to work for quite some time." Then, I followed Amma to Switzerland, Italy, and many different places. That phone call was the best thing I have ever done in my life.

In the beginning, Amma draws us in. She was really sweet to me, and I enjoyed her healing touch, looks, *bhajans* and *satsaṅgs*. My hunger for the Divine was born. As Amma says: "Just as a person needs air to breath, the soul needs to be nourished with love and care." After my first *darśan*, I never touched alcohol again. When I went back home, I again saw my therapist. As I entered her office she said, "The whole room is full of light!" I knew that it was Amma's light. Later this therapist came to meet Amma.

I went back to work, but I started to think about taking a break and traveling to India for a year. Soon, I quit my job, cleared my flat and booked a flight. I reached India 25 December 1994. When I stood on Indian soil for the first time and inhaled the Indian air, I felt I was entering into my heart. The energy was so touching it brought tears to my eyes.

My plan was to travel around India. I would start in Amma's āśram and say hello to Amma, then leave after a few days. Crossing the backwaters on the ferry, I was amazed at the sight. Amma was giving *darśan* in the Kali Temple, and I had a powerful feeling that I had reached home. My plan to travel dissolved. I stayed with Amma the entire year and travelled with her during the North Indian Tour in 1995.

During the tour, I saw Amma give *darśan* to thousands. And she traveled with us and bathed with us in rivers. She fed us and guided us through India. Indian culture was so new—so much color, the saris, the temples, the *pūjās*, the spiritual heritage. So much heart.

My first āśram *sēvā* was toilet cleaning and dishwashing. I was absolutely *not* a good *sevite*. Whenever Amma came to the Temple or sand *sēvā*, I ran to be with her. I wouldn't even show up for my assigned *sēvā*. I apologize to everyone because that happened quite often.

Once, during sand *sēvā* with Amma, instead of helping to carry sand, I just stood watching and chatting with another woman. Amma turned, looked at me and said, "Either you do *sēvā* or you go." Wow! That hit me hard and went deep inside. It was a shock treatment. Thus, slowly Amma changed me. I learned that *sēvā* is worship when we offer the fruits of our actions to God.

A whole year with Amma wasn't enough. No matter how long we are with Amma, it's never enough! I asked Amma if I could become a renunciate and she said, "You try." In 1997, I joined the āśram.

I am so grateful to Amma for her guidance. Before receiving her teachings, I never heard that the body-mind complex is not real. Amma says, "The divine is present in everyone. In all beings, in everything. Like space is everywhere, all-pervading, all-powerful, all-knowing. The Divine is the principle of life. The inner light of consciousness and bliss. It is our very own self."

I never knew about the bondage of *samsāra*. It was even hard for me to understand that I am bound in worldly life. Only after hearing again and again, and praying, did I understand, "Yes. I am bound. Yes, I am in darkness. Yes, I have a scattered mind. Yes, I need guidance."

When I heard there is a life after death and about the law of *karma*, it felt so true to me. Only when I came here did I learn and understand that everything is made from the Divine. We are instruments; only the ego is ours. Only through *satsaṅg*, Amma's books and speeches and the *Bhagavad Gītā* did I hear that I am *not* the body-mind complex.

When Amma sings, '*Manō Buddhi*,' I start to get an idea. I feel like an onion: Amma is peeling away the outer layers one by one. In the end, there are no more words; only the essence remains. The longer I am here, the more I know that I don't know anything. This makes my need for the *Guru* absolutely clear.

My family still doesn't accept my life. They only believe in their religion. They do not even like to talk about this topic. I do not blame them. Their beliefs are just the result of their upbringing. This is what happens when one doesn't have a *Guru*. Amma says, "There are many religions, but God is One." My family has not received such teachings. We are so blessed to be guided by a living realized master who removes our ignorance.

In 1997, whenever I spoke to my parents, they made me feel guilty because I live here in Amṛtapuri. Once I went running to Amma and told her that I don't know what to do. Amma said, "Whenever they say such negative things, just hang up." In the beginning, I was scared. I didn't want to hurt my parents. But I did what Amma said. Each time they said something negative, I hung up the phone. After a few times, something changed. They stopped trying to make me feel guilty. Amma also said to me, "If you are with Amma, she will help your whole family. Both, the generations before and after you."

One year, my parents agreed to meet Amma. My father was too proud to come for Amma's *darśan*. Instead he stood at the side of the hall. When Amma was leaving, she walked straight up to my father and hugged him! He was shocked. After that, he came for Amma's *darśan* every year I was in Germany with Amma. Each time, Amma gave him an apple. When he watched Amma give *darśan* to thousands of people and saw all her charities, he said, "Well, I guess Amma is not an ordinary woman." I have seen Amma's words come true. Even though they do not fully accept my choice to live here, Amma's grace has reached them. They live happy, healthy lives.

I am so thankful to Amma because she reminds us over and over again that no one is our own. The body is burnt to ashes, the near and dear ones come to the funeral fire and then go away. Their love is selfish. Only God truly loves us and is with us forever. Every night, in the *satsaṅg* and *bhajans*, we are reminded of what is real and what is unreal.

Amma helped me begin to understand why we are born and about our duty in life. We have to take responsibility for ourselves. Slowly, I understood, "Oh, if I want to attain God, then I will fulfill the purpose of this human life. If I want to strive for the goal, there is really some work to do." From then onwards, I took *sādhana*, meditation, the classes and *sēvā* seriously. From balancing myself with the right mixture of *bhakti-yōga*, *jñāna-yōga* and *karma-yōga*, I feel more content and complete than ever before.

I would like to run to Amma and ask her, "How sick am I? How deep are my wounds? How much more pus do you have to squeeze out? Please, Amma, don't stop! Even when it's painful. Amma, please heal me." I like to see Amma as Mother Kali because she wants to make her children feel happiness from the inside. One of my favorite things about Kali is her hands. She has such beautiful big hands. I'm lucky she has extra hands so she can slap me back onto the right path when I go astray. Even if it hurts a bit, I know it's for my own good. Kali has shown me how my *vāsanas* create suffering.

When I came here in 1995, there was no āśram shop yet. We had to go all the way to Vallikavu junction to shop. One day, I was craving tapioca chips. I walked to the backwaters to the ferry. As was boarding the ferry, the boatman was looking at the other shore and didn't see me. He pushed the ferry forward, and I fell into the backwaters. Instead of tapioca chips, I got a mouthful of backwaters! I climbed out and ran, fully drenched, to my room.

I wish I could say that I learned Kali's lesson. I wish I could have told myself, "Those chips won't bring me closer to God!" Maybe then I could have gone to the Kali temple and sat in blissful meditation. But I *craved those chips*! So, I changed my clothes, ran again to the backwaters and took the next ferry to Vallikavu.

The fight against my lower nature is constantly going on. I try to offer my negative feelings, emotions and thoughts to Amma's Feet, and I try to pull out the roots, but I fail often. Then the negative thoughts overpower me. The mind is like a wild horse. But Amma helps us overcome our *vāsanas.*

Years ago, I was doing veggie chopping after *Dēvī Bhāva*. We used to take all the fruits left over from the *Dēvī Bhāva darśan* and make a salad for breakfast. Every renunciate got one serving. But I loved it so much I secretly took some *before* breakfast. And then I took a *second* portion when breakfast was served.

When I went back to the Kali temple, I had to pass under Amma's room. When I looked up, can you guess who stood at the window? It was Amma, looking down at me with a serious gaze. I froze. Amma stared at me for a long time. Then, she turned away from the window.

Immediately I could feel that I had taken what was not mine. This pained me, but it is only through such experiences that we learn. After that, whenever I feel a strong craving, I remember Amma's face. My cravings are not over, but they are less than they were before. Amma's divine presence is weakening my negative tendencies.

Amma constantly advises us to be helpful. Even if we can't give something we should give a smile or a kind word. I try to practice this. All I want is not to hurt anyone, and to be calm and friendly. I am far away from this; but, Amma says our effort brings fruits. Even if I fall, I just get up and start again.

Once, when I was a bit down, I mentioned it to Amma's Swāminī Kṛṣṇāmṛta Prāṇā. She told me, "Now is your chance to be with Amma. Take advantage of this time." That helped me. Whenever I am a little sad or depressed, I say to myself, "What a gift it is to be here with Amma and to imbibe good qualities and Amma's teachings." I pray that I appreciate what deep healing happens here.

Earlier this year, I went to renew my passport. When I came back, I was in quarantine for *four* weeks. When I finally returned to the āśram, I really understood how much energy is here.

Every atom is filled with positive power. Amma is helping us to be happy.

I am constantly inspired and thankful to all of you. Often, when I forget to chant my *mantra*, I see someone chanting their *mantra* and I am reminded. Or I see someone sitting in a corner reading a spiritual book, and I am inspired. Or, when I am too extroverted, I see someone with an "in silence" badge, and I am reminded to speak only when necessary and to think before speaking.

Something really unique about Amṛtapuri is how many different types of people stay here. We are always meeting people who think differently from us. Over time, I have learned to open my narrow mind by adjusting with people who think in ways that I could never have imagined.

One of my *sēvās* is to decorate *arcana* books with Amma's photo. In the beginning, we made *arcana* books with Amma's photo only on the right side. One day, a lady doing *sēvā* with us put Amma's picture on the *left* side. I did not like it and said she should follow the instructions and put Amma's photo only on the right side. Later, the lady explained that some people look first to the left side, and medical studies have proven this is quite common. Didn't I want to give these people a chance to find the right *arcana* book?

We had never done this before, and I was not fond of it. But I contemplated and realized that I am not the only one who has to like these books. So, we changed our way of making the books. Now some have Amma's picture on the right side, some on the left side, and some in the middle. And our sales have increased! Now we can serve even better.

I became more flexible through this contemplation. My thoughts are often only from habit or a concept. When I just let go of my way of thinking, I can see things more as they really are. I can discriminate about what thoughts bring me closer to God. Like this we learn to use our mind as an instrument to reach God.

One day I was feeling sad while sitting in the Kali Temple. Suddenly, someone came to me and said, "Amma is calling you." I went straight to Amma, and she took me in her arms like a baby. When I came out of her arms, she took the end of her sari and the end of my shawl, and she tied the two cloths in a knot. Then there was only one piece of fabric. I don't even remember what Amma said. I only remember the image and the feeling. Amma is with me, guiding me and holding me close to her. And she will never let me go.

I pray for Amma's Grace, that she uplifts us all and brings us to the goal—the place where there is no sorrow nor any negative feelings. The place where there is only pure Love, Light and Peace. What a wonderful world! What a wonderful world! I offer my Words to Amma's Lotus Feet.

10

Start Smiling

Ambujam Keyes (United States)

Amma often says, "Sorrow is the greatest doorway to God." In my case, this door was a long, dark tunnel filled with tears. But for some time now, Amma has been telling me, "OK, you have reached Me now, so you can stop crying - and start SMILING!"

In the seventies, when awareness and practice of spiritual traditions from India was new and rare for the west, I was blessed to be born to Kṛṣṇa devotees. My mother used to tell me she read sacred scriptures, like the Śrīmad *Bhāgavatam* and *Bhagavad Gītā*, while I was in her womb; and, my father told me that he prayed to Lord Kṛṣṇa, when I was born, "Oh Lord, please save this child from *māya*."

My first five years were full of the bliss of love for God in the forms of Radha and Kṛṣṇa, Sita and Rama, Lakshmi and Narayana. Because of their love for Kṛṣṇa and Indian culture and spirituality, when I turned five, my parents put me in an austere "*Gurukula*" in an isolated Kṛṣṇa commune.

Though everyone there had good intentions and tried their best, they lacked understanding and proper guidance. As children, we had the bright light of worshipping Kṛṣṇa and learning high values, but we endured extreme *tapas* and hardships. I would cry myself to sleep, praying for Lord Kṛṣṇa to rescue me.

One of my childhood idols was the five-year-old *bhakta*, Prahlād, who had so much faith in Lord Vishnu that, even when his own demon father, Hiranyakashipu, repeatedly tried to kill him, Prahlād would just fold his palms together in *pranāms*, with a smile full of faith, and chant *Jai* Śrī *Hari*, *Jai* Śrī *Hari*. I tried, but I could not follow Prahlād's example. I didn't have Prahlād's full faith and determination. I could only cry and pray. When neither Kṛṣṇa nor Lord Narasimha came to rescue me, I stopped believing in God.

We had no TVs or radios there, so I knew nothing about the outside world except that I had been taught it was all "demons". Traumatized and disillusioned by the hypocrisy, I ran away when I was 13. I got a crash course in the suffering that many youths face due to lack of love and values. In my rebellion and confusion, I did everything I had been taught not to do. I ended up living with other lost and angry, inner-city kids in abandoned buildings and parking lots, addicted to drugs and alcohol to numb the pain. I tried everything to escape my suffering, but, it only made things worse. Still, no matter what dangers I threw myself into, somehow, I survived.

When I was 15 years old, Divine Intervention came when I was run over by a car, and my right leg was shattered. Unable to walk for six months, I couldn't go out to party anymore. I was forced to look inward and think about the purpose of my life. As part of my recovery, I received massage therapy. Later, I learned this therapy to help others.

Amma often tells us, "A smile, a sympathetic glance, or a word of solace, can change one's life." When I was 16, I put myself in therapy. My therapist was the first person who ever showed me kindness and understanding. Instead of judging me as bad, she said, "It's natural for you to feel this way after all you've been through." Then I thought, if my therapist could understand me and not condemn me, then surely God must also understand me. *Maybe God even loves me!*

I wasn't ready to believe in Kṛṣṇa again, so instead I honored Nature and the Universe as God. As soon as I started to open up to God's Love, my life changed for the better. I was on the road to healing. Amma says, "Faith and self-confidence are interdependent."

With the insurance compensation from the accident, I studied massage therapy. I was 18 years old. All the pain I'd suffered enabled me to have compassion for others' pain. In my 20's, I had a successful massage therapy business and was getting high marks at university. I was also seeking pleasure and attempting to enjoy the world. I still felt empty inside and "partied" with friends almost every night to escape my pain and my desperate need for love.

Just before I met Amma, a good friend suffered a severe brain injury, which wrecked everything about him, making him unrecognizable and dysfunctional. Witnessing this made me ponder deeply. I thought, "The brain is just like a computer, processing inputs and impressions. If brain damage can change someone so entirely, then *who are we really? Is there anything inside of us that does not change?*" This question catapulted me into self-inquiry. With a little food and a tent, I ventured out to a remote beach in Hawai'i on a 'vision quest' fervently seeking answers to the question: WHO AM I?

For days, I cried despondently to Mother Ocean, begging her to help me know my true self, experience pure love, and give me a teacher and a mother! "You can't make a child without a mother!" I cried. "Where's my mother? Where's my teacher?" Well, Amma heard me because one night, I noticed a fire burning some distance down the beach. I walked there and saw a young man gazing at the fire, chanting... "Amma... Amma... Amma..." I asked, "Who is Amma?" He gave me some *prasād* flower petals and a book about Amma's life, which I took back to my tent to read with a flashlight.

I was astonished to learn that Amma had also loved Kṛṣṇa, and how much she also had suffered as a child. But Amma never lost her connection with her Self or with God. She used her hardships to cultivate more devotion for God, dispassion for the world and compassion for others. My pain had shut down my heart. I had retreated from God, and from the world, too.

After nine years of relieving other's pain through massage therapy, I finally had to stop because feeling all the physical and emotional pain of my clients had become unbearable. But here was Amma going beyond her own pain and taking on everyone else's pain by the millions. And yet, remaining completely unaffected, fully established in Divine Love.

One morning, after reading Amma s biography, I woke up with a strong message in my heart: "If you want to meet your teacher, you have to go back to the mainland US." I used the last of my money to book a flight to LA, even though I didn't know anyone there. This seemed totally crazy, but I couldn't resist this mysterious inner call. Upon arriving, I opened a local magazine straight to a notice that Amma was in town.

It was *Dēvī Bhāva*, June 2001, when our Divine Mother first took me in her arms (in this life). Amma pressed me to her heart. With a pumping, shaking motion, she chanted loudly and soulfully in my ear, "Mā Mā Mā Mā ..." and filled me with light and love. Suddenly, all the pain, guilt, and sin that had ruled my whole life started flushing out through the palms of my hands. Shhhh... "Mā Mā Mā...Shhh..." When Amma finished, I stood up in a daze, feeling light as a feather. *"Is this love?"* I wondered.

When I learned Amma was offering *mantras*, I decided to receive a *mantra*, too. I wanted whatever Amma was giving. At the orientation, they asked me what form of God I believed in, so Amma could give me a *mantra* to strengthen my faith. "Wow," I thought. "Amma is not trying to convert people to a particular religion. She supports everyone's unique experience of God! How Profound!!" I had seen a quote from Amma: "The essence of all forms of God is the same - Pure Love." I answered excitedly, "PURE LOVE!"

As I sat close to Amma waiting for my *mantra*, she was shining with divinity in her red silk sari and crown. For the first time since I was five years old, I was in my heart. I saw Amma as Lakṣmī Dēvī, the nurturing mother goddess who takes care of devotees and grants Pure Love and Devotion.

I was instantly, forever transformed by just this one *darśan*. I had struggled with substance addiction from the tender age of 13. But, from the moment I met Amma at age 27, I lost even the *slightest* craving, as if Amma had awakened me from some bad dream. Amma has saved hundreds of thousands of other people from drug and alcohol addictions by filling our hearts with what we were so desperately thirsting for, and, literally, dying for: Pure Love.

Amma says, "Love is the only medicine that can heal the wounds of the world. Love can accomplish anything and everything. Love can cure diseases, heal wounded hearts, and transform human minds. There is no problem that love cannot solve." That November, I ended up in San Ramon with Amma. As she pulled me into her mystical eyes, I knew Amma was my spiritual master. I heard myself saying, "Ok, I'm ready to try to do things your way now. My way is *not working*."

I came to Amṛtapuri that December 2001. Finally, I found my home after searching my whole life! My first time here, Amma gave me a rare opportunity to massage Her. After that I was miraculously able to go back to massaging people again because I was able to feel Amma in them. I was also able to meet their pain with the blueprint of perfect wholeness which Amma had let me feel in Her divine body

I joined Amma's Indian tours, all the while bathing in a river of cleansing tears. Amma's presence was like a turbo-flashlight on my impurities, and I kept having deeper realizations that Amma was not only God and a true *Sadguru*, but also the real mother I had never had.

When I told Amma about my childhood, she said, "Sadly, those people don't have the Mother... but..." Amma said, "It brought you to Me, didn't it?" "Yes Amma!" I said, gratefully, standing next to God and realizing my childhood had been the express path to the Divine. Amma also said, "You're not that affected, are you?" When I tried to say "Yes," Amma said "No!" She always encourages me to be strong and to rise above the limitations of my mind.

Then Amma said, "Just because a diamond is soaking in a bucket of oil doesn't mean it is not a diamond." Over the years,

Amma has patiently been helping me rescue the big, beautiful diamond of *dharmic* values and devotion to God from the oil of my *vāsanas*, ego and conditioning.

Once, I asked Amma, "What did I do in my past life that I had to be separated from you and crying for you for so much of my life?" Amma smiled and said, "Let's not think about that! Just know that Amma will be with you now and in every life to come."

Since I joined the āśram in 2005, Amma has continually tried to teach me how to relate to God from Love rather than from fear. Love is God and fear is ego. Her every glance, touch and movement demonstrate love in action and shows us that the path to Love is Love. True freedom comes from discipline, and true discipline comes from Love.

When Amma first opened my heart, I was surprised to find undying love for Śrī Kṛṣṇa, and a treasure box of memories of living with my parents in Vṛndāvan when I was four years old. My inner child felt that Kṛṣṇa was still in Vṛndāvan, and that he must be waiting for me. I was often sad that I'd missed seeing Amma in Kṛṣṇa *Bhava*.

One year, during the North Indian tour, I couldn't ignore my longing anymore. At a roadside lunch stop before Delhi, I asked Amma if I could go to Vṛndāvan. She looked long and deep into my eyes, understanding my need, and said, "OK. But come BACK!" I asked, "Amma, will you come with me?" She gestured around to the group of devotees sitting around her, nestled together like Kṛṣṇa's cowherd friends (*gopas* and *gōpīs*), and answered with a huge smile, "*This* is my Vṛndāvan!"

Still, silly me, I went. On the train, I prayed, "Amma, I know Kṛṣṇa's still in Vṛndāvan waiting for me. I'm going to bring him back for you. I'll find a sign and bring it back for you, even if it's just a leaf that reminds me of Kṛṣṇa."

In Vṛndāvan, at the sacred *rasa* dance site, I sat down and closed my eyes, trying to feel the energy. Instead, I recalled how many times Amma has danced so beautifully with us. I reflected on how Kṛṣṇa multiplied Himself to dance with each *gōpī*. Actually, isn't this what Amma does, giving us each a unique, personal relationship with her as she teaches us how to dance with the Divine through our lives? I went to meditate by the Yamunā River but could only think of Amma.

After many experiences like this, I thought: *Wait! Vṛndāvan is sacred because Kṛṣṇa was here 5,000 years ago. But Amma is here with us now! Amṛtapuri is the portal to the spiritual world. Wherever on earth Amma's lotus feet have touched is sacred. Amṛtapuri is the most sacred place on earth. There, all of humanity can experience Amma's awakening love and guidance and come home to the Self. How many opportunities have I wasted by not tuning into this?*

Some monkeys broke my reverie. I picked up a big stick to protect myself. Walking defensively with this big stick, I realized I'd been on guard like this most of my life. No wonder I hadn't fully seen Kṛṣṇa in Amma. My monkey mind was too active, and my heart was too closed. But I knew that Amma's constant love and purification, through *sēvā*, were gradually removing my ego, training my mind and softening my heart.

Still exploring Vṛndāvan, I found a field with some cows. Nostalgically, I imagined Kṛṣṇa playing his flute as he herded them. Suddenly, a brown cow with big horns butted me hard on my arm. "Kṛṣṇa!!" I cried out, just like I did when I got hurt as a child. When leaving Vṛndāvan, I remembered I'd promised to bring Kṛṣṇa back for Her. I felt the bruise on my arm. The bright blue mark reminded me of Kṛṣṇa's blue skin—my only souvenir of Vṛndāvan.

A few days later, on the Singapore tour, I was near Amma. She looked up and gave me a sparkling smile. She told Geetha, "She went to Vṛndāvan looking for Kṛṣṇa," as if it were a noble and brave but pretty silly venture. Amma put up her hands mischievously, showing they were empty, and asked, "So, where is He? I thought you were going to bring him back for me!"

How in the world did She know that I had thought that!? I hadn't told a soul. But Amma let me know she is the indweller of my heart, the *paramātmā*. As if on cue, I took the opportunity to respond. I said, "Amma, I wanted to! But all I brought back was this blue bruise from the cow." Amma laughed. Full of concern, her eyes mirrored the sadness I felt at not finding Kṛṣṇa in Vṛndāvan. She then astounded me by repeating, word for word, all the thoughts I'd had in Vṛndāvan. *She had come with me!!* Then Amma said, "You have to go to the Vṛndāvan in your heart. It's not about the outer Vṛndāvan. The Vṛndāvan of your heart is always there for you."

During the Reunion *Dēvī Bhāva darśan*, Amma applied *chandan* (sandalwood paste) and a *Vaishnava tilak* to my forehead — marking my body as the temple of Kṛṣṇa. Her face took on the most attractive, delightfully divine mood of Śrī Kṛṣṇa as she rhythmically pressed big *gō*pī dots of *candan* all around my eyes. Somehow, with each press I felt Amma was giving me downloads of all Her Kṛṣṇa *Bhāvas* I had missed.

Looking in the mirror afterwards, I was amazed to see the face of love looking back. I looked four years old again. The *tilak* looked exactly like I used to put it on as a child—wide, a bit messy and a little slanted. Amma was not just with me in Vṛndāvan.

She has been with me my whole life. She, the indweller of my heart, was the one applying my *tilak* back then and the *gōpī* dots we used to wear during festivals. Amma was reminding me to celebrate every day with Amma as a festival, just like the *gōpīs* did with Śrī Kṛṣṇa. Also, she was reminding me that I need to see everyone as the Lord's beloved *gōpīs*, uniting with them in harmony, through devotional service.

At the airport, Amma laughed when she saw me. She said, "Candana yesterday!" I had not washed it off. "*Candana* every day, Amma!" I said. "I'm never washing this off!" Then she told everyone, playfully, "She went to Vṛndāvan looking for Kṛṣṇa. So, I had to give her Kṛṣṇa." Gesturing with her finger, Amma made the *gōpī* dots in the air, smiling at me like Kṛṣṇa, and chanting, "Kṛṣṇa, Kṛṣṇa, Kṛṣṇa..."

On the next tour, I was getting some eye pillows blessed and showed one to Amma that had Baby Kṛṣṇa embroidered on it. Amma surprised me by saying, "You - Kṛṣṇa!" My jaw dropped. "Huh?" Waving her hand in a circular gesture, encompassing the whole room, Amma said, "All my children are Kṛṣṇa!"

In Malayalam, the pupil of our eye is called *kṛṣṇamaṇi*. The purpose of our pupils is to receive light. Imagine if we could consciously see Kṛṣṇa's divine light in everything and everyone we looked at. And if, just like the *gōpīs* who saw Kṛṣṇa in everything, or Amma who sees the Divine in everything, we could see Amma dancing as the Divine Light of Love in everything.

Amma gave me that sweet experience of Kṛṣṇa Love to restore my childlike faith. She has also given me many sweet and fierce heart-opening experiences with Kālī Mā. Amma has shown me many times that God is not limited to any particular form. And, as we all know, thousands, or maybe even millions, of people have been blessed to experience their beloved Deity revealed through Amma.

God is the blissful, pure love Consciousness dancing within everybody and in all of creation. This Divine Love that came to earth as Kṛṣṇa, Rāma and Buddha has returned, as our beloved Amma. Amma says, "Kṛṣṇa's greatest miracle was his smile." But Amma's smile is the Mother of all Miracles.

In this *Kali Yuga*, a mother is what we need most. Our Amma is not just mothering us and guiding us with her pure love. She is awakening universal motherhood in us to restore *dharma* to the planet. Amma has given me so many experiences, but I still forget what a wondrous, glorious grace it is to live in the loving care of *Mātārāṇi*, the most supreme embodiment of Divine Love ever to walk this earth!

> *tasmāt praṇamya praṇidhāya kāyaṁ*
> *prasādaye tvām aham* īśam īḍyam
> *pitēva putrasya sakhēva sakhyuḥ*
> *priyaḥ priyāyārhasi dēva sōḍhum*

Bhagavad Gītā 11:44

> Therefore, O adorable Lord, bowing deeply and prostrating before you, I implore you for your grace. As a father tolerates his son, a friend forgives his friend, and a lover pardons the beloved, please forgive me for all my offenses.

Amma says, "The sign of a true devotee is that they always have a smile on their face." Why? Because they trust God and have optimistic, childlike faith. The gratitude and surrender that they all experience is their beloved Lord's *prasād*. Like a child, they trust their Mother always to guide them, feed them, nurture them, protect them, and even play with them. A mother only wants to see her child happy. Amma wants so desperately to free us from our desire, anger, fear, sorrow, and pessimism so that we can join her to play in her land of *amṛta* (immortal bliss).

Amma tells us to decide, "No matter what happens, I *choose* to be strong and happy. I am not alone. God is always with me." Amma keeps telling me to smile, to celebrate this great fortune of having such an infinitely loving, compassionate, wise, omnipresent, and omniscient mother, father, beloved and *Guru*, all in one.

Amma also says, "Spirituality is the ability to face any obstacle with a smile." Often, when I am tested, this seems impossible. But Amma patiently keeps trying to teach me to find the inner balance and bliss within. May *Mātārāṇī* be victorious. May our hearts expand and our smiles merge in her Divine Love, so that we can joyously love and serve all of creation as God, just like Amma does.

11

Children of Immortality

Śivānand Mousely (United Kingdom)

The *Upaniṣads* state that all suffering is born from a deep-rooted and primordial misunderstanding. We may feel there are many causes for our sorrow; all our fears, attachments, emotional and physical pain we go through. But, at the root of all of it, there is only one problem. We do not know who we are.

Why does this cause us to suffer? For one simple reason: we seek happiness *externally*, from objects — experiences, places, people and things. All of these are finite, ephemeral and temporary in nature. Thus, we fail to look within, to recognise our true identity, the ever-present foundation of every experience — the Self (*sacchid*ānanda), pure being, pure consciousness and eternal bliss.

In Amma's words,

> Children, what you are seeking is within you. Stop running after the objects of the world and turn inward. There you will find what you are seeking. You are both the seeker and the sought. You are searching for something you already have. It cannot be found outside. Therefore, every search for happiness outside will result

in failure and frustration. It is like the dog chasing its own tail.

We are all familiar with the story of Karṇa from the *Mahābhārata*. Adopted at birth, he was unaware that he was Kuntī's first-born son, the eldest of the Pāṇḍava princes, of royal blood and heir to the throne. He realised his true identity only when Kṛṣṇa told him. Amma, like Kṛṣṇa, reveals something previously unknown to us: not that we are royal, but, as she sings — *oṁkāra-divya-poruḷē varū,* ōmana *makkaḷe vēgam* (Come quickly darling children, *you who are the divine essence of oṁ*). Amma echoes the words of the *Upaniṣads*, which address all of humanity as *amṛtasya putrāḥ* (children of immortality).

The life of Karṇa illustrates well this principle of a mistaken identity and its eventual revelation. There is a similar story in my own family, though, due to Amma's grace, the outcome was quite different.

When my mother was young, she gave up her first-born son for adoption when he was less than a year old. Another family adopted him, and he grew up believing that they were his real mother and father.

As life went on, this created a lot of pain for my mother. She wanted to contact him, but the law didn't allow it. She thought about him often, hoping he had a good life, wondering sometimes if he was still alive. Over 54 years went by. Then the law changed. Through the adoption agency, my mother discovered that her son was alive, and she could try to contact him.

At this point my mother became very anxious. She was worried and could not sleep. What would his reaction be? Would he be angry? Would he reject her? Did he even know she existed?

What kind of life had he had? So many thoughts burdened her mind.

My mother asked me to tell Amma. Amma said that she would make a *saṅkalpa* (resolve) and indicated that everything would be ok. This relieved my mother very much, and she began attempting to contact her son.

Soon, he received a letter from the adoption agency saying that his birth mother wanted to contact him, and if he wanted to meet her, he should call them. He called the agency and told them there must be some mistake. He was not adopted. His mother had recently passed away, at 82 years old, after a long illness.

They informed him that there was no mistake. Only after he saw his birth certificate which proved he was adopted did he finally accept the reality. This was a huge shock. His whole life he thought his adoptive mother was his biological mother. Now, just a month after she had passed away, he was being told he was adopted, and his biological mother wanted to meet him.

He and my mother have now been happily reunited after 54 years of separation. He is so grateful to discover his birth mother and brothers — all of whom he never knew existed. My mother is ever thankful to Amma, for lifting this life-long burden. Moreover, his adoptive mother died peacefully, knowing that *in her mind,* she had been his mother, and he her son. The adoption case worker commented that they had never seen a more perfect outcome in all their years working there. Only Amma's compassionate *saṅkalpa* could resolve the situation in such a beautiful and perfect way, with everyone involved at peace.

This experience brought to life the story of Karṇa for me, making me contemplate and reflect. Are we not all "adopted" children, unaware of our true origin? Taking this body of flesh and blood and mind of desires and fears to be our parents and guardians in life? Have we not all forgotten our real identity? Are we not all, as the *ṛṣi*'s proclaim and as Amma sings, "The sons and daughters of immortality"? The divine essence of ōṁ, the Self, the very foundation of all that exists?

My mother's eldest son did not *become* her child upon hearing the news that she had given birth to him. Though unknown to him, he had always been her son. This is an indisputable fact. In the same way, we will never *become* the Self; we *are* that, even now.

Amma and the scriptures tell us this truth again and again. Yet, like Karṇa, even after hearing it, we cling with pride and loyalty, to our false identity, this limited ego born of "I" and "mine," unable to let go, due to our timeless attachment to a misapprehended reality. That is why it is said *tyāgēnaikē amṛtat-vam-ānaśuḥ* (by renunciation alone one attains immortality). Only through *tyāga* (giving up, letting go) of what we are *not,* can we recognise what we already *are*. Though this may be the final truth, to make this a living reality is not so easy.

Enlightened masters like Amma, and the scriptures, unanimously declare that to discover our real identity, we must have the grace to come to a living *Sadguru* like Amma, one fully established in the Truth.

As Lord Kṛṣṇa says in the *Bhagavad-Gītā*, chapter 4:34

tad viddhi praṇipātena paripraśnēna sēvayā |
upadēkṣyanti tē jñānaṁ jñāninas-tattva-darśinaḥ ||

> By humble prostration, questioning and service to the *Guru*, know that truth. Those *jñānīs*, who are seers of truth, will impart knowledge unto you.

The beauty of Amṛtapuri is that Amma has created the perfect environment for this purification and discovery to happen. We are given the space and opportunity to develop humility and devotion, unprecedented access to Amma, and the freedom to ask her questions. Moreover, we have countless opportunities to engage in *sēvā* and other *sādhanas* (spiritual practices) like meditation, *arcana* and *bhajans*, helping us to develop the mental purity and inner stillness required to imbibe the knowledge that Amma transmits to us, day after day, through her every word and action.

I first saw Amma on television when I was 20 years old. The presenter was in Kerala visiting the āśram. She went for *darśan* and described her experience. I remember asking my mother, "Who is Amma?"

My mother replied, "She is the Hugging Saint." She knew a few people who had met Amma in London in the early '90s. I asked her why she hadn't gone to meet Amma and taken my brothers and me along? But I already knew the answer: my mother had her own *Guru* and spiritual tradition in which my brothers and I were raised.

My parents had met their *Guru* in the early '70s. My brothers and I were brought up in the community that he had founded in the UK. Along with a normal education, our school also taught meditation, *yōga*, Sanskrit, the *Bhagavad-Gītā* and the basics of *Sanātana Dharma*.

During my teenage years, I became rebellious. I did not reject my childhood spirituality completely, but it fell into the background as my desire to explore the "world" grew and my priorities changed. A turning point came when, at the age of 19, I visited India for the first time and traveled to various holy places such as Vārāṇasī and Gaumukh (the source of the *Gaṅgā*). Somehow, my experiences at these places awakened a deep longing, and I regained interest in the spirituality of my childhood.

Upon returning home, I read some spiritual books about the lives of various *mahātmās*, and I began to long to meet a *Guru*. This was when I saw Amma on television. Later the following year, Amma visited London, and my younger brother and I went with some friends to the program.

I remember my first sight of Amma. She glided into the room as if floating, very small and beautiful. The first time I saw her, I knew she was the Divine Mother, *Devī*. After *darśan*, I was dazed, even unaware I had received *prasād*. After realising that others had been given *prasād*, I spent a few minutes crawling around on the floor looking for mine, which I had obviously dropped in my stupor. I then sat the rest of the day, sinking deeper and deeper into a blissful silence. I left the venue feeling very happy to have met Amma, a real *mahātmā* like the ones I had read about, that she was definitely *Dēvī*, and that maybe she could help me find my *Guru*?

The following year I returned to India for one year. I was restless, seeking someone to guide me. Looking back, truthfully, in my heart, the recognition had already taken place; but, due to my mind's superimpositions and delusions, I continued to search.

As Amma says, "We all live in our own world of imagination and preconceived notions." Perhaps, due to my upbringing and the books I had read, I had a very strong concept about how *my* Guru should be. And, yes, in my preconditioned and ignorant mind, *he* was definitely a "*he*" and not a "*she*."

He would be sitting in a cave somewhere high in the Himālayas. *He* would be like Śiva, with a long beard and matted hair, very stoic and austere. I would have to struggle through many hardships to meet *him*, climbing over crags and rocks, to the ends of the earth. And at last, upon reaching *him*, *he* would announce that *he* had been waiting for me. And *he* would impart the secrets of the universe to me and a few other disciples.

Yes, I was a fool. Though I am still quite foolish, I was much more so back then. Our own mind is the biggest trickster there is. The *Upaniṣads* say we weave this universe like a spider weaves its web — dreaming a dream and then living in it. During my travels through the web of my own creation, I eventually ended up here, in Amṛtapuri.

I explained to Swāmī Śubhāmṛtānandajī that I was looking for my *Guru* and wanted Amma's guidance. Though deep within, beyond my mind and its delusions, my heart already knew. Thankfully, I was compelled to ask him to ask Amma — just in case — if she was my *Guru*. He must have thought I was highly confused, and he was probably right.

When I went for *darśan*, Śubhāmṛtānandajī explained my situation, my background and that I was seeking to find my *Guru*. He also asked Amma if she was my *Guru*? Amma looked at me and joyfully replied "Yes!" in English, as if it was the most obvious thing in the world. Then she told me to sit next to her. Śubhāmṛtānandajī later told me that Amma had said to him, "I am his *Guru*; there is no one else."

Like the beat of the gong that Amma sounds during meditation, the *vedānta-ḍiṁḍima,* (drumbeat of *vedānta*) with these words, I awoke from my ego's delusions. I knew that whatever Amma said was the truth. Her words silenced my mind and its superimpositions. My heart had already recognised the truth that could now shine, unobscured.

Amma says, "The *Guru*-disciple relationship is the only eternal relationship there is." This ego of ours is a false and temporary identity. Our meeting with the *Guru* signals its impending annihilation. Darkness cannot exist in the light of the sun. Amma was always my *Guru*. My preconceptions had blinded me to the truth. Only her words could dispel my ignorance and shine light in my clouded mind. From that moment my life began to transform dramatically, as if a glowing ember that had been smouldering quietly in my heart, had been ignited by the winds of grace. Upon reaching the feet of the *Guru*, a world previously unknown to us opens up, and we begin to walk the path they lay before us.

A few years ago, when Amma was in Finland, it snowed heavily. I and some friends decided to make a Śiva *liṅgam* out of snow and offer it to Amma. As part of the sculpture, we also made a small snow statue of Nandi, the bull.

Amma looked happy when we gave her the snow *liṅgam*, along with Nandi. After feeling the snow with her hands and examining what we had made, she noticed Nandi had no ears. Amma pointed this out and began to construct them herself. I explained that we had not made the ears because they were very small and difficult to create. Amma continued carefully sculpting them. Only after Nandi had ears was she happy. Then she blessed the statue with flowers.

What was Amma telling us? The disciple, Nandi, needs ears for śravaṇam—to hear the words of Śiva, his *Guru*. The divine sculptor, Amma, teaches us through her every word and action. We must learn to listen deeply to fully imbibe the knowledge she is imparting. One of Amma's most incredible qualities is that she accepts everybody, not just those who have this capacity in full. Due to her infinite compassion, if we lack fully formed ears, or even if we don't have them at all, she will patiently help us to develop them. Amma says, "The *Guru*'s patience is the disciple's liberation."

Like the mother who keeps trying to feed her child even when the child turns away countless times, Amma patiently continues to impart her wisdom until we are finally able to hear what she is saying. To truly listen to the *Guru* with an open heart, we must cultivate faith. Only if we have faith in the *Guru* will we value their teachings, put them into practice and assimilate them until they become our experience.

During the first tours I went on, Amma gave me many experiences that deepened my faith in her. She showed clearly, many times, that she is the consciousness within me and within everyone and everything.

During the 2010 Australian tour, I asked Amma for a name. Śiva had always been my favourite form of God, and I hoped for a name associated with him. This desire grew when I met a man Amma had named Śivānand. I thought, "If only Amma could give me *that* name; that is the *only* name I want." It felt like a nice fantasy and then I dropped the idea.

On the first day of the Gold Coast retreat, I waited in the name line with fear and anticipation. When I reached Amma's chair, Swāmijī was there with a bowl of small papers with names written on them. The person in front of me received his name, and he seemed happy. I told myself I should also be happy, whatever name Amma gives me, even if I don't like it. In truth, I didn't want any name but Śivānand.

I watched Swāmijī shuffle through the names and then select one. Can you imagine my shock when it said "ŚIVĀNAND" in capital letters, the exact name I had wished for. I was speechless. He showed it to Amma. She smiled and nodded that it was the right name. I managed to mumble, "Thank you," my mouth still hanging open. Amma burst out laughing, knowing the whole story. Turning to Swāmijī she said, "I have seen him in the āśram."

Indeed, Amma had seen me, but not just my physical form. She had seen *inside me*, into the depths of my heart. I had told no one of my desire for this name, yet Amma knew. How is this possible? Because Amma is not only the five-foot body we see before us. Amma is the all-pervading consciousness, the Indweller of every heart, the Seer behind all seeing.

Such experiences, sculpted by Amma's compassionate hands, remove our misconceptions and strengthen our faith, so that we can move forward on the spiritual path. The layers of ignorance and wrong notions seem endless as we progress, and the obstacles become more subtle. Our identification with our false self (ego) is so strong, it is very difficult to grasp that it is *not* our true identity. But we learn that, since it is perceived by us, it cannot be our True Self, the very one who perceives.

To conclude, I would like to share how Amma healed an emotional affliction of mine. During *Dēvī Bhāva* in Dallas in 2011, I was sitting in the *darśan* line thinking about a problem I had wanted to tell Amma about for a long time. It was embarrassing, but I really wanted share it. For many years I had been unable to cry, no matter how sad I was, no matter what the situation. As I approached Amma, both my fear to express myself and my desire to do so increased equally. I thought, "Anyway, the *bhajans* are very loud. If I just whisper to Amma no one will really hear."

To my horror, when I arrived at Amma's chair, the song abruptly ended. It felt like pin-drop silence. Amma looked at me as if saying, "Do you want to tell me something?" I felt like everyone around Amma was waiting for me to speak. Finally, I just blurted out, "Amma... I can never cry!"

Everyone started laughing. Some were saying "*Awww*, he can't cry." I felt so embarrassed. Just when I thought it was over, Amma looked at me compassionately and told me to sit there while she continued *darśan*. She asked someone to bring an onion and then said, "Don't worry; I will help you to cry."

The next thing I knew, someone gave Amma a lemon, not an onion. She looked at it, assessing if it would be adequate for her purpose. After ascertaining that it was, she bit into the lemon and peeled back some of the skin.

She then beckoned me to come close to her and to open my eyes wide. I moved forward happily and held my right eye open with my fingers. Amma stared seriously into my eyes, examining them like a doctor assessing the malady of a patient. After checking with me if it was ok to go ahead, she slowly and very gently touched the inside of the lemon peel to my eye.

Nothing happened. Amma looked concerned and a little surprised. She said, "Something is wrong with your eyes." I shrugged and motioned for her to try my other eye, opening my eyes even wider. Same result. No tears, no reaction. Amma looked even more concerned. "Something is wrong with your eyes," she repeated. "Your tear ducts don't work."

At this point I also became very confused. I knew that I could not cry, but I did not know that my eyes were impervious to lemon juice and physically incapable of producing tears. I thought deeply for a moment, and then came the moment of clarity. I had discovered the obstacle. I said, "Amma... I'm wearing contact lenses."

She began laughing, and I also laughed. Both of us realised what the problem was. I usually remove my glasses before going for *darśan* and often wear contact lenses to see Amma's face clearly, something I had totally forgotten. Realising that I was about to lose my chance for Amma to help me cry, I removed my contact lenses there and then, threw them on the ground and said to Amma, "Please try again."

She seemed reluctant and said, "I don't want to hurt you." I said "No, no, it's ok. I don't mind; you won't hurt me. I want you to do it; please try again." I leaned forward again, pulled my eyelid down and opened my eyes wide, watching Amma's concerned face. She stared into my eyes and very slowly, very gently she touched the lemon peel to my eye. Then, after a moment, my eye finally began to water. Amma looked pleased that my eyes were working. As I got up to leave, she said, "Now you will cry."

By Amma's divine intervention and *saṅkalpa*, later, during *bhajans*, when a song touched me, at last I was able to shed tears. Since that day, I can cry freely, with an open heart, whenever something moves me.

ajñānatimirāndhasya jñānāñjanaśalākayā |
cakṣurunmīlitaṁ yēna tasmai śrīguravē namaḥ ||2

> Salutations to that *Guru* who opened the eyes of one blind due to the dark cover of ignorance, with a needle coated with the ointment of knowledge.

We approach the *Guru* to remove our ignorance, that which obstructs the knowledge of our True Self. Like the contact lenses, some aspects of our ignorance that cover, filter or obscure our perception are very subtle and difficult to recognise, let alone remove. Only a *Sadguru* like Amma can see what obscures the ultimate reality. Only such a one knows if the "lenses" of our perception are the wrong prescription and need changing, or if they should be discarded completely.

By listening to the *Guru*'s instructions, and through introspection and effort, we come to see the Truth they are pointing to. Then we can shed our false identification, our ignorance, our wrong notions, and the *Guru* can apply the ointment of knowledge, opening our eyes, at last, to the recognition of our True Self.

I pray that we all make the best use of our time with Amma, and that by her infinite grace, we are all given the eyes to see, the ears to hear and the mind to realise our oneness with the ever-present reality that Amma is the living embodiment of. I pray that we all may become pure instruments in her divine hands, serving this creation and all beings in it as expressions of our own True Self.

12

The Promised Land

Sulma McCollom (United States)

Amṛtapuri is like a *Gurukula* (the teacher's village). Amma is creating Amrita Village Communities all over the world, where we can work together to learn what is real spirituality and selfless, unconditional, divine love. By Amma's Grace, all these small children are coming up so brilliantly; and we big children are also improving a lot.

Amma says, "The reason why we practice spirituality is to learn how to forgive others for their mistakes, and to love them and not reject them. Anyone can reject others; but to accept everyone — that is difficult. Only through love can we lead others from wrong to right." With Amma's *saṅkalpa* (resolve), let us unite, and follow Amma's sacred path wholeheartedly.

In 1973, when I was 15 years old, I heard about this concept of "The Goddess," God in a female form. I loved Mother Nature, so seeing and feeling her as God was very natural for me. I was raised in a small town of 500 people, near the Pacific Ocean in America. Our whole family would spend all our spare time in Nature. The sea, the rivers, the forests, and mountains — Mother Nature was always our friend.

At age 17, I packed my backpack, took my best friend (my guitar), and my $50 (3500 rupees), and went to a big "Back to the Earth" commune in California, called "Mama Mountain." In the middle of the pristine wilderness, like a deer, I was running. Like a fish, I was swimming in the fresh, clean river that flowed at the bottom of the land. I made my campsite alone, close to the river. My love for Nature and The Goddess could now grow freely.

A new friend gave me a book: *Autobiography of a Yogi*, by Paramahansa Yōgananda. I was very impressed by the love and dedication he had for his *Guru*. All the mystical saints he met, especially the female saints, sounded fascinating. Seeing the date (1920), I was very disappointed. "Back then, people were good," I thought. "Now most people are so materialistic. But it would be so cool to meet a real female saint."

After four months of bliss on "Mama Mountain," a big forest fire damaged the neighbor's property. They filed a case against us, and we were left totally homeless. For lack of anywhere else to go, most of us went to a four-day music festival nearby. There we sat, very sad. Then, one person started talking loudly. She said, "We are the blessed!!! We are the chosen people!!! The Goddess will provide us with a Promised Land! Don't give up now! We have to search for that Promised Land!"

A small crowd gathered to discuss many ideas about how to get to the Promised Land of the Goddess. One person said, "No problem! We can simply drive to Mexico and search for some land there." A second person said, "Where east meets west, on the remains of the lost continent of "Mu," (in Hawaii), there the Goddess lives." Another person said, "In Guatemala, on the Caribbean coast, there is a small Rasta village that can only be reached by boat. That place is very good." Yet another said, "In

Belize, there is a small Garifuna (African people mixed with Red Caribbean Natives) village on the seashore, opposite a big coral reef with many, many islands." A practical person said, "Just go to the city and get a job. Make more money to buy a different land. Ok?" Someone else said, "The Goddess is great. She has whole solar systems, just waiting for us...all we have to do is go to the Arizona desert and wait under the clear night sky, with a campfire. She will come and pick us up with her big UFO (Unidentified Flying Object) space ship!" "Unidentified Flying Object Spaceship!" I thought. "Wow, if it's true, this sounds very easy."

After four days, I got in a van with some of the younger members of the group and drove to the middle of the desert in Arizona to wait for the Goddess's space ship. If Amma had been there, she would have told us the Promised Land is actually *inside* of all of us. In Amma's words, "The real source of Grace is within you." Instead, it took me the next 19 years to try everything on the above list, and more, until I could meet Amma.

In 1978, after three years of traveling to Arizona, Mexico, Hawaii, and assorted communes in Oregon and California, I landed in "Livingstone" (Guatemala) where some Garifuna elder women befriended me. They were my new role models, and were happy to have me help in their farming projects. After two years in Livingstone, I had learned how to make a canoe, build thatched huts, do tropical farming, and herbal medicine.

And I learned what it feels like to go to sleep hungry. After too many nights without food, I seriously started to wonder if I was on the right path to find the Goddess. This thought troubled me a lot. One night I spent the whole night praying to The Goddess to *please* show me a sign. In desperation, I launched my canoe into the dark, calm sea and lay down, hoping I would miraculously merge into Nature. Staring up at the stars, I wondered tearfully, "Where are You?" Finally, as dawn approached, I returned to the shore.

Looking east out to the sea through the coconut trees, suddenly, my whole vision was filled with a huge beautiful Black Face. Silver, mirror-like diamonds encircled her Head. The Great Black Mother had answered my prayers. This profound experience, showed me the power of prayer, and gave me so much faith and strength. After trying to live in the jungle for two years without money, I knew it was not practical, and was, sometimes, even very dangerous. The Garifuna women encouraged me to get a job in America and come back later to purchase a small piece of land.

Back in America, as a woman, I had a hard time finding carpentry work. Often, men would make rude comments. But when I finally got work, I learned fast to act tough, work hard, face everything with a smile, come in early, stay late, and never give up.

In 1988, a friend told me, "A great saint has come to Santa Fe. She is a *Guru* from India. We met her last year, and you should really meet her." I said, "That's nice, but I am very busy. I have to get a new job." Little did I know that Amma would give me my dream job, but it was simply not my time yet.

Finally, In 1994, the day came to meet Amma. We drove to a beautiful forest that is now the Santa Fe Āśram. We arrived just as Amma came into the big white tent. Amma looked so saintly, so young, and so very gorgeous. We stood in awe. The *bhajans* transported me to another world. My *heart* knew for sure that "Amma is the Goddess." But hours later, my interfering intellect scanned the crowd, and asked, "But why does Amma have so many weird people here?" Later I understood that I am also odd, and Amma truly loves everyone and never rejects any one.

Amma says, "Spiritual bliss cannot be experienced by the intellect. The heart is needed. The intellect cuts things apart like a pair of scissors, but the heart sews things together like a needle." As we reached Amma for *darśan*, Amma held me very close and spoke in my ear like an echo, "Mā, Mā, Mā." "Wow," I thought, "Amma gave me a *mantra* already!" Then Amma, with a lightning move, put some sandalwood paste on my forehead. I felt so good. I bowed down to Amma with gratitude, and sat in deep meditation for the very first time.

The next day, after work, I hurried to the program. When I reached the big tent, nobody was there. I had the very best seat when Amma came to the hall. Amma looked straight at me. Sitting so close, I could watch Amma's each and every move. I don't know when or why I started to cry. Tears rolled down my face for no known reason. The *darśan* had started. I sat crying until late in the night. But I was not sad.

The next day, early morning, before the *Dēvī Bhāva*, I came for the first time to volunteer in the kitchen. The people there were really very nice. The main cook was Kamala *cēcci*, a super-happy Indian lady from Tamil Nadu. To my surprise, she immediately got up and gave me a hug, as if she knew me. "Welcome to Amma's kitchen," she said.

Suddenly someone said, "Look Amma's coming!" In the bright morning sunlight, Amma was walking gracefully down the hill smiling, holding out her hands to touch everyone on the way. Then, abruptly, Amma stopped to discuss something with Kamala.

After Amma left, I saw tears of joy in Kamala's eyes. "You know," she said smiling, "Amma told me, 'To feed the devotees of the Divine Mother is one of the greatest boons we can receive from the *Guru*.'" Soon I experienced this truth for myself. By Amma's Grace, in all tours, I get to help with *sēvā* (selfless service) in the kitchen.

In June 1995, I got a chance to make a garland to put on Amma during *pāda pūjā*. That sounded very exciting, until I met the official garland lady. "*ōm namaḥ śivāya*," she said. Immediately, she reminded me of my grumpy, 10th grade math teacher. "Have you ever made a garland?" "Oh, yes of course." I lied confidently, becoming the bad student who flunked math.

She tried to explain to me how to make a garland. "First, you should take a shower in the morning." I confirmed; "I *always* take a shower in the morning, ok?" "Making a garland for Amma is very special," she went on, "so we should chant our *mantra* while stringing the flowers." "OK," I said. "Do you have a *mantra*?" she asked me, as if I was a small child. "Oh yes of course." (Actually I didn't have a proper *mantra*, just, "Mā, Mā, Mā.") "You can use what flowers you like, but *don't use those dark red ones*. They are too old." "Yeah, ok," I said.

"You come early. Make sure the garland is ready by 9am. Amma's comes at 10am." "I know, I know," I said. Finally, she said, "Now don't forget, above all, we should make the garland with *love*." "Ok, I know that," I answered, thinking, "What does this lady know? I love Amma the most."

The next day, at 5:30am, I reached the āśram. It was silent. I started making the garland. Faithfully I was chanting my mantra, "Mā, Mā, Mā." The red flowers weren't *that* old, so I decided to add a few. Slowly, carefully, the garland took shape. "Mā, Mā,

Mā." I had almost finished the garland, and was thinking, "My garland will be super."

Just then, a terrible, bad thought crossed my mind. I was so shocked. "How could I *think* like that *now*? Oh Goddess, this is a disaster! I cannot give this garland to Amma. I have to throw away the whole garland, and start over! But there are not enough flowers! And, there's not enough time." I started to panic.

Just then, the grumpy lady walked in. Oh no. "ōm *namaḥ* śivāya. So, you haven't finished yet? And what is *this*? I told you *not* to use these red flowers." She coolly ripped the red flowers in half, and threw them in the waste. "Come on, fast. Fast. Amma is never late."

Fighting back my tears, I started adding flowers fast and finished the garland. That lady took me to the hall and said, "You stand here. Amma is coming in five minutes." A few tears rolled down my face, out of fear and shame. I thought, "Amma is the Goddess. She knows everything. I cannot pretend anything." I was in *high* tension.

The big crowd was pressing close all around where Amma would enter the hall. I had nowhere to hide. Deep guilt flooded me as Amma came through the crowd, with the sounds of the conch, bells, and chanting. As Amma arrived, the āśram was transformed into a joyous festival. Amma stood as an innocent, pure, divine angel, right in front of me, her eyes closed. With deep remorse and shivering hands, I placed the garland on Amma, and fell at her feet.

When I finally stood up, Amma was already on the stage. My eyes met hers from across the room. Could it be that Amma didn't notice my offering was completely tainted with ego and bad thoughts? Maybe Amma didn't care? But Amma *did* notice, and Amma *did* care. My conscience was burning; I could not face Amma. Before anybody could tell me how wonderful the *pada pūjā* was, I escaped through the forest, and drove home, and collapsed. Since I could not fall asleep, I contemplated the disastrous events of the day.

I began to recollect my life. How I had always blamed everybody, everything, and the whole of society for all my problems, and the problems of the world. But, from this intense experience, it was clear that, because of my impure mind, lack of love, and arrogant ego, *I* was completely to blame for all of my problems. Amma had just started to press the poisonous snakes of ego, jealousy, greed, and anger out of me. It was the perfect time, the time when I thought I was pure.

Amma's words rang true for me: "Only when we become aware of the burden of our own ego will we be able to remove our faults. At present, we cannot bear someone else's ego or mistakes, but *ours* are all right. '*My* ego is beautiful, but *his* is ugly.' This is our present attitude, and this attitude should go."

The next morning was *Dēvī Bhāva* day, the last program, and my only chance to tell Amma I was sorry. Feeling very sad, I got in the *darśan* line. Seeing my condition, without words, Amma gave me an all-knowing beautiful smile and made some hand gestures, as if to say, "Hey, why are you crying? What exactly is your problem anyway?" Expressing her unconditional divine love, Amma hugged me very tight. Amma had forgiven me. My heart soared like a bird. The whole *Dēvī Bhāva* night, I happily served food and chai, and tried to sing along with the music.

Just after Amma left the āśram, I heard a loud voice, "Your garland, your garland! Hello!" It was the teacher lady. "Your garland is here, you have to take it!" "No need." I said, "It's not that great. You can just keep it," and, like, whatever. "No, no!" she insisted, "The garland is Amma's prasād. It is sacred. You made it for Amma. It's very special. While Amma's away, it will help you to remember Amma. Please take it." She held out an old paper bag. "Please take it." Reluctantly, I took the bag with the garland and said, "OK. Thanks a lot." I managed to give her a smile, thinking, "I should have been nicer; after all she was just trying to help me."

I went home and put the crushed, half-dry garland around Amma's photo on my altar. A week passed. One night, I was relaxing, looking at Amma's photo. Suddenly, Amma was standing in the place of the altar. Around her neck was that old garland. I was totally surprised to see Amma there, but I was more surprised to see that the old, damaged, useless, bad, garland, was now *fully fresh*. All the colours of the flowers had come back to life. Amma smiled at me lovingly. Then, just as suddenly as Amma showed herself, she disappeared. Amma had resurrected the garland from the dead.

Amma's unconditional compassion was on the way to resurrecting me also. In June 1996, I went to see Amma in San Ramon. Kamala *cēcci* welcomed me to the kitchen. Since I had full time kitchen *sēvā*, they gave me some chances to give *prasād* and sit close to Amma. At the end of *Dēvī Bhāva*, when Amma threw the flower petals, I was just at Amma's feet.

Amma looked so radiantly, divinely beautiful. She smiled and threw a lot of flower petals on my head. Spontaneously, I threw two handfuls of flowers onto Amma's feet, again and again. Amma was laughing at me, and when the curtain closed, I sat, full of bliss, in a big pile of flower petals.

My attachment to Amma was growing. In 1997, at the insistence of some friends, I managed to escape from America to go to Amṛtapuri, for "just one-month vacation." When we arrived in front of the magnificent Kali temple, people told us to run to the green roof. We took our offerings and ran upstairs. Amma was sitting on a cot, lovingly and innocently smiling and hugging people, like a small girl. Amma was so very happy to see us and insisted on tasting everything we brought. My life-long search was over. I knew Amma's Amṛtapuri was the Promised Land!

There was a small carpentry workshop under the new "B" flats. I had brought some tools and started *sēvā* immediately. After a week, Amma left for the North India tour. I stayed back, cheerfully working. One by one, people would come with requirements, and I would try to help them. Since my youth, I had wanted to help people. Now was my chance. Amma says, "Even if we can make someone happy for just a moment, our life will be truly blessed."

But part of me would often get angry, like when people cut the "Q" for chai. Sometimes there was no electricity in the workshop. That *really* made me mad. I angrily complained to Radhika Cēcci, "This is a total waste of my time! Maybe I will just change my flight ticket, and go back!" Luckily for me, just in time, the electricity would come back. Because of my anger, I came close to leaving and *losing everything*. One night, I read in *Awaken Children*: "By acting and thinking with anger, you lose a lot of good energy."

I went to the *arcana* and the workshop every day. The weeks flew. Sometime in March, when I came for the *arcana*, a big, beautiful photo of Amma was resting on a silk cloth on Amma's *darśan* chair. Above that was a shining, decorated umbrella.

During that *arcana*, in an instant, I was floating waist-deep in the middle of a calm, vast, rippleless sea. All around me, no land, no boats — only the blue sea and the clear blue sky

My mind was totally clear. Everything was Amma. My whole, small world was gone, and Amma was everywhere. That night was *Śivarātri*. After that, I decided to ask Amma's permission to join the āśram. When Amma returned from North India, I got my letter translated:

> "Dear our most Beloved Amma, this unworthy daughter seeks your permission to renounce, wishing only to serve Amma for all time, Koti Pranāms."

Amma held me on her chest, slowly reading the letter. Taking a deep breath, Amma gave a sigh of relief, as if finding her child that was lost for a long time. Amma softly said, "OK." Since that lucky day, Amma's divine love and great patience have guided me to become a better person.

Amma has blessed me with chances to help with a few of her international charitable projects in the fields of construction, women's empowerment, education and music. I experience great contentment and joy living in the āśram. With Amma's Grace, I could help in some small way at AIMS Hospital, at Mata Amritanandamayi Centers in America and Canada. Also, in schools in Kerala, especially Paripally orphanage, and Amma's school and orphanage in Kenya.

Living around Amma and seeing millions of people come forward enthusiastically to volunteer and support Amma's worldwide humanitarian projects gives me so much hope for this world. I hope that, someday, this whole world will become The Promised Land for each and every one.

Here are a few of my favorite Amma's Teachings:

"Selfless service and utter dedication are the two things that make one fit to receive the *Guru's* Grace."

"Even if all the people in the world love us, even then, we would not get an infinitesimal amount of the bliss that we get from God's [or Goddess's] love."

"Real prayer includes being compassionate and humble towards others. Smiling at someone and saying a kind word."

"Children, you should all love one another. No one should get angry and break away."

"We should live on this earth for the upliftment of the soul. Let each breath of ours carry a message of peace to the world."
I offer these words, and everything, at the Lotus Feet of my Most Beloved Amma.

13

From Helplessness to Humility

Dr. Arvind Perathur (India)

I grew up with a materialistic and westernized outlook even though I was born in a Tamil *brahmin* family. We lived in Goa, a famous "party town," and I spent many school and college days in bars and restaurants. So, to have come to Amma and be living here in the abode of 'The Divine Incarnate' is a *huge* miracle. Giving *satsaṅg* today is an almost bigger miracle. If a mute could recite a poem, and the lame could climb a mountain, why couldn't I give a *satsaṅg*, with her grace, in her divine presence?

My ideas about spirituality, the meaning of life, and the existence of God, have been strongly influenced by my years of medical training and practice in India and the US. Caring for patients suffering in the ICU, and supporting their families, and constantly confronting death, gives me daily chances to practice Amma's teachings.

When I was younger, my parents sometimes complained about my small mistakes. I would always answer with the analogy of a small black dot (my bad behavior) on a big white board (all my good behavior). Then, in the early years of our marriage, I even used it on my wife when she complained about my tardiness, or missing an important event, or not taking her out on our wedding anniversary. I would say, "My dear, look at all my *good* qualities. I am a doctor and good-looking. I eat the food you cook without complaining too much. I even help you with the dishes, sometimes. So, don't complain about such trivialities!" (Isn't this a most common husband-wife tale?)

In life, we often see only others' black spots (faults), and we miss the big white background (their good qualities). Amma is so different. She nurtures and nourishes our microscopic white spots of goodness and helps us erase our black spots. She can do this because she is not limited to her five-foot frame. She is the all-pervading Consciousness, the same Consciousness in each one of us.

One winter morning, I walked into the ICU to find a 44-year-old man on the ventilator (breathing machine). He was wide awake but was completely paralyzed below his neck. His eyes were open and filled with despair. His wife and three teenage kids stood nearby. After studying the case, they saw the hopelessness in my eyes, and they burst out crying. The father had been playing with his kids on a snowmobile and had fallen. His neck injury severed his spinal cord. Usually, the first snow of the year is a fun time — skiing, snowboarding, preparing for Christmas. While others were enjoying the season, this family was devastated. As Amma always says, "Even the next breath is not in our hands."

Tests confirmed that this millionaire businessman would probably spend the rest of his life in a nursing home, paralyzed from the neck down, completely dependent on others for eating, breathing and passing stools, etc. So sad! The day before his discharge, he asked me for medicine to end his misery, since there was no hope of recovery. I cried with him and consoled him that miracles do occur, and that he should pray.

One year later, he was on a motorized wheelchair, having recovered some strength in his fingers. He was living with his family, rather than in a nursing home, but they had to do everything for him. Yet, the family was happy to have their dad home for Christmas. Not the best outcome, but better than expected, given that he wanted to kill himself a year before.

At AIMS, I remembered this patient when I took care of a 19-year-old Muslim girl with a congenital muscle defect. She was so weak that she used a motorized wheelchair. Despite her severe disability, she aspired to become a charted accountant and was in her first year of Bcom. She was in the ICU on a ventilator due to pneumonia. The family was very poor.

Amma was on her foreign tour, so the family could not meet her in person, and I was unable to reach Amma. All I could do was say silent prayers. The patient developed one complication after another, and I started to lose hope. But, miraculously, after 30 days in the ICU, she went home, promising to come back and do my taxes once she was a CA. That was a huge win, compared to the other case, and our patient services had subsidized her hospitals bills.

A few years before moving to India, during one Christmas season, I was distributing gifts in my neighborhood. That year, I bought myself ear mufflers because the wind chill was close to 10C. At one neighbor's house, I fell down, hitting the back of my head on the step. I lay still for a few seconds, telling myself I should have been more careful. Then I got up and finished distributing the rest of the gifts. Back home, I felt some pain in my lower back rather than on the back of my head. This surprised me, until I examined the ear muffler. I was shocked. It was cracked right at a spot over the nape of my neck. Had it not been for the muffler, this might have been a very different story.

Several questions arise from these three scenarios. What is fate? Who decides fate? Was an unseen hand protecting me that evening? Comparing the two patients: Why was the overall outcome of our AIMS patient so much better than the other patient, against so many odds? Our AIMS patient was much sicker, almost on the verge of death. And the resources available to the US patient vastly exceeded what was available to our patient? Is it all just chance or timing?

Before I met Amma (in this life), I believed in fate, like luck, good or bad! Since meeting Amma, I am convinced there is no point in discussing fate. Amma says time and again –

EFFORT (good actions) + FAITH (in HER/GOD)→ Invokes GRACE (Changes Fate)!

After all, she is our very own, most compassionate Mother, exalted in the *Lalitā Triśatī*, '*ōm kaṭākṣasyandi karuṇāyai namaḥ*' (One whose eyes drip with compassion). We see this at the end of *Dēvī Bhāva*, and even during the "*ārati*." She is also the one who distributes the fruits of our past actions, as in the *Lalitā Triśatī*, '*ōm karmaphala pradāyai namaḥ*'. So, we have nothing to worry about. We are safe in her hands.

When I was doing my medical training, in India, before I met Amma, a teacher once scolded me in front of everybody. He said, "If you cannot feel your patient's pain, you are no good as a doctor." It hurt then, but now I recognize the power of compassion and its urgent need in society today.

I heard about Amma's *darśan* and compassion from my wife during our many pre-marriage Yahoo chats in 2000. (We were early users of online dating!) My bucket list included social service and wanting to give back to India. AIMS hospital was almost new.

Usually, in India, the groom goes to see the bride (*pōnupārk-arude*). But my would-be bride decided to fly from Australia to meet me in NYC. She made a secret pit stop in California so that the Director of our play (Amma) could bless our life script! Can you guess the first engagement gift I received at our first meeting? Amma's biography! Before our marriage, I thought that this 'Amma thing' would go away. I was wrong!

Typically, we listened to *bhajans* in our car, because, as you know, while the chauffeur drives, the wife controls the music in the car, as well as the music in his life! Amma's calls to Kṛṣṇa and Dēvī sounded as real as if she were one with them, and she was not going to take her next breath between the calls. I had never heard such devotion-soaked music. Unintentionally, my eyes would well up, which I would try to hide.

In 2003, I met my most glorious Mother in NYC. My wife and I were doing ā*rati* to her. What a blessing! Her compassionate, mesmerizing eyes smiled right into mine, and the memory is etched deep in my heart. But it took another 13 years of many *darśans* and many, many apples to finally come home. In the early years, I would get an apple every time, and my wife would be jealous! I would offer to share it, but she would refuse. Now, if I get one, which is very infrequent, forget sharing. I don't even tell her I got an apple.

But honestly, at the time of that ārati, I was thinking, "Why am I doing ārati to a total stranger? I am not into all this spirituality stuff. I am only here to impress my newly-wedded wife." To further impress my wife, I even took a *mantra* at the first *Dēvī*

Bhāva. The three-day program was nice, but I never imagined that, years later, I would live in her āśram. As our family grew, we met Amma more often, and slowly this became our family vacation, because the rest of the time I was working.

Timing is everything, isn't it? Right from hitting a cricket ball, to making the right move in life or career, or investing in stock market. Things can play out so differently, based purely on the timing. A tragedy can even become a blessing! Say one is destined to lose Rs. 1,000 in the stock market out of an initial investment of Rs. 2,000. That 50% loss would be a shock. But, if a year after that loss of Rs. 1,000, the same investment had grown to Rs. 10,000, it would not hurt at all. Moving the same event to a different time changes its effect.

A few years ago, my aunt came to AIMS for a checkup. She also wanted to ask for Amma's blessing for her 35-year-old son to get married. He would be an ideal groom, but his horoscope was unfavorable for marriage. Amma told my aunt that she could not do anything. Then she said to me, "Amma cannot change *prārabdha*, but she *can* change *kāla* (time)." Who controls time? *KALI*! I sincerely believe that Amma has engineered the timing in my life more than once to work in our favor.

Our decision to move to India was made in five minutes during Amma's California program in 2015. Out of the blue, Amma told us to move. After convincing me, Amma warned my wife, Anita, "If you don't move now and something happens, don't come and complain to me." We decided then and there; but, when we returned to our hotel room, I could not believe what I had agreed to. Next day, I told Amma about my big house, my new job, and my retirement investments which had already lost half their value. And, on top of that, what do I tell my parents about our reason for the sudden move?

Amma answered all my questions, even correctly quoting prices of the stocks I owned. Her ever-flowing grace, constant encouragement, and the faith she instilled, helped us settle our mortgage, clear all our debts with minimal losses, and move to India. Most surprising of all, my family was thrilled that we came back to India, though our choice to live in the āśram was a hard pill to swallow. During the move, I complained more than once about all the aggravating issues. Amma replied, "Aren't you moving to India to be with Amma?" I still contemplate that sentence.

Uprooting from the US was hard. Adjusting here was harder. One time, I confessed that I was unable to surrender. Amma's response was, "What can Amma do then?" I replied, "Amma, you are the only one who can do something. I am helpless." Amma responded, "Then be like a patient in the ICU." Patients in ICU give consent to be sedated, and let the doctor perform lifesaving procedures. Consent translates to the patient's surrender to the doctor to do what is best. I am working very hard to be an obedient patient under the care of Dr. Mātā Amṛtānandamayī Dēvī.

Amma insisted that I travel back and forth to AIMS by train every day, chanting and meditating during the journey. This was a *torture* for me. Even Amma's public praise and encouragement for the travellers did not help me. I also was not contributing much at work. I struggled and complained. Amma repeatedly advised, "Acceptance!" I even wrote a 23-page thesis analysing all the hospital's shortcomings. All I got for my frustration was Love, Love and more Love. Like a perfect magician, Amma cast her spell and kept me distracted — with travels to Ernakulam and to the US for advanced training. Remembering Amma's own lung health helped me develop acceptance to events that would happen later.

At 45-yrs-old, with over 17 years of medical training, including several fellowships, and 10 years of clinical practice, Amma asked me to train in the field of Interventional Pulmonology at Harvard Medical School in Boston. I was *not* happy, but this would help establish our program at AIMS, and we would be able to train other doctors. We are now among the top three programs in India, and probably the most affordable one in the private sector. Absolute Grace! The message is very clear: Amma alone is the doer.

At the World Association of Bronchology and Interventional Pulmonology Conference 2020, AIMS won the First Prize for most innovative and cost-efficient management of multiple tumors in the lung. By Amma's infinite grace and compassion, AIMS is able to provide world-class care at a fraction of the cost, thereby fulfilling Amma's original mission for the hospital: "...where the poor can have access to advanced medical care in an atmosphere of love and compassion." AIMS serves not only Kerala, but all of India, and many impoverished neighboring countries.

In December 2019, we learned that Anita had cancer. The COVID pandemic was just starting. We were shocked, but then we understood why Amma had insisted we come to the āśram. When we told Amma, she assured us that everything would be ok. Amma advised us to proceed with all the treatments at AIMS, and to be strong and to face it bravely. When she gave us *darśan* that day, I cried, and she comforted me. In my childhood, when I was sad, I would lock myself in my room and cry out for "Amma."

My crying to "Amma" was not to any particular goddess or to my biological mother. I believe Amma heard my cries and came into my life way back then, and she has been with me ever since!

By Amma's grace, Anita's surgery, chemo and radiation were completed very quickly, and Amma was with us throughout. Post-surgery, Anita was in excruciating pain despite multiple different medications. Just then, Amma called and asked if she was in a lot of pain and assured her that the pain would resolve. The next medication worked, and her pain improved.

Amma says, and I have also noticed, that the patient's faith in the treatment is absolutely necessary for it to work. Amma's call, right at that moment, reinforced our faith that Amma is always with us. We hadn't told Amma the date or time of the surgery. The only explanation is that Amma, herself, is Time.

Initially, the tumor board recommended eight cycles of chemo; but, halfway through, due to increased COVID cases, they reduced it to four cycles. Amma did not agree. She insisted that we move to Ernakulam to finish the chemo and the radiation. A few days after we returned to the āśram, a cluster of Covid cases was reported right around where we had stayed in Ernakulam. That was my worry from the beginning, but when Amma insisted on the additional cycles, we never hesitated. Even with Amma's physical presence, this has been one of the most challenging times in my life. I have learnt so much about relationships, about myself, and the Truth of Amma's words.

I would like to return to the black dot on the white board analogy. White board now represents gratitude, and black spot is the cancer. Despite all the difficulties, I have a lot to be grateful for. If we had been in the US rather than in India, I would have had to work in the hospital to keep our health insurance going. Imagine if one of us had gotten Covid!

Everything that Amma utters is significant. During the treatment, staying away from our kids shielded them from seeing their mother suffer. The whole āśram came together to support our every need and take care of our children while we were not here.

Aneesh and Adi have complained to Amma many times, since moving to India, that I am never available for them. They even call me a 'Virtual Dad'. Amma fulfilled their wishes this year by letting me stay in the āśram and spend time with them. My complaint about missing *bhajans* while in Kochi was also resolved this year.

Amma, the divine logistician, is always showering her grace! We just have to be open and accept, with innocence. Amma's stern warning was a blessing for us. I bow down in reverence and gratitude. At times of such helplessness, questions fade away. Humility dawns and hopes give way to certainty that you are not alone. The Universal Mother takes the oars of our broken boat and shows us the light at the end of the tunnel.

The day before the Kurukṣētra war, trees were being felled to level the battlefield. Accidentally, a sparrow's nest with its four babies got knocked right onto the field. The sparrow mother was helpless as her little ones were too young to fly away. That night, while examining the battlefield with Kṛṣṇa, Arjuna saw the nest, but he did not act. Later, the sparrow approached Kṛṣṇa and cried, "Lord! Please! Save my children." The all-knowing Lord shrugged helplessly and said, "It is the law of Nature. I cannot change the course of this war. Anyway, stock up enough food for three weeks."

The next day, just before the conches were blown, Kṛṣṇa asked Arjuna for a bow and arrow. Arjuna hesitated, because of Kṛṣṇa's oath not to take up arms. Kṛṣṇa then shot at an elephant, and he told Arjuna that this elephant had felled the tree with the sparrow's nest. The arrow only dislodged the bell from the elephant's neck without harming the elephant.

After the war, Kṛṣṇa and Arjuna were surveying the battlefield and paying respects to the dead. They came across a large bell that must have fallen from some elephant's neck. Kṛṣṇa asked Arjuna to move it. Lo and behold, the sparrow and her four now not-so-little sparrows flew out. Arjuna was awestruck! That one shot that Kṛṣṇa took 18 days before had protected the whole sparrow family all through the war. Surrender and unending faith in the Lord is always protective.

Bhagavad Gītā 18:66 says:

> Abandon all varieties of *dharmas* and simply surrender unto me alone.
> I shall liberate you from all sinful reactions; do not fear.

The sparrow and her young ones were insignificant to the war, but not insignificant for the Divine, for whom nothing is insignificant. They mother sparrow surrendered helplessly to the Lord, with full faith, and thus invoked the Lord's grace. That year, I felt like that helpless sparrow. The difference is that the sparrow asked for help. In my case, the compassionate Divine Mother even saved me the trouble of asking.

The world has produced millions of teachers, only a few disciples, and, very occasionally, *Gurus*. The teacher instructs about the external world. The *Guru* guides deserving disciples to turn inward to the Self. Only an *avatār*, or God Herself, can transform undeserving into deserving disciples, guide them inward, and lead them to her own feet, the seat of *mōkṣa.*

Swāmī Vivekananda said: "The *Guru* is the bright mask God wears to come to us. As we gaze steadily, gradually the mask dissolves, and God is revealed." I bow to my *Guru*, the embodiment of Bliss, the personification of highest knowledge, the giver of greatest beatitude, who is pure, perfect, one without a second, eternal, beyond pleasure and pain, beyond all thought and qualification, transcendental.

No wonder the disciple looks upon *Guru* as God himself, and trusts, reveres, and obeys him, unquestioningly. This is the relation between *Guru* and disciple. I pray we all assimilate those qualities and stay devoted to her lotus feet for this life and all our future lives.

14

Who Am I?

Salma Jetha (United States)

> "Where am I? Who am I? How did I come to be here? What is this thing called the world? How did I come into the world? Why was I not consulted? And If I am compelled to take part in it, where is the director? I want to see him."

I had this quote on my wall for many years. It was written by Soren Kierkegaard, a Danish Existentialist who lived in the 1800s. I learned about the Existentialists when I was in high school. I was about 15 years old. I loved these philosophers. I would quote them all the time, and my friends would make so much fun of me. These philosophers were asking the questions I was wondering about myself. I admired them for that, but as much as I read and looked, I realized they didn't have answers to these questions either. We had not heard of *Sanātana Dharma*.

I grew up with a *Guru* and learned many of the practices Amma teaches us. Meditation, selfless service, *bhajans*, *satsaṅg*. I learned about great Sufi saints like Mansur Al-Hallaj who went around Persia proclaiming, "*Anal Haq, Anal Haq*" (I am the Truth). He was eventually gruesomely killed for making such a proclamation. I even learned about the concept of *Tawheed* (the oneness of God), but I never included myself. Until I met Amma.

The basis of Amma's teachings is the answer to this great question, "Who am I?" EVERY action of Amma tells us, "YOU are the DIVINE." She enters the hall and, even before she sits, she bows down to all of us whom she calls 'the embodiments of Pure Love and the Supreme Consciousness'. Really? Me? And in the west, many times Amma will say, "You don't have to believe in me; believe in yourselves." Over time I realized Amma was not just saying those words. That is ACTUALLY what she sees when she looks at us — Embodiments of Pure Love and the Supreme Consciousness.

My parents were great examples of *Guru bhakti* (*Guru* devotion). They're both gone now, but their *Guru* is still alive, and my family still follows him. Somehow, I always knew that he was not a *satguru*. My mother's love for the *Guru* expressed in service — to her family, the community, and the poor. I often saw my mother giving food and clothing to people who were less fortunate than us. And I would see my father wake up early every morning and meditate for hours. They would even wake us up at 3am to go to the Prayer Hall for the early morning meditation from 4-5am. I think I was five or six years old and would ask my parents, "What am I supposed to do for an hour sitting in that dark room?"

My mother was super strict. One little sound from us and we would get first the evil eye, and then a beating at home if we were really naughty. She was a typical Indian mother — so much love and so much strictness. I am so thankful for that now because when Amma scolds me or gives me that look with her Divine eyes, I am so filled with joy that she is REALLY my mother.

Sitting in that dark prayer hall early in the morning trying not to fall asleep, I would recall my parent's instructions, "There are a thousand names of Allah. Just pick one you like and chant that and pray silently. There must be *one* name that you like."

So, I would sit and silently chant, '*Allahuakabar Allahuakbar*' (God is Great). But I was not very convinced that God was great. I saw so much sadness and suffering around. I would visit my friends and their parents would fight and have so many problems, just like mine. I remember wondering, "Is there even one happy married couple that I know?"

Then came a big turning point in my life that made me leave the *Guru* and the religion. My mother was diagnosed with cancer when I was 17. I was the eldest daughter, so I took care of my mother both in the hospital and when she got home. People would come visit my mom and tell me to pray. Pray to what? To Whom? I had been taught that God is loving and benevolent. How could a loving, benevolent God do this to my mom? It made no sense to me. I had little understanding of the concept of *karma*.

Both my parents were also great examples of how to die. When my mom was in the hospital, literally on her deathbed, the doctor had said it would probably be just a few days. I remember she was on morphine because of the pain. She opened her eyes, looked at him and said, "How do you know? You're not God."

I remember, during that time, asking my mom, "Aren't you scared?" "Scared of what?" she said. "There is nothing to be afraid of." Her close friend was there praying the whole time.

When she passed, I had pretty much left the *Guru* and the faith. I was 20. I was very angry with God, and my father worried about me. I became focused on my studies, career and all these material things. It's easy to get lost in the world, as we all know.

Then, after some years, I became settled and calmed down a bit. I started to do *yōga* and meditation with a group of people who followed Paramahansa Yōgananda. My mind and my heart started to open again. I read *Autobiography of a Yogi* and was impressed by the book but not attracted to him as a *Guru*.

One day these friends of mine showed me a postcard of Amma and said, "We're going to see Amma on Sunday, do you want to come?" I looked at the picture of Amma, and she looked so sweet and gentle. I said, "Sure, I'll come with you guys." It was June 18, 2006.

We somehow got a seat inside the temple in San Ramon for the *Dēvī Bhāva* pūjā. There were ALL kinds of people there, all races, ages, backgrounds, rich, poor, EVERYONE. That really attracted me. I had never been in a religious/spiritual gathering that was so diverse. I really liked Amma's *satsaṅg*. Everything she said resonated with me. The pūjā for World Peace was powerful, and the holy water reminded me of the holy water called *Niyaz* that my parents used to make us drink every morning when I was a kid.

We waited for our *darśan* token numbers to come. I, like most first timers, was anxious. I had to work the next day. Around midnight our turn came. As soon as I had *darśan*, I knew Amma was a *sadguru*. I don't know how I knew but I knew. Amma's blessing in my ear that night was very distinct, and she has not repeated those same words since then. They must've done the trick because I didn't want to leave. It was after 1am, and my friends were perplexed, "We have to go Salma," they insisted. We lived about an hour away from the āśram on the Pacific Coast. I reluctantly left with them.

That was the beginning of my journey with Amma, and it has been beyond words amazing. Each and every step with Amma has been an incredible journey within myself. She has answered that question that puzzled me for so long on so many levels. "Who am I?" And the focus of my inquiry changed from "Who am I?" to "Who is Amma?" In the beginning, I knew Amma was a *sadguru*, but I realized that that was just the tip of the iceberg. And, as I began to understand more who Amma really is, I began to understand who I really am. Amma never forgets who she really is, but we constantly have to remind ourselves, "I'm **not** this body, I'm **not** this mind... **Stop it**." We have to control our mind, but Amma is ever established in her infinite nature.

One story from the book *The Timeless Path* is indelibly etched in my mind. Amma and the Swāmīs were at a TV studio in America. The station was doing a special on world religions and had invited Amma as the representative for Hinduism. The producer told Rāmakṛṣṇānanda Swāmī, "We would like Amma to introduce herself, saying, "Hello my name is Mātā Amṛtānandamayī, and I am a Hindu spiritual leader." The swāmīs were totally confounded. They had never heard Amma make such a statement and were doubtful that she would agree to say such a thing. They told Amma the producer's request, and as expected, Amma was reluctant. Finally, this is what Amma said: "This visible form people call 'Amma' or 'Mātā Amṛtānandamayī Dēvī' has no name or address. It is all pervading." (p 49 *The Timeless Path*)

After meeting Amma in 2006, I started to go to the San Ramon āśram for Saturday *satsaṅg*, *sēvā*, classes, *arcana*, *pūjās*. I learned so much about Amma and the āśram. I also started to read Amma's books — the *Autobiography* and all nine books in the *Awaken Children* series. Amma's infinite nature began to dawn within my mind.

But it was really Sugunanandan *acchan*, Amma's father, who helped me to understand Amma's infinite nature in my early days in the āśram. When I first came to India in 2007, I didn't come to the āśram; I went to AIMS to do *sēvā*. During that US Summer Tour, I had asked Amma if I could do *sēvā*, and she had told me that I could do anything I like. So, I somehow got connected with Ronji and Dr. Prem and landed up at AIMS in the Quality Assurance department.

Amma had even hinted to me, "Who is there for you at AIMS?" And I said, "You are Amma." I didn't feel fit or qualified for spiritual life and thought, "What am I going to do in the āśram all day? I should do some service that is of use." So, I went to AIMS to help establish some key quality metrics in the hospital to monitor patient satisfaction, waiting times, etc. Quality Assurance was my area of expertise, and I had a business helping companies design, develop and commercialize medical devices in accordance with international standards. I would come to the āśram as much as I could. One time, I was here for *Viṣu* (Amma was not in the āśram), and Sugunacchan gave a beautiful *satsaṅg* (2008 *Viṣu*).

He wanted a nice watch and he told Amma his desire. Sugunacchan and Damayanti-amma lived on the way to the backwaters in a small house with a porch that faced south. You could almost always find them sitting out on the porch. I always got the feeling that they were awestruck by all the people going by and what the āśram had become. One day while he and Damayanti-amma were sitting on their porch, an eagle came and dropped a nice watch on the ledge of the porch. Sugunacchan knew it was from Amma, but he was so upset. Why did she have to send an eagle? Why couldn't she come herself? He was so upset he went to Śaraṇāmṛta Swāmī's (Raju) old cloak room to speak with Amma, but finally Raju calmed him down.

Haven't we all felt this way? Why couldn't Amma just tell me? But that is not our Amma's way. She is not confined to this beautiful five-foot form, and she wants us to know that, to understand that, to experience it, so that we never forget.

Then Sugunacchan told the story of when Amma peed on him when she was a baby, but he didn't remember this incident. It was Amma who reminded him many years later. How could she know? How did she remember?

In Amma's 108 names, the 16th verse (*Om dūrīkṛta-ṣaḍūrmayē namaḥ)* means, "She who is devoid of the six modifications of life" (birth, existence, growth, change or evolution, degeneration, destruction). I always wondered about this; how does Amma transcend these phases?

She is so subtle and careful not to show her true divinity. When you watch *River of Love* (a beautiful movie on Amma's life), Suganacchan is talking about Amma, and he says, "She wasn't like my other children. After six months, she started to walk and soon after to talk normally. She never did any baby talk." All these stories and incidents made me realize Amma is not just a *Sadguru*. She is an *avatar* who came here with full awareness of who she is and a clear purpose.

In those early days, I would be so confused when I chanted *arcana*. (Well, I didn't chant then...I actually just tried to read the names while the *brahmacāriṇī* in the Kali temple was chanting.) But I would be so confused. How can Amma be Śiva, Śiva's wife, Śiva's Śakti and then be described as beautiful *Dēvī* and then as the Absolute? Oh, this is so confusing. Who is she? How can she be all these different things? This *arcana* was giving me a headache. I just didn't understand. It took me many years to begin to understand.

Some of you might remember when Amma used to sing to Soham when he was young, "Soham Soham, you and I are one." I used to watch Amma and wonder what does she mean? I feel that everything Amma does in front of all of us IS for all of us to learn something.

Remember when Thumban first came to sit with Amma during bhajans? He walked up to the front of the stage and looked at Amma and waited. Then after some time Amma gestured that he could come up. And then Amma looked at all of us and said, "Look at this dog. He has more śraddhā than all of you. He came and waited for permission to come up. How many of you wait for me to give permission?"

And then later, when he got older, Amma used to take the leash and tie it around her foot, and he would try to run away. And I would wince... Ayo! Amma's foot. Then I thought about what does that represent? That's my mind that Amma has tied to her foot. She needs to hold me so close to her as well, so my mind doesn't run away. And how many times has my mind run away during *bhajans*? He only tries to run once or twice!

Coming back to this song... "Soham, Soham you and I are one." It was not just for Soham. But how could Amma and I possibly be one? And then I realized, Amma is not talking about my body. She is talking about my soul — that part of me which I am completely ignorant of and with which she is intimately familiar. We are so identified with our bodies that we can't even fathom this reality of who we really are.

I lived in the *brahmacāriṇī* building for many years and heard Suma Cēcci refer to Amma as *parāśaktī.* What does that mean I wondered? And only recently, during this Corona *Kāl*, when we have had time to contemplate and read some books, have I finally understood. Amma IS ādi *parāśaktī.* The *arcana* (Śrī *Lalitā sahasranāma,* 1000 names of the Divine Mother) describes Amma in a thousand of her various aspects.

In *The Hidden Wisdom of the Goddess*, the author describes the Supreme Goddess (ādi *parāśaktī*). Through her power (*māya*), the Divine Mother gives birth to everything and fills it with her presence. She is the mother of the gods and men and every living creature, from the exalted to the lowly. Everything emerges from her and has its being in her. Everything returns to her in the end, for hers alone is the power to create, sustain, and dissolve. (Page 21)

That's why Amma's *darśan* touches us so deeply — because SHE IS OUR REAL MOTHER. Each of our souls came from her and will return to her. When she whispers in our ear, "*Ende mol, meri pyari beti, meine liebe*" (my daughter, my daughter, my love), we feel it on the soul level, on the level that is beyond the grasp of our minds. And many of us just start to cry because she has touched her own child in a way that only ādi *parāśaktī* can. Only she can say to us, "You're my child, I created you, I know how many lifetimes you've come and gone, how many bodies you've dwelled in, how many times you've run away from me, like Sītā chasing the golden deer, forgetting me in my own *māya*, but this time..." And that's when we completely lose it. By her Grace alone we know she has finally caught us and is not going to let us go. And this time we don't WANT her to let us go, EVER.

My first tour with Amma as a staff member was in March 2008 when she went to the Andaman Islands, Singapore, and Malaysia. I flew from AIMS to Calcutta and joined the group. The first stop of that tour was the Andamans. I will never forget that night. I had been to a few of Amma's programs in India before the Andaman Islands, but not enough to understand how things work. There were less than 50 staff members going to the Andamans.

As you all know, usually for a public program in India there are 500-1000 people traveling with Amma to do all the *sēvās*. There were less than 50 of us. I was given the task of changing the token numbers on BOTH the gents' and the ladies' side of the venue. It was a large venue and a huge crowd, and there was no one to help me. You can imagine... I kept getting called to the stage, and Amma was very upset with my performance. I just couldn't keep up with her, AND I had this mistaken notion that the token number on both the gents' and the ladies' side had to be the same. That's how it is in the West but NOT in India. The crowd was huge, and just getting back and forth from one side to the other took me 10-15 minutes. I kept getting called to the stage, and Amma was scolding me severely. I didn't understand much Malayalam then, but it was amazing. I kept looking into Amma's eyes. I could hear her yelling, but all I felt was this *śakti* (energy) from her divine eyes. It was indescribable. I did the best I could, but you can all imagine. Madhubala was translating, and I kept getting called. At one point, Amma looked at me as if to say, "You're still coming back?" Finally, Amma told Madhubala to take care of the numbers on the ladies' side and let me do the gents' side.

In the morning I had to go to the stage for something. Then Kripa Prana called me and told me to hold Amma's umbrella to block the sun. Okay, I did what I was told, but then I got worried. Oh no, Amma is going to see me here and not at the number board. Oh no... She's going to get really upset... But that didn't happen. Actually, the energy was sweet and soft, and I realized what an amazing grace it was that I got to hold Amma's umbrella... until she went to her car. After Amma left, I was in another *lōka* (world).

Amma had told me to tour with her, and I thought, "Oh, so this is tour." And I realized how crazy it was to ask to go to AIMS. From there, we went to Singapore, and I had a chance to ask Amma if I could come to the āśram, but she told me to stay at AIMS. I had a project there to finish. After five to six months, I came to stay at Amṛtapuri.

I would like to thank Amma for this Corona *Kāl* in the āśram. It's been an amazing time for me, and I imagine for many of you. I don't remember a time ever in my whole life not getting on a plane for this long.

You could say I'm a true ABCD (American-Born Confused Desi), but I am not American-born. I'm African-born. I was born in East Africa, in a place called Dar es Salaam, Tanzania. Then, after a year and half, we moved to Europe and lived in France for four years. Then we moved to Canada for a year, six months in Montreal, then six months in Vancouver. Finally, my parents bought a business with an uncle, and we settled in Los Angeles, California where I grew up. But my family is originally from Jamnagar, Gujarat which is on the road to Dwaraka. They were *lōhana* Hindus, a *kṣatriya* (warrior) class that defended India's Northwest Border for centuries. But then they started to get converted to Islam. My family was converted 500-600 years ago. I never know what to say when people ask me where I'm from. At least here and now I can say I'm from Amma, and I'm praying that I go back to her when all is said and done.

I pray that we can all merge back into ādi *parāśaktī* when this chapter of her divine play is over. I'd like to end with a poem from Hafiz, one of my favorite Sufi poets.

I Have Learned So Much

I Have Learned So much from God
That I can no longer Call Myself
A Christian, a Hindu, a Muslim, A Buddhist, a Jew.
The Truth has shared so much of Itself With me
That I can no longer call myself
A man, a woman, an angel Or even pure Soul.
Love has Befriended Hafiz so completely
It has turned to ash And freed Me
Of every concept and image
My mind has ever known.

15

Amma, the Divine Gardener

Haran Macindoe (New Zealand)

I grew up in New Zealand, enjoying friends and doing stupid things like riding motorcycles in the snow in the middle of winter. While studying economics at university, I realized I wasn't ready to spend the rest of my life stuck in an office, so, I decided to travel. I spent almost a year in Taiwan, teaching English to 200 Chinese kindergarten kids. In Nepal, I hiked in the spectacular Himalayas. Before heading to Europe, I decided to visit India. India's past and present fascinated me... monuments and temples, forts, museums, palaces and castles, and just wandering the streets. In South India, I heard about a saint named Amma. Another interesting experience to add to my collection, I thought.

Crossing the backwaters that evening, the only sound was the water slapping the side of the boat as it glided towards the āśram. It was January 1992, and I was 25 years old. I planned to stay a week or maybe two. I checked in and slept in the men's dormitory in the Kali temple. The next morning, I went down to the *darśan* hut. Seated on a simple cot, Amma was receiving visitors. People sat on either side of the aisle watching Amma or meditating. A solitary musician played a harmonium and sang sweetly.

I had no idea what to expect. When my turn finally came, she embraced me lovingly, looked at me, and asked where I was from. When I said, "New Zealand," she mimicked the long beak of the Kiwi bird and we both laughed. I wondered how she could have known what a kiwi bird looks like. My *darśan* was pleasant, but Amma hadn't blasted me into the stratosphere. I did not feel any change.

Traditional spiritual masters were mostly like florists who arranged small bouquets of talented and worthy disciples around them. I was neither talented nor worthy. For someone like me to stay on the spiritual path, Amma couldn't be a florist. She would have to be a farmer—someone who would till the soil, add nutrients, plant seeds, build a fence, water daily...and even be the sunlight itself, radiating the life-giving presence that nourishes and gives direction.

The āśram atmosphere was (and is) a unique blend of peace and quiet punctuated with noise and activity. Or...maybe it is noise and activity punctuated with peace and quiet. Whatever it was, I quickly felt very comfortable. Life was simple and rustic and always revolved around Amma. I was a high-energy, physical guy, and there was always work (*sēvā*) to do: blocks, bricks, sand to move. Piles here to move there; and piles there to be moved back here. Hand-mixing cement, chopping wood, cleaning toilets, washing pots...on and on...

Amma didn't fit into any category. She was some kind of a divine being, but she seemed so down-to-earth. She would give you a blissful *Dēvī Bhāva* darśan in the evening; and, the next morning, during sand *sēvā*, she'd eagerly fill your bag with sand!

Amma never put on superior airs. She worked hard along with everyone, and she was very careful and joyful—always looking out for others and making people laugh.

Sēvā with Amma was like a party—and she was the perfect hostess. She showed how even the most mundane labor is a chance for focus and fun. Her joy was infectious, and everyone loved to be around her. Feeling Amma's loving presence, for the first time in my life I felt I was really living.

I moved to one of the grass huts that had been built. Often the āśram bell would ring very late, and a few of us would gather for late-night sand *sēvā* with Amma in the open area outside my hut. After *sēvā*, we would sit with Amma in the sand. As she chatted with us under the star-studded sky, in the cool night air, she would hand each one a glass of sweet black coffee and a handful of peanuts. These were magical moments, and everyone knew it.

Around this time the āśram was trying to drill a bore-well outside my hut. The whole place was a complete mess of dirt piles and ponds of sticky mud. As the truck drilled, the sand kept collapsing into the hole. I guess the project didn't look very promising because, one day, the drilling truck left.

Then, late one evening, word came that Amma had gone to the seashore to meditate and wanted to be alone. Later, I heard a splash outside my hut. Amma was standing in one of the mud ponds. Another āśram resident arrived, and we helped Amma out of the pond. I brought a bucket of water, and, as Amma leaned on me for support, we washed the mud from her feet.

That night, I lay in bed, completely sleepless, reflecting on the great blessing to have washed Amma's feet, even under such humble circumstances. Of course, (miraculously!), a few days later, the drilling truck returned and started drilling right where Amma had stood. And the project was, suddenly, a success! It became the main well for the āśram, giving thousands of gallons of water every day!

At that time, there weren't more than 40 westerners in the āśram. Most mornings, Amma joined the westerners for meditation on the roof of the Kali temple. Amma sat absorbed and immovable under the open sky, and it seemed like our very own Arunachala Mountain. You didn't even need to close your eyes to meditate.

Amma made every day special. We had plays, festivals, celebrations, *Dēvī Bhāva* every Thursday and Sunday, daily *darśan* in the hut, group meditations, group *sēvā*. We could sit very close to Amma when she sang evening *bhajans* as she sat on the floor of the Kali temple. Amma's presence had made my life so full that, instead of continuing my travels to Europe, I decided to join her 1992 American Tour and come back here for another year.

One of the many powerful—and challenging—aspects of being in Amma's presence is that it awakens awareness in you. Before meeting Amma, the idea of observing my thoughts was completely foreign; but, becoming aware of my thinking became uppermost in my mind, especially once I realized that Amma *knew* what I was thinking. Sensing that *she* noticed what I was thinking, *I* started noticing what I was thinking. The upside of this is that I began to see the thoughts in my mind. The downside of this is...I began to see the thoughts in my mind.

It was very difficult to reconcile that, no matter how hard I tried, I could not turn off my old ways of thinking. I sometimes felt I didn't belong here. But, whenever I went for *darśan* or saw Amma around the āśram, she always welcomed me with her compassionate smile. This showed me I could completely trust her, even with my most private thoughts—and that her Love is truly unconditional.

By showing me the ditch water in my mind, Amma made me WANT to clean it up. I began the painstaking process of adding pure water, drop-by-drop, to the ditch water. I began to meditate, do *japa*, *yōga* and *arcana*. I got an Amma-name. And I read every spiritual book I could find...even when I didn't understand any of it. Amma was slowly replacing my desire for worldly experiences with longing for inner unfoldment.

Sometime after this, I started dividing my time between Amma's California āśram in San Ramon and Amṛtapuri. Finally, in 1995, with Amma's blessing, I settled in San Ramon as the facilities coordinator, and I called it home for the next 18 years. Each evening, we would gather in the *pūjā* room, like a family, with Paramatmananda Swāmī, to hear his classes on the *Bhāgavatam*, *Mahābhārata* and the *Rāmāyaṇa*, and to sing *bhajans*. We loved when he would reminisce about the old days with Amma, or his years in Tiruvannamalai. With Amma coming to San Ramon every year, and time to meditate, and wholesome and engaging *sēvā* on the land and in the community, my life felt complete. The āśram community became the close-knit family I never had.

Amma gave me some advice. She said, "Haran, perform all your actions like they are flowers with which you can make a garland, and offer that garland to Amma." I still treasure this beautiful image. But I wasn't able to follow her advice. I didn't offer my actions to her as a flower garland. I did lots of *sēvā*, but I didn't have the mindset of a *karma yōgī*.

I enjoyed helping people and overcoming challenges, but I loved the praise and the validation that came with achievement.

All the successes and accomplishments were *mine*. I didn't try to feel that Amma was working through me. I wasn't trying to be her instrument. "*I*" was doing the work, not Amma. Amma gave me a lot of room to imagine that I was the master of my destiny. As you know, on the spiritual path, we all need to begin to introspect and surrender to life. For me, this required a shock.

Sudden failure came in June 2000, during Amma's San Ramon program. Just after lunch, an enormous "BOOM" shook the āśram grounds. We looked up and saw a huge orange fireball rising about 100 feet in the air above the kitchen. It was a nightmare. A 20-gallon propane tank had exploded. Then five more tanks exploded, one after the other. All we could do was stare.

A lot of people had been in the kitchen, but by Amma's grace, almost everyone escaped before the main explosion. But, several close devotees, who are also my dear friends, did get badly burned. The cause of the fire proved to be faulty propane tanks, but *I* felt *a lot* of guilt and shame for the disaster.

The local government officials and fire department required us to completely upgrade the facility before they would let Amma visit San Ramon again. The final list of required improvements was overwhelming. We had to:

- Repair and upgrade the damaged 6000-square-foot *mandapam* and make it a fire-proof "refuge" with exterior walls and fire escape doors, fire-proof wall and ceiling coverings, cement floor and fully upgraded electricity.
- Install a complete fire alarm and sprinkler system.
- Construct two more 10,000-gallon concrete fire water tanks.
- Install about 1000 feet of buried water line with two fire hydrants.

- Construct a 3000-square-foot temporary, code-compliant commercial kitchen.
- and many other tasks.

We were just a small handful of volunteers and had only a few months to finish this before Amma was due to arrive for her 2001 summer visit. This was the biggest challenge of my life, and I was not confident. Looming failure caused a lot of fear and stress. The problem was *I* felt that the burden rested on *my* shoulders—not on Amma's shoulders; and that the outcome depended on *me*, not her.

After months of hard work, worry and stress, the final inspection was scheduled for the day before the first San Ramon program in 2001. After looking at everything, the inspector issued the permit for Amma's program. Exactly when the inspector's car drove out of the property, Amma's car arrived from the airport. Their cars literally passed each other. But I was not able to celebrate Amma's arrival. I couldn't even bring myself to look at Amma. I had never offered my positivities to Amma; and now, I didn't know how to offer my negativities to her.

Being an instrument is like an insurance policy against stress and anxiety. I had dug myself into a deep pit of negativity. I didn't know how to surrender and reach out to Amma to beg her to pull me out of myself into her light.

I couldn't climb out of my pit, so she jumped in, and stood there alongside me. Shining her loving presence into my mind and heart, Amma showed me things I needed to acknowledge and surrender but couldn't: low self-esteem, doubt, fear of failure and rejection, desire for praise and acknowledgment, cravings, anger, sadness, shame, and so on. It felt like the old sand-sēvā days, but a kind of "inner" sand-*sēvā*. The poet, Rumi, describes this process beautifully:

> I have come to drag you out of yourself
> and take you into my heart.
> I have come to bring out the beauty
> you never knew you had,
> and lift you like a prayer to the sky.
> If no one recognizes you, I do,
> because you are my life and soul.
> Don't run away, accept your wounds
> and let bravery be your shield.
> It takes a 1000 stages for the perfect being to evolve.
> Every step of the way, I will walk with you
> and never leave you stranded.

Amma said: "Remember, the Self is even-mindedness: the same in pleasure and pain, hot and cold, success and failure." And: "Haran, it's the "*I-ness*" in you that must dissolve, like a salt doll trying to measure the depth of the ocean"

I understood that it's not the "*doing*" that causes suffering; it's the "*doer.*" I also saw that the everyday ups and downs of life could teach me even-mindedness, and reveal the nature of this "*doer*", this "*I-ness*". I realized that, if I continued to live an unaware life, I would never be free from old habits, never know even-mindedness, and never know my true nature.

A basket-full of ocean crabs never needs a cover because, even as one crab is climbing free, the others drag him back down. Amma says our "likes and dislikes," are like these "crabs." The actions in our past lives have formed *samskāras* and *vāsanas (karmic* patterns) in us that become our thoughts and our feelings, and then manifest as our words and behavior. I'm helpless until I become conscious and begin to discriminate. Amma helps me to see this, which frees me to live in the present moment. *Amma* is the director of all experiences. Every place, every event and possession, every interaction with everyone and everything is an opportunity to become more conscious.

Traveling with Amma, both in India and abroad, has deepened my enthusiasm for the spiritual journey. I see again and again how her beauty makes every place she visits beautiful. Amma's sanctity makes every place she goes a holy place—whether an enormous program tent in Bordeaux, France; or at the UN in Geneva or New York; or at the Parliament of Religions in Chicago, or conferences at the Vatican or Abu Dhabi, even Saint Francis' *portiuncola* (a holy Christian pilgrimage site) near Assisi in Italy.

Touring with Amma has ups and downs. So many people come to Amma's programs. The blinding pace and super-long hours seem to shift the ground under your feet. You can't hang onto anything except Amma. She alone is reliable. She holds everything together while she shows us the things that prevent us from being fully present. I feel that Goddess Kālī should have a fifth hand—one that holds up a mirror that reflects our reactions to us so we can learn from them.

Speaking of Kālī, I have learned a lot about myself through my wife Rasya, who never compromises on what she feels is right. While living in San Ramon, Rasya and I take occasional walks along a trail that passes through some wealthy neighborhoods. On one such walk, I suddenly realized that I was walking alone. I looked back and saw Rasya eagerly picking used glass bottles from the public rubbish bin. The āśram runs a recycling program, and it gets a few cents' refund on each bottle for Amma's charities.

While I support this project *in theory*, I was embarrassed because I felt that the locals would think *we* were poor and desperate for those few cents. I tried to convince Rasya to stop. I said, "Let's come back next week with bags to carry them." But she just kept picking the bottles out of the rubbish.

I tried bribery—$20 if she would put the bottles back and just keep walking. But Rasya is Amma's daughter. I was afraid of what others might think of us, but Rasya is fearless about *dharma*. I stared at the ground as people passed, but Rasya grinned from ear to ear as we walked back carrying our sticky, smelly loot.

You can see the genius of Amma's teaching about even-mindedness. I might imagine I'm spiritually superior in meditation and understanding, but what happens to my "spirituality" when I'm in a situation I don't like? Training my mind was the goal, but even after years, the same old endless procession of thoughts is still there. Amma says the mind swings endlessly, like a pendulum, between happiness and sorrow. How do we break free from the movements of the pendulum?

Are the thoughts themselves the problem? I asked Amma, "Do people who have attained liberation have thoughts?" She replied, "Yes, *jivan muktas* have thoughts, but they understand the nature of those thoughts and are not bothered by them." So, what does Amma mean when she says, *'not bothered by the nature of thought'*? The second chapter of the *Bhagavad Gītā* answers this question:

nāsato vidyate bhāvō nābhāvo vidyatē sataḥ
ubhayōr-api dṛṣṭō'ntaḥ tvanayōs-tattva-darśibhiḥ

> Enlightened ones understand that anything that changes is not real.
> Only that which never changes is real.

And so, the way to even-mindedness, to 'not be *bothered* by thoughts,' is to understand that thoughts have no separate reality. A thought can never know itself. Thoughts have no life, no power over me other than the power I give them—by entertaining them. And so, to be free of thoughts means simply to accept the mind and life as it is... to understand that the pendulum swings back and forth.

Acceptance is transcendence. Amma accepts the world as it is, so she is unaffected by it. She floats like a lotus on the surface of a pond. She can love us unconditionally because she doesn't judge us. She accepts us just as we are. All growth from unconsciousness to consciousness happens because of Amma's loving presence—she is like the sunlight that nourishes a plant.

Amma has no likes or dislikes, no sense of limitation or confusion. She doesn't need anything from anyone. The world doesn't bind Amma, so her words and actions are always perfect. She acts; she never reacts. Amma is Supreme Being. She exists infinitely in the present yet remains completely untouched by experiences. Her every action is always perfectly aligned with Supreme Being. She is like a bird flying freely through the sky, leaving no *karmic* trail.

I once asked Amma, "When you look at the world, what do you see?" She said, "Amma is like a honeybee in a garden. She doesn't look at the flowers; she only sees the honey." For Amma, there is never any sorrow. She knows only the sweetness of the changeless reality that is the substratum of everything. Amma brings awareness and understanding to our experiences so we can learn to taste that same sweetness. May the sweetness of Amma's radiant presence continue to bring solace and happiness to the entire world for generations to come.

16

Faith and Surrender

Anita Raghavan (Australia)

Once upon a time, Śrī Buddha visited a town that had prepared for weeks to receive him. When he arrived, everyone gathered in excited anticipation of hearing him speak. However, when he reached the venue, he was silent. His attention was diverted towards the road outside the program venue.

After a long wait, the elders of the town asked, "For whom are you waiting? All of the important village members are already here. Please start your discourse." Śrī Buddha responded, "I cannot start because the one I have come so far to meet is not here yet." As he gave this reply, a 13-year-old girl entered the hall and fell at his feet. She said "I am a little late, but you kept your promise! I knew you would keep your promise because I have waited for you for ten long years, since the first time I heard your name."

Buddha responded, "You have not waited in vain. You are the one who attracted me to this village." At the end of the lecture, the girl approached the master and said, "Please initiate me and take me to live with you." Śrī Buddha replied, "Yes. You must come and stay with me. This town is too far out of the way, and this body is growing too old to travel so far."

At night, as they were settling down to sleep, Ānanda, Śrī Buddha's chief disciple, said, "Master, before you sleep, I want to ask you one question. Do you feel a certain pull towards the places that you visit?" Śrī Buddha replied, "Yes, Ānanda. That is how I decide my journeys. When I feel someone is thirsty... so thirsty that, without me, there is no way for them...I have to move in that direction."

In 1991, when I was 12 years old, my most glorious Amma visited my hometown of Melbourne, Australia, and gave me the good fortune to meet her. Like Śrī Buddha in this story, our compassionate mother has traversed the globe tirelessly, for so many years, quenching the spiritual thirst of longing hearts. It's not that Amma needs devotees, or that she likes travelling to far off places. She is *pūrṇa-brahma-swarūpiṇī* (complete within herself). But, out of her infinite compassion, she travels far and wide to rescue so many souls who are crying for her divine touch.

When I was five years old, my baby brother passed away from a rare form of cancer. My parents lost their drive for worldly pursuits and went on a spiritual quest. They took me to many temples and pilgrimage centers. I prostrated at the feet of countless *swāmīs*, and slept through countless spiritual lectures. Also, I used to attend Christian Mass every day at school. I longed to understand the mysterious entity called God.

From the moment I entered the program venue on that blessed day, and saw Amma ecstatically calling out to Kṛṣṇa and *Dēvī* during *bhajans*, I was mesmerized. My father was amused that I did not fall asleep during the program and asked, "What are you thinking about?" I responded, "Up till now, you have taken me to so many masters who spoke about God; but here, finally, you have brought me to someone who can *see* God."

What makes Amma so attractive to all kinds of people is that she truly walks her talk. Her every moment, every word and every action are perfect and complete. And her every moment, word and action awaken us to see God (or her) within ourselves. However, we must purify ourselves to receive her ever-pouring grace.

Growing up in Australia, I was often confused about where I belonged. Was I Indian, the way I was being brought up at home? Or, was I Australian, the way that I was treated at school. In the *Lalitā Sahasranāma*, Amma is venerated by the *mantra*, *ōm sampradāyēśwaryai namah* (the one who preserves traditions). When I was growing up, Amma used to affectionately call me *paṭṭatti* (*brahmin* girl). Because I grew up in Australia, I had no idea what a *brahmin* was. My world was tidily categorized into brown people, white Australians, and Chinese. I had no idea how vast Indian culture is. Because of Amma's encouragement, my love for the culture of my ancestors was awakened.

Amma always encouraged me to speak in my mother tongue (Tamil), despite my poor command of the language. She encouraged me to sing *bhajans* and attend *satsangs*. Because of Amma, not just I, but thousands of children growing up abroad, have awakened to the ancient culture of *Sanātana Dharma*. It is because of Amma that my own children can experience the culture of this ancient land. Amma is indeed *Bhārat Mātā*.

Self-confidence (ātmā *viśwāsam*), faith and surrender are qualities every seeker should cultivate. Amma often compares Self-confidence to a booster rocket. She also says we should be strong like mighty lions, not meek like kittens. The Self-confidence that Amma speaks about is not from the ego. It refers to our confidence in Amma who is, in fact, our own true Self.

I was very shy, as a child. To help me overcome my introvert nature, and to teach me about Indian culture, my mother enrolled me in *bharata nāṭyam* (Indian dance) classes when I was six years old. By my dance teacher's own words, I was the worst student she had ever seen. I had two left feet, a crooked smile and hunched shoulders. She kept telling my mother not to bring me to class. And she would never let me perform at important events; but, my mother persevered. I had no choice but to take all of my teacher's scoldings and abuse, week after week.

Someone had given me a small idol of *Naṭarāja*, and I used to bargain with him desperately. Either he should give my mother the sense to end my dance classes, or perform a miracle by making me dance properly. When I was around 13 years old, I got a chance to perform for Amma. Nearly everyone who had ever seen me dance remarked about how terrible I was. I was hoping to perform quickly, and that Amma would not see anything.

In those days, Amma used to give *darśan* sitting with her back to the stage. To my great astonishment, when I started to dance, Amma kept turning around and clapping her hands. When I went for *darśan* later, she kept remarking about what a wonderful dancer I was. I had no idea that *Naṭarāja* would answer my prayers like that.

After that, I never missed a chance to dance for Amma whenever she visited Australia. In fact, on the occasion of my dance *arangētram* (graduation), my teacher remarked that I was her greatest success story. She felt her career was complete after turning someone so hopeless as me into a good dancer. Of course, we all know that it was not my teacher's success. Only Amma's grace let me develop this skill. By making me do what seemed impossible, Amma awakened the Self-confidence that I lacked.

Faith in the *Guru's* words is essential for every spiritual seeker. However, the *māyā* surrounding Amma is so powerful that sometimes we forget Amma's greatness and think she is confined to her five-foot, adorable figure. In *Bhagavad Gītā* 7:14, Lord Kṛṣṇa says,

> *Mama māyā duratyayā*
>
> *Māyā* is as powerful as himself, and difficult to cross through our limited self-effort.

At the end of the *kurukṣētra* war, Kṛṣṇa asked Arjuna to descend from his chariot first, and then allow the Lord to descend. Despite hearing the entire *Bhagavad Gītā* and seeing the Lord's *viś*war*ūpa darśan*, Arjuna forgets, and thinks that Kṛṣṇa is "just" his cousin and friend.

Initially, Arjuna refuses to get off the chariot. However, upon further persuasion, he does get off before Kṛṣṇa. As soon as Kṛṣṇa gets down, the magnificent chariot bursts into flames and is reduced to a heap of ash. Everything Amma tells us is only for our own good; but, because of *mahā*māyā, we often forget Amma's glory, and, trivially, brush aside her words.

When I was 16 years old, I longed to live a spiritual life here in Amṛtapuri, and I asked Amma to let me come and stay with her. She said, if I studied well, I could definitely come. I was thrilled that she had given me her promise. Somehow, I used to persuade my parents to let me spend at least a part of every summer holiday here in the āśram. I would save up my pocket money for flight tickets and travelling with Amma. However, when I was 21, my parents, fueled by the prediction of an astrologer that an early marriage would be the only option for me, decided to look for a suitable match and get me married.

I had studied well and had a good job with a multinational company. I thought that Amma would support me since she had said earlier that I could live with her. Instead, Amma encouraged my parents to pursue an ideal groom. I felt betrayed when Amma told me, strictly, to listen to my parents. My father searched for six months but did not find even one suitable horoscope that matched mine.

I was just getting hopeful that he would never find anyone when the horoscope of an unsuspecting young doctor, living in the United States, fell into his hands. Amma was convinced that this was the right choice for me and would not tolerate any of my protests. She assured me, with love, that this was the best path for me. She promised me that this groom, selected by my parents, was also her devotee. He had never even heard about Amma at that time.

Amma gave me so much love leading up to my marriage, choosing a *sāri* and a piece of jewelry for me. Unfortunately, in my limited and immature thinking, I still felt betrayed that she had broken her promise to me. When I relocated to the US after marriage, I struggled to adjust. My husband was a self-confessed workaholic and was grappling with the demands of residency and fellowship. He had very little time or energy to entertain me. Only through Amma's *satsaṅg* in New York could I gain some stability and get on with my life.

Due to visa issues, we eventually had to relocate to Iowa, and I found myself in the middle of rural, midwest America, a complete misfit. To cope with the isolation and surrounded by affluent people, I started to lead a worldly life, and I prioritized worldly pursuits over spiritual life.

Thirteen years after we were married, my husband became Amma's devotee, just as she had predicted. We were visiting San Ramon, California, during Amma's summer program. While Amma was giving *darśan*, I was chasing our two little boys outside the program hall when a lot of people came looking for me. They said Amma was in a very serious conversation with my husband, Dr. Arvind. When I went to investigate, Amma explained that she thought we should move to India. She had a job for Arvind at AIMS, and I should live with the children in Amṛtapuri.

I couldn't believe it. Amma was going to fulfill her promise of nearly 20 years before. In fact, in my worldly pursuits, I had completely forgotten my desire to live in Amṛtapuri. I asked Amma how I would live in India after spending my entire life in the west. Every word that Amma utters is only for our good. She is the *kalpavṛkṣa* (wish-fulfilling tree). We forget this.

It took us nearly a year to wind down our opulent life in the US and move to India. The adjustment was not smooth. My children had to downsize from a 4200 sq. ft. house to a 200 sq. ft. room. They were not happy about the sudden loss of creature comforts. Having already attended school in the US, they both decided that they didn't like the education system here and would constantly scheme to skip school. Amma, in her infinite patience, counseled us through each meltdown and reassured me that everything would be ok.

Once, my younger son, Adi, concocted a plan to get out of school by putting a *manjāḍi* (flower seed) into his ear and telling me that a classmate did it. Amma uncovered his naughty scheme and gently sent him back to school. When my husband had difficulty establishing a practice here, Amma suggested that he return to the US for further training, and establish a practice in interventional pulmonology. Every time one of us faltered, Amma reassured us and gave us love and comfort. I am so grateful to Amma for keeping us here.

Surrender is the most important quality for a seeker to cultivate. Surrender is such a simple word; but it is so difficult to actually practice. A few years ago, I had an opportunity to visit Kapistalam, (in Tamil Nadu), my ancestral temple from my father's side of the family. A beautiful story of surrender from the *Bhāgavatam* called *Gajēndra Mōkṣa* is said to have taken place there.

Gajēndra was a mighty elephant who was the king of the forest. He was a happy elephant and a well-loved king, but he was very proud of his strength and valor. One day, he was roaming the forest with his fellow elephants. It was extremely hot, and he entered a cool lake for a bath. A crocodile who lived in the lake was irritated by the disturbance, and sunk his teeth into *Gajēndra's* legs.

Gajēndra mustered up his own strength to free himself from the crocodile's grip; but, despite repeated attempts, he could not. Finally, realizing he was completely helpless, he cried out to the Lord to save him. Immediately, Lord Viṣṇu appeared on his mount, *Garuḍa*, and cut off the head of the crocodile with his discus, thereby rescuing his dear devotee.

Life's struggles are only opportunities to practice surrender. Only when we feel totally helpless in the face of sorrow can we realize that Amma is our only refuge. Amma says, "With *Dēvī's* grace, we can overcome the *karmic* fruits of our past actions. When a child is afraid, he will cry out to his mother, and she will come to his rescue.

This year, I had an opportunity to practice helpless surrender. While details of covid were just emerging in the world, I was diagnosed with breast cancer. Initially they thought that surgery would be sufficient, but further tests showed it was a rapidly growing tumor, and the tumor board recommended aggressive treatment, including surgery, chemotherapy, and radiation. I was numb with shock, and my husband took me to Amma to explain all the details.

Amma advised me to undergo the full treatment. I had lost my brother, my father and my uncle to different forms of cancer, and I knew all too well the horrors of cancer treatment. I was filled with dread. The night I had surgery to remove the tumor, I suffered agonizing pain, and the pain medications were not helping. In those moments, I thought, selfishly, that I should just die. I prayed to Amma to release me from this torture.

As I was thinking these dark thoughts, Amma called. She said four simple sentences: "Don't be sad. The time will change. Be brave. Amma is always with you." The faith and self-confidence from so many experiences in her divine presence carried me through pain; but, more importantly, helped me to surrender helplessly to her will and accept it.

I received my full treatment at Amma's own hospital where Amma's beautiful smiling photos hang on every wall. The surgeon and chemotherapy nurses were devotees, and full of love and compassion. Previously, I thought I was very strong and independent. Then, suddenly, I found myself needing the help of others for even the simplest tasks. I often felt frustrated at my physical weakness; but with time, started to accept the situation.

At the end of my treatment, my oncologist told me that the biggest issue for cancer patients is that cancer will leave the body but not the mind. It's true. Memories of intense pain continued to haunt me days after treatment ended. In the end, it was Amma's words that gave me solace. When I returned to the āśram after three months of treatment (during the lockdown period), Amma looked at me and said, "Ellām śari ākum." (Everything will be ok.)

I recently read a story about gratitude. A poor blind boy sat on the steps of a building with a hat by his feet. He held up a sign that said: "I am blind, please help." There were only a few coins in his hat. A gentleman, who was walking by, took a few coins from his pocket and dropped them into the blind boy's hat. Then he took the sign, turned it over, wrote some words, and placed the placard so that everyone walking by could see the new words.

Soon the hat began to fill up with coins. That afternoon, the man who had changed the words on the placard returned. The boy recognized his footsteps and asked, "Are you the one who changed my placard this morning? What did you write?" The man said, "I only wrote the truth. I said what you said, but in a different way." I wrote, "This world around you is so beautiful. You can see it, but I can't." Both signs told people that the boy was blind; but, the first sign just stated the boy was blind. The second sign reminded people how lucky they were not to be blind, and to be grateful for the gifts that we often take for granted.

Amma often reminds us that life is fleeting. She tells us to be like birds perched on a twig that may snap at any moment. My experience with cancer let me experience the truth of Amma's words. It has taught me to be grateful for each and every thing, and to see life as a cup half-full rather than half-empty. Amma's words are so precious. When she says she is always with us, she truly is.

When my son, Aneesh, was three years old, he was standing outside the Sandown Race Course in Melbourne when Amma was leaving the hall after *darśan*. He was a baby growing up in America. Instead of saying, "*Namaḥ śivāya*" as Amma passed him, he shouted, "Bye Amma." Amma stopped for a second and looked at him very seriously. She said, "Bye? No bye." It seemed so trivial; but later, I realized Amma was promising that she would never ever forsake him, and that he could never say good-bye to her.

To this day, the sweetest moments in my life have been Amma's *līlas*. In the *Tulasi Rāmāyaṇa* is a beautiful story of a *kēvaṭ* (boatman). When Rama reaches the *Ganges*, during his travels, he asks the *kēvaṭ* to ferry him to the other shore. The *kēvaṭ* says he will do it on one condition: If Rama allows him to wash the dust off his feet. The Lord says that his feet are clean enough, and that he should be able to enter the boat without washing. But the *kēvaṭ* is adamant. He had waited so many lifetimes to wash the dust off the feet of the Lord. He would not miss this opportunity.

At the end of the boat journey, Lord Rama asks the *kevaṭ* how he should pay him for the trip. The *kēvaṭ* answered, "It is not customary to ask those of the same profession for payment for their services." He then asked the Lord to return the favor and ferry him across the ocean of *samsāra.*

When I heard this story in my childhood, I had an intense desire to receive the dust from Amma's lotus feet. Many years ago, Amma fulfilled my desire when I was doing line monitoring *sēvā* next to Amma. I was not doing a very good job, and people were complaining about me left, right, and center. Amma looked at me compassionately and asked me to massage her feet rather than monitor the line, if I wanted to be close to her. I don't know how much time passed, but I am forever grateful for the gift she gave me. Since my illness, I pray to Amma that, for however long she has extended my life, my mind should always dwell on her. And that, when this life ends, she should take me across in her divine boat.

I want to end with this Tamil prayer from Abhirāmi Paṭṭar, the great poet saint and *Dēvī bhakta* of the 16th century.

> The Goddess, in all her compassion,
> showered her grace on me,
> Undeserving though I am. How to thank her?
> Whatever situation I am in,
> even if I am in the middle of the ocean of *samsāra*,
> I know that she will take me to the other shore.
> She is the Supreme Consciousness that lives in all *jivas*,
> and the formless, my very own mother.

I offer all these precious memories at her lotus feet.

17

Amma's Love

Sudhamayi Schoenmeier (Germany)

In 1997, āśram*ites* were giving *satsaṅgs* in the Kali Temple while Amma listened from her hut below the temple. Then was the first time I gave a *satsaṅg*. In 2001, this practice had shifted to the green roof of the Kali temple. Amma would listen on the side roof, without seeing the person, and we also did not see Amma. One night, I was asked to give a *satsaṅg* in **English**. Afterwards, when Amma came to serve *prasād*, she asked, "Who gave a *satsaṅg* in **German**?" Now, almost 20 years later, I have the great grace to sit **next** to Amma, and I *hope* to sound **English** this time.

Many of us have known each other many years and have walked this path together. Hearing our life stories connects us even more deeply and leaves us in awe of how powerful Amma is. Actually, these talks are like a flower garland woven from Amma's glory and our gratitude. Today let me weave my little flower into this garland strung on the thread of Amma's Love. Amma's Love is my topic today.

It is astonishing how all of us have come here, from so many different backgrounds, countries, religions and social groups.

Some come from far corners of the world. Others lived as close as a two-hour bus ride away. Amma's grace alone brings us here.

Amma knows our hearts, and what each of us needs for our spiritual growth. She is established in Supreme Consciousness in which all names and forms arise. Amma is like a huge ship that can carry countless passengers. She shows us how to realize our true nature, the Self. To persevere on the path requires our effort, but Amma's love even more so. Her love lets us feel protected and safe and gives us confidence that we can reach the goal.

Amma's love is infinite. One of the greatest visible testaments of this love happened on Amma's 50th Birthday. More than half a million people came from all over the world to celebrate. On the last day, Amma announced that she would give *darśan* to *all* her children. The crowd was huge, and people were pouring into the program venue. When I saw Amma's eyes, blazing with the fire of her divine power and enthusiasm, I understood that nothing in this world could stop Amma from showering her love through her *darśan*.

I will never forget Amma's eyes. She was ready to "eat up her children." We should also have the urge to "eat up our Amma," meaning to completely merge in her. We should long to dissolve into her. Our ego should disappear. Amma says: "Love can easily consume the *Guru*. Love can easily consume your ego. Once your ego is fully consumed, the *Guru* will simply enter into you; or you can simply enter into him. This flow of love goes both ways and becomes one. The *Guru* is flowing and overflowing with love."

Amma's love has the power to heal. Most of us carry deep inner wounds and so much pain. Amma says, "The inner wounds and pain give others the power to hurt you again and again.

Words cannot heal you, nor can intellectual knowledge. But the unconditional love and compassion of a perfect Master can heal your wounds and give you the strength to prevent you from being hurt again."

During my first visit to the āśram, I got very sick. I lost a lot of weight and could hardly eat anything. I was mentally very clear but slept barely four hours at night. One night I had a vivid dream. Amma came to me in the form of Kali and was breastfeeding me. It was so incredible that I woke up. Soon after, I was completely cured.

The deep message of the dream was: Amma will take care of me and everything. This was very healing because I always suffered from feeling deprived of what I needed. Throughout my life, I felt left out, neglected, rejected. After this dream I understood why. After I was born, my father was supposed to pick up my Mom and me from the hospital. For some reason he was delayed, and the wait gave my Mom such a shock that her breast milk stopped. She could never breastfeed me.

Many ask Amma how to overcome certain strong emotions. Amma says that, if the mother experiences trauma, it will affect her child. Amma says, to overcome a negative emotion, we have to go to the root of it. This dream helped me to do that.

I haven't overcome this problem completely, but I am no longer such a helpless victim. When these emotions arise, I remind myself that I am Amma's child, and Amma takes care of me. In fact, the attitude, "I am Amma's child" is the qualification that grants me entry into this "divine university." To graduate, I need to allow Amma to be my mother and receive her love and her discipline.

My father was very strict and had a bad temper. My four siblings, my Mom and I always just had to bear it. We could never explain ourselves. As a result, I got stuck in my faults and weaknesses and felt good for nothing. Fear and guilt always weighed me down.

Amma says, "Guilt is like an infected wound that gnaws at you from within. The best way to get rid of it is to become fully conscious of it. This can happen only in the presence of a true Master." Standing close to Amma to help in crowd control has been a good playground for Amma to discipline me. If I lacked śraddhā (attention), I would hear, "Sudhamayi, you go!" These words would pierce my heart and trigger the agony I used to suffer when my father scolded me, and I could not explain myself. The hurt of his words would fester inside me.

In the beginning I took Amma's scolding personally. But slowly, I understood that Amma only wanted me to become conscious about these past experiences and overcome them. I am very grateful to Amma for disciplining me like this; because, along with her words, her love was penetrating deep into my heart to help awareness dawn. Her love sheds light into the hidden corners of our mind to reveal our negative patterns and replace them.

One time, in Coimbatore, a devotee almost fell while leaving Amma after her *darśan*. Amma scolded me, saying, "If the person fell on her back, it would be very, very bad." For the next three days she did not allow me to help with the *sēvā*. It was a torture. I kept thinking about the incident. At first, I felt I didn't even touch the person; the person behind me was at fault. Then I started to realize that there must have been *some* carelessness on my part. This was a warning to be more careful in future.

Also, Amma had to remove my big ego. I was thinking that *I* was doing such a great job. I had to realize that only by Amma's grace did I have this opportunity.

When we introspect like this, our ego crumbles. Amma only wants our spiritual progress, so sometimes she has to give a show of anger. I learned to receive it as an expression of Amma's Love and a blessing to help me grow.

My upbringing was traditional Bavarian country life on a farm. We had to work hard harvesting, tending the animals and in the house. My father was strict about doing these chores at the right time. The only thing my Mom was ever strict about was attending Sunday church. There was no excuse whatsoever to miss it. She firmly believed that "Without God's grace, nothing can be attained in life." What a good training for āśram life!

I had an excellent job with benefits, good working conditions and job security. I would have continued to work there my whole life, but I felt dissatisfied and bored. I kept thinking: This *cannot* be all there is to life. Living only for myself seemed meaningless. In the best case, I would take care of a family. What's the sense to spend all my energy to earn money just to fulfil my desires? In my search for fulfilment, I started practicing *yōga* and meditation.

On New Year's Eve 1990, my elder sister, Annamaria, and I were on our way to India. One month before we departed, each time I closed my eyes to meditate, I heard a voice inside my heart calling very distinctly and clearly, "Mā Mā Mā." This was very unusual. Also, despite my fears of travelling in a tropical country, I felt a strong certainty, deep inside, that I would find my real home in India.

Our stay in India began with a Yōga Teachers' Training at Shivananda āśram near Trivandrum. There, a fellow student told us about "a woman in white who hugs everyone." A strong longing arose in my heart. I knew this was where I wanted to go. We arrived on February 15, 1991.

We were brought to the *darśan* hut. Before I could see anything around me, a powerful mass of *shakti* hit me in my heart. I sat down right at the entrance, crying. I continued crying, for no reason, for the next four weeks. My sister started to get worried. One day, while I was crying like this, suddenly my heart became light and free, and a blissful laughter burst from deep within. Later, I read in one of Amma's books that this type of crying is "untangling the knots in our heart." Amma says, "In the atmosphere of unconditional love, the closed dam of the mind opens up, allowing the hardened mind and its emotions to soften and flow unhindered."

The only thing I remember about my first *darśan* is that Amma whispered in my ear, "Mā Mā Mā," exactly as I had heard in my heart before I left for India. I understood that Amma was already calling me then, and that I was always searching for Amma. Finally, I had reached my real home. Till today, every time the plane lands in India, I feel so happy and grateful to return HOME.

Amma says, "A spiritual aspirant should be alert and vigilant in every action. *Śraddha* includes both love and faith. When you have love and faith, awareness in all your actions will automatically follow." Growing up on a farm, I was used to working hard, fast, and efficiently. Combining work with meditation and love was completely new. I used to do my work out of necessity, or else I would get scolded. Amma gives us the gift of *sēvā* so we can experience working with love and dedicating every action to God. A spiritual aspirant should remember God with every breath.

In Amma's words,

> The *sēvā* of a spiritual person is also his *sādhana*. His aim is to be free of all bondage. He serves others to purify his mind and to become detached, so he can realize the supreme goal. If you love God and surrender to him, you can perform any action perfectly well, without any sense of doer-ship or notion of 'I' and 'mine'. Making the effort and leaving the results to his will should be your attitude.

Before moving to the āśram, I took part in Amma's San Ramon program in June 1994. There, Amma orchestrated my permanent *sēvā* in the āśram. One day I was looking at the Amma dolls in the bookshop and commented to the dollmaker: "These are beautiful, but there are not very many. I hope there are enough for the Europe tour." To my utter surprise, the next day, Amma called me and said, "You make the dolls!" Later, I found out that the dollmaker took my concern to Amma. I did not consider myself fit for this *sēvā* at all. It was purely out of love for Amma that I obeyed. When I was young, I dreamt to study medicine. Now, Amma made me a doctor, nurse, surgeon, and midwife in the "Amma Doll Hospital."

Whenever a new doll is finished, everyone in the doll room admires and enjoys it, like a newborn baby. It is a real celebration of joy and unity. After people have had their dolls for many years, the doll sometimes becomes worn out from so much love. So, we perform surgery on her. I even give anesthesia to the Amma doll by praying in her ear, so she goes into *samādhi.* During the surgery, my *mantra* is most necessary to avoid complications. Otherwise, the thread will break, or the needle will prick my finger.

The crowning moment is putting on her sparkling nose ring. Only if I surrender any doer-ship notion at Amma's feet, do I succeed. Otherwise, the glue will stain her face and I have to start all over. After completing the surgery, I say another prayer to heal her wounds. Then, Amma looks so beautiful and fresh, as if she has just taken a bath. Seeing her fills my heart with joy and peace.

I think this is what Amma meant when she told me years ago that making Amma dolls is a high, high, high meditation. I am so grateful for this beautiful *sēvā*. It is always a meditation on Amma. All *sēvā* and everything we do with the right attitude is meditation. Recently, Amma told us to use this lockdown time to remember our beloved Deity in all we do. For example, when we take a shower, we can imagine we are bathing our beloved deity. Like this, our life can become a meditation.

During a chai stop on one North Indian Tour, Amma asked whether we could remember a trying situation when we did *not* react with anger, jealousy, or any other negative way, but stayed calm and untouched? All of us shook our heads no. Then Amma said, "That means not one of you has done any proper *sādhana.* The fruit of *sādhana* is not a tickling experience or *samādhi*, bliss or anything else. Rather, it is remaining calm in any situation."

Not reacting negatively is not easy. In 1997, on tour with Amma, we had a long overnight layover. In the evening, Amma called us to meditate at the beach. After meditation, we enjoyed listening to Amma joke and laugh with some of the Indian members of the group. As I was able to follow the conversation, I translated to a few people near me. One sister, sitting a few rows back, wanted me to talk louder so she could hear. I obliged, but she was still unable to hear. Out of respect for Amma, I didn't want to speak louder. The sister said, "Louder!" again and again. Finally, I got angry and replied in a strong voice, "I am already talking too loud."

Amma stopped talking and laughed. Pointing at both of us, she said, "Both saaaame!" Two words only. But they made me reflect. We had had repeated conflicts, and I felt provoked and treated unjustly by her. Amma's words made me introspect: What is my part in the tension between us? I started to observe myself and saw the same behavior. Gradually, I stopped reacting; and slowly, the tension dissolved. Today we have a respectful and sisterly relationship. Amma's two words still ring in my ears. Introspecting enables me to overcome my preconceived judgements.

When I was about nine years old, I felt this extremely strong and vivid inner calling to become a nun; but the dark robes and stiff head covers of the Christian nuns made me afraid. When I met Amma and saw the white robes here in the āśram, I knew this monastic life was possible for me.

Soon after I joined the āśram in 1994, I realized I wanted nothing else in life, and I asked Amma to become a renunciate. Her answer puzzled me: "But how will you be able to travel with me? Oh, you can go and find a temporary job." I was shattered. My "German" mind expected either yes or no. After some inner turmoil, I decided to jump into the ice-cold water and become a renunciate. This was the best "jump" ever. No boredom ever since. And my life is full of meaning and purpose.

Amma keeps reminding us not to worry about our family, but to fully immerse ourselves in our practices. This is like how watering a tree at the roots benefits the whole tree. In May 1998, I was going to Germany to work before joining Amma for the US Tour. My Mom was perfectly ok before the tour, but when I reached the US, I got the message that she was in a waking coma with a brain infection from a tick bite.

I was shocked and worried, but I did not want to leave the tour. My four siblings lived nearby and could take care of her. Feeling guilty and full of turmoil, I sat near Amma. Suddenly, Amma turned to me and said: "You don't have to take care of your Mom; Amma takes care of her!"

Soon after that, my Mom woke up with a clear memory. After a few months, she completely recovered. A young man was admitted with the exact same condition in the same hospital. He woke up with brain damage and will spend the rest of his life in a care facility. I asked my Mom if she wanted me to come stay with her. She said she feels I help her much more being with Amma than if I were physically there in Germany.

Amma has done many miracles for my family. Most recently, my younger sister, Sabine, told us she had breast cancer. I prayed to Amma for help and got the idea to give her the "White Flowers of Peace Meditation" CD. Sabine was depressed; she looked and spoke as if her fate was sealed. I gave her the CD and suggested she do this meditation every day. A few hours later, she called me and said that, for the first time since she learned her diagnosis, she felt some peace. She continued doing the meditation three times every day. Like this, she went through chemotherapy and 28 radiations with almost zero side effects; and she returned to work. She says this meditation is her saving grace.

She also confessed, that, because of her Amma doll, she did not need a psycho-oncologist. She brought her doll along for her treatments. She says her Amma doll radiates peace and love and prevents her from getting depressed and removes her fear of recurrence of the cancer.

The greatest miracle is Sabine's inner transformation. She always expected only the worst and put spiritual life last. This precious meditation, her Amma doll, and above all, Amma's grace, carried her through the cancer, and will be part of her life forever. Amma's miracles are not for their own sake. They are meant to instil faith and open us to deepen our spiritual life.

Amma says the *Guru's* only goal is for the disciple to realize his divine nature. For this alone Amma showers her love on us "disguised" as discipline, as trying situations, as healing. Amma wants us to realize that we are embodiments of supreme Consciousness. She says, "The *paramātmā* is not a distant entity. It is 'nearer than the nearest.'" As long as there is ignorance, the Self will seem far away, "farther than the farthest." Once the misconception that we are the body-mind goes, we realize that what seems "farther than the farthest" is "nearer than the nearest."

Let us open our hearts to receive the shower of Amma's love, however it comes—whether it comes as white flowers of peace falling softly on us, their sweet scent soothing our mind and heart; or as Durga Dēvī, taking up her neem-leaf broom to sweep the world clean of covid and our minds of negativities. Let me end with two lines of a German *bhajan* I wrote for Amma:

Amma, Du bist mein, zeig mir wie werd ich Dein.
Amma, Du bist mein und ich bin Dein.
Ganz Dein Eigen will ich sein,

komm zeig mir wie werd ich Dein.
Jai Ma Jai Ma Jai Jai Ma.

Amma you are mine, show me how I become yours.
Amma you are mine and I am yours.
Entirely yours, I want to be,
Come, show me how I become yours.
Jai Ma Jai Ma Jai Jai Ma.

May this prayer come true for all of us.

18

A Star in the Sky

Devapriya Marks (United States)

A few years ago, we were traveling with Amma on her South India tour. We stopped on the side of the road, and, after meditating, Amma began to serve dinner. Serving food is one of Amma's favorite activities. She says, when she feeds others, her own hunger is satiated.

Imagine Amma's reaction when Br. Ōmkārāmṛta came to Amma and whispered that we didn't have enough food. Very concerned, Amma turned towards us and conveyed the bad news. Seeing Amma's distress, the people sitting close to her held out their plates, and said, "Amma! Feed someone else with my food!"

Amma held empty plates in her lap. She reached out and took a little food from each person's plate. A *dōśa* (Indian savoury pancake) from one, some curry from another, and passed it to the remaining people. In no time, everyone was fed. I marveled at the miracle Amma performed. She fed many people with a small amount of food. But she didn't manifest more food. She did something much more miraculous. She manifested compassion in the hearts of those present.

Right now, it feels as though humanity is stumbling through a very dark night. Everyone tells me: "I can't bear to read the news anymore. There is so much selfishness, so much suffering, in the world." People feel hopeless. When we turn our eyes up to the sky, we only see darkness.

But Amma is ever hopeful. She doesn't give up on humanity. She just gives love. Amma keeps showing us that her love is actually our true nature. For Amma, compassion is the ultimate expression of Advaita Vēdānta. The Upaniṣads tell us there is only one Self. It manifests in all the various names and forms. Amma gives the example of the human body: If my right hand gets hurt, my left hand immediately reaches out to help, because it understands this is one body. Likewise, Amma says that if we understand that everything is our own Self, we will see others' pain as our own pain.

When Amma explains it like this, I understand the theory. When I read in the *Gītā* that a *jñānī* (knower of the truth) "sees the Self in all beings, and all beings in the Self," it sounds beautiful! But, for ordinary people like me, these are just abstract concepts. Fortunately, we don't have to look far to see a practical application. To see Vēdānta in action, all we have to do is watch Amma. Amma brings the scriptures to life. She makes these principles visible.

During darśan, Amma becomes one with each person. When a student comes to Amma with their diploma, she becomes their joy. If the next person has been diagnosed with cancer, Amma becomes their grief, shedding tears. Amma says that looking at us is like looking into a mirror. She sees her own Self reflected. Even when there is a huge line, have we ever heard Amma say, "Enough! I need a break?" Never! For Amma, there is no "me."

During darśan, people constantly grab and touch Amma. On the right side, someone taps her to ask a question. On the left side, someone pats her arm to get something blessed. Meanwhile, someone pokes her from behind: "Did you read my letter yet?" This doesn't bother Amma! It's as if there is no point where her body ends and the other person begins. Watching Amma's love is like watching a miracle. But, perhaps the greatest manifestation of this miracle is when Amma awakens *our* capacity to love.

Once, someone asked Amma: "Is it ok if I feel that Amma belongs to me alone?" Amma said, "Yes. You can have Amma as your very own. But, that is not the point. The point is not to own Amma, but to become Amma. If you see a banyan tree in the desert, you can enjoy the shade of the tree. Or you could become a banyan tree, offering solace to others."

When I hear this, it is very inspiring! I want to be like Amma! However, practicing this ideal is not so easy. Let's say I wake up in the morning and pray: "Oh Amma! I want to be just like you! May I love and serve everyone just like you do." When I pray like this, I feel really good about myself. I feel warm and fuzzy inside; oxytocin fills my body.

Then, I leave my room.

I go down to the café. I plan to have a nice big breakfast and then start my day of selflessness. But, on my way, someone asks, "Can you step in to cashier?"

"Oh... Of course." (I'm here to serve, right?) I put on my apron and go to the counter. There's already a huge line, and I am the only cashier. Everyone is staring at me, tapping their fingers. They haven't had their coffee yet. And the only thing between them and their coffee is me.

I am really hungry. So, I decide to take their orders as fast as possible so I can have my breakfast.

I ask the first person what he wants. He says, "Ummm...... I don't know.... what do you think I should have for breakfast?" The next person is "In Silence." She is trying to place her order by drawing pictures in the air. While I'm trying to understand what she wants, when someone taps my right arm: "Can I just get a chai?" Someone else pats my left arm: "Excuse me, where do you guys keep the forks?" From behind, a friend pokes me and asks: "Did you read my email?"

All this time, my stomach is growling, and I think: "Doesn't anyone care about me?" Then I wonder, "What happened? Back in my room, I couldn't wait to serve food. Now, I wish everybody was fasting!" What is the difference between me cashiering and Amma giving darśan? Why is my hunger not satiated by feeding others?

During my years in the āśram, this question has been my *manana* (contemplation). I watch Amma and ask myself: How can I go from being this bubble of selfishness to prioritizing others' needs before my own?

Once, a psychologist studied the benefits of meditation. Research shows that meditation makes people more calm, focused and productive. He wanted to know if meditation could make someone a better person.

He studied a group of people. Half practiced meditation for eight weeks. Half did nothing. Then, all the candidates were put in situations where a stranger needed help. He observed that those who meditated were three times more likely to help the stranger. The author concluded that meditation increases awareness, so people can see others' needs more clearly.

Obviously, this psychologist hadn't met Amma. Amma tells us that "love is our true nature." Amma gives us *sādhana* (spiritual practices) to purify our mind. Doing sādhana is like wiping a dusty glass. As we remove the dirt, the light starts to shine through. We are still in the cleaning process. When I introspected after my cashiering shift, I didn't like what I saw. Instead of progressing, I felt like I was regressing.

Amma says, "Spirituality is not a journey forward; it is a journey backward. In that process we pass through layers of emotions and thoughts that we have accumulated through many lives." That psychologist was right. Compassion *does* begin with awareness. But it's not awareness of *others*; it's awareness of *ourselves*.

Witnessing our selfishness is painful but essential in developing empathy. If I think I am perfect, I will easily judge others. But when I see all my own faults, how can I judge anyone? Now, if the café cashier is grumpy, I sympathize. Just like me, everyone is facing their negativities. We are all going through this human experience together.

Around Amma, we don't need to go looking for situations to develop this awareness. Amma brings them to us. She has a delivery service.

One of her favorite "delivery vehicles" are the buses on North India tour. The bus drives you from one city to the next, while the people on the bus drive you crazy. I'll never forget one very hot travel day. The person in front of me wanted the window closed. The person behind me wanted it open, and they were arguing over my head. My seatmate alternated between snoring at the top of her lungs and falling over and drooling on my shoulder. To top it all off, it was more than an hour past 4 o'clock, and I wanted my afternoon chai.

Finally, we stopped by the side of the road. Amma's camper slowly pulled up behind us. Everyone jumped into the aisle. I had my āsana in one hand and my chai cup in the other. When the driver opened the door, we exploded out of the bus. Imagine the scene: people running, āsanas flying, everyone pushing to get the best spot.

When Amma arrived, she made a little space for someone to sit next to her and then asked for the microphone. Amma then described to us what she had just witnessed.

In front of one bus, there was a big rock. Some of her children saw it and ran around. Others leapt over it. Because it was dark, some tripped and fell. But, even those who fell just jumped up and kept running. Amma asked, "Why didn't any of you stop to warn those behind you?"

This never ocurred to me. I was so intent on getting a good spot that no one else even existed. Amma said, "When a normal mother has a baby, she constantly wonders, 'When will my baby turn over? Did it sit up yet? When will it say its first word?'" In the same way, Amma watches all of us and wonders, "When will my children grow up? Are they thinking of others? Have their hearts opened?"

Amma said that wanting to be near her is very good. But Amma longs to see compassion awaken within us. Amma said we all think that compassion is something abstract, like "serving the poor." But, actually, it is an attitude we can practice in each moment.

Amma then told us that one person did stop when he saw the rock. He pulled out his torch and stood by the rock, shining light for others. Everyone had already taken their spots when Amma arrived, except this man. Amma understood that he had sacrificed sitting near Amma for others' safety. So, she took his hand, and walked with him all the way to her chair. She made a space and asked him to sit right next to her. Amma told all of us, "When you think of others, God comes rushing towards you."

Ever since that day, whenever I see a big rock in the ground, I stop and look around to see if I can warn anyone. Previously, this would never have occurred to me. But after hearing Amma's words, I now ask myself: "What would Amma want me to do?" This is how Amma's love expands us. We have all received so much of her love. Trying to be more compassionate expresses our gratitude to her.

I first received Amma's love in 1996, when I was 12-years-old. My parents were always interested in spirituality and liked to meditate. In India, people generally have good *samskāras* (values) and respect their parents. But I was not like that. Whatever my parents said, I did the opposite. I wanted to be "normal" and "cool" like the people I saw in magazines. When my mother told me we were going to meet "a saint from India," I said, "No way! I'm staying home. Alone!" My mother responded by throwing me into the backseat of the car. I cried the entire three-hour drive, kicking my mother's seat, and screaming, "I don't want a hug!"

When we arrived at the program, I sat in the very back corner of the hall. Watching Amma, I started to calm down and thought, "Well, she is pretty. Actually...she's beautiful." After a few hours, I changed my mind about the hug. When Amma took me on her shoulder, she smelled so good. Her arms were so soft and tender. During my darśan, Amma was speaking to Swāmijī. I couldn't understand, so I assumed she was saying really good things about me. When Amma smiled and gave me two chocolate kisses, I decided that she was not only "normal." She was actually very "cool."

My plan was to love Amma with a small corner of my heart, and be normal in the rest of my life. My plan failed. I went completely crazy. Gradually Amma's photos replaced the posters of movie stars on my wall, my music changed from pop to bhajans, and instead of looking forward to fashion magazines, I anticipated getting "*Matruvani*" in the mail.

Amma had stolen my heart. All I wanted was to come to India, but first I had to finish school. I looked forward to Amma's US tour all year. In my last year of high school, Amma's first program in Seattle fell on a school day. I really wanted to go, but had a very strict English teacher. She yelled all the time, and all the students hated her and loved to make fun of her. She was a new teacher, and probably insecure, but she was very rigid and insisted we could not miss any classes.

The first day of Amma's program, I went to school. I sat in my English class feeling sad and resentful. I knew that Amma says, "I am the 'I' in you, and you are the 'me' in me," but I couldn't experience it. The teacher was lecturing when the phone rang, and she went to answer it. All the kids started talking and passing notes. Suddenly she said, "Mom, I can't talk right now," and hung up the phone. The class fell silent. We were shocked. What was going on? She turned to us and said, "My mother just found my father, dead, in the bathtub. She didn't know what to do so she called me." She walked out of the classroom, shut the door, sat down in the hallway and began sobbing. Everyone froze in their chairs. We listened as she cried and cried and cried. I looked around the room and saw that every single student—all the girls, all the boys, everyone—was crying.

Finally, the principal came and dismissed the class. We all went out to buy cards and flowers for the teacher and piled them up on her desk. When she returned, she found a mountain of compassion on her desk. Before that day, all the students hated that teacher. But, when we imagined how we would feel to get that call, we felt deeply connected to her. We care about others only when we can see ourselves in them. Every human being suffers. Realizing this is the source of compassion. Just as I want love, everyone just wants love.

That night, I couldn't stop thinking about my teacher. I knew there was nothing I could do to alleviate her pain. At the same time, I was sad that I wasn't physically next to Amma. I fell asleep, torn between these two emotions. During the night, I had a dream.

I dreamt I was walking through the empty halls of my school. I went into my English classroom and found my teacher crying. As I walked towards her, something strange happened. My body became smaller and smaller. Around it, Amma's body appeared. My arms became Amma's arms, and I was inside Amma. My teacher laid her head on 'my' (now Amma's) shoulder, and cried, releasing all her pain. Amma's darśan comforted her completely.

When I woke up, my pillow was soaked. I had been crying in my sleep. But they were tears of bliss. I felt so close to God. I actually felt jealous of Amma, thinking, "She gets to do that all the time."

This is what Amma taught us at our chai stop. "When you think of others, God comes rushing towards you." This dream taught me a secret I meditate on even today: I can experience Amma's love by expressing it to others.

When I think about the darkness of today's world bearing down on us, I remember a question someone once asked Amma. She was a nurse in an ICU, in a very dangerous neighborhood. Most patients came to her hospital suffering from violence, addiction, and drug abuse. She told Amma that she saw only the darkest side humanity, and had only a few moments with each patient. She asked Amma, "What can I do in that short time to help them?"

Amma said: "The only real wealth is love. There is a never-ending spring of love within us. We should tap into that and express it to them. This is the only thing that will help them." Amma says that love is the inner experience, and compassion is the outer expression. If I want to become that banyan tree that offers shade to others, I have to express that love within myself. Amma guides us to do this in every moment.

We will never fully know the ripple effect of Amma's effort. This is her invisible miracle and her greatest miracle. Amma says, "We are not isolated islands, but are interconnected, like links in a chain." So, when Amma awakens love in one person, it does not stop there. Like this nurse, many of Amma's devotees ask themselves: "How can I bring Amma's love into my work? To my family? To strangers who need help?" Quietly, in hidden ways, Amma's love ripples out into the world. What greater miracle could there be? Right now, Amma's love is what the world needs most.

I moved to the āśram as soon as I finished high school, after waiting a long time. I assumed that, once I lived in Amma's physical presence, everything would be easy. I would feel blissful all the time and live happily ever after. You all know how the story actually unfolded. Amma had stolen my heart; now she wanted my ego, too.

My first few years were an absolute shock. I couldn't believe how much negativity I saw within myself. I was restless during bhajans and sleepy during meditation. My enthusiasm for sādhana disappeared, and I became very depressed. Then, I went with Amma on one of her foreign tours. The tour was a convenient excuse to stop spiritual practices. I was "too busy!" But as the tour wore on, I started to get tired and fight with my coworkers.

On the last day of the tour, on the last Dēvī Bhāva, I sat down, exhausted. At that moment, a friend came and sat next to me. They said "Wasn't this a wonderful tour? I did so much sādhana. I feel so blissful!!"

As soon as he left, I burst into tears. I thought: "Everyone else is such an advanced seeker. I am a spiritual failure." Amma says we are all inside of her. I felt like I was a grain of rice stuck between her teeth.

When I went into the hall, Amma was calling everyone for darśan. I joined the line, and wrote a short note to Amma: "Dear Amma. I am jealous of people who do lots of spiritual practices. Whenever I go within, all I see is darkness."

When I came in front of Amma, I handed her my note, trembling. She read it and burst out laughing. Then she started talking and making hand gestures. She pointed something imaginary towards my chest and spread her arms in the air like a dancer. I waited for the translation. Amma said: "Shine light inside. The darkness will go. Keep trying. If you do this, you will become so full of light that you will shine like a star in the sky. This star will give light to the whole world."

These words inspire me to keep trying. When things get tough and I lose enthusiasm, I remember that this effort is not just for me. Ultimately, it's for the benefit of the world. I am far from this goal, but I dream about it. Sharing Amma's love is how I can express my gratitude to her.

During the white flower meditation, I like to imagine all our brothers and sisters practicing, simultaneously, everywhere in the world. Through her children, Amma is casting a peace net over the earth. I pray we all become Amma's stars, full of her love. When Amma looks up at the night sky, may she see her children shining light to the whole world.

19

Stretched by Guru's Grace

Lakshman Winn (United States)

A while back, a group of us was sitting near Amma. She was looking into my eyes and smiling, and I was smiling, and I felt full of love and peace. Then Amma said, "You should give a *satsaṅg*!" My peace vanished. I thought, "That's *a lot* of people. Who am I to teach anything?" But what can you do when Amma tells you to do something? I just said, "OK."

Maybe I looked shocked. She said I should talk about knowing Amma as a little kid. I could talk about my experiences with her and try to make it spiritual. That calmed me down a lot. I'm not here to teach anything. I just hope something I say will remind you of what you already know.

One of the nicest things about the last few months was hearing so many stories about meeting Amma for the first time. Unfortunately, I can't tell you that story because I don't actually remember meeting Amma. My family met Amma in America in 1989, when I was three months old, and every year since we were lucky enough to see Amma when she was touring the US.

I cherish that time when I was little. Amma was a mother and a friend to all the kids. She played with us and swam with us in the hotel pools. She gave me extra chocolates when I went for *darśan*. Sometimes Amma sat outside on the grass for the meditation and *satsaṅg*, and she taught all the kids to respect nature and not pull out the grass.

I learned about *dharma*: how to treat other people and the basics of right and wrong. But I knew nothing about spiritual philosophy. I learned a lot of spiritual jargon from my parents. I knew enlightenment was important and that Amma was enlightened, but I had no clue what that meant. It seemed boring. I used to pray every night, "Please make me enlightened... But not until I'm old so I can still have fun!"

Amma made clear that, for this *satsaṅg*, I should talk about playing with Amma as a little kid, and how I used to pretend to shoot arrows at her. You might wonder, "Why would a little boy pretend to shoot arrows at his *Guru*?"

When I was three years old, my parents got the 1987 Hindi *Rāmāyaṇa* miniseries with English subtitles. I fell in love with this story. I watched the whole 78 episodes of this series three times in a row—39 x 3=117 hours!! Because I was three and couldn't read, my father read the subtitles to me for 117 hours!

My favorite part of the *Rāmāyaṇa* is Śrī Rama's *dharma*—that he gave up the kingdom to uphold his father's honor. His grace and even-mindedness inspired me. Rama was the *dharmic*, reasonable one. But his brother, Lakshman, had a fighting spirit. I liked him! He went out and fought all the time. He defeated the demon, Indrajit, who had literally defeated the gods!

So, I used to imagine I was Lakshmana and run around pretending to shoot everything and everyone with arrows. The only one that ever shot back was Amma. That became our game. I'd go for *darśan* and pretend to shoot arrows at Amma, and Amma would shoot arrows back. One day Amma asked me, "What are you doing?" I said, "I'm Lakshman!" And Amma said, "OK." And that's how Amma gave me my name. I was playing a game, but Amma was shooting me in the heart, planting the seeds of love and devotion. She completely captured me, and I sincerely *cannot* thank her enough.

At the end of the *Dēvī Bhāva darśans*, my father put me on his shoulders and carried me to get showered with flower petals. I had long, curly hair at the time, and it was hard to get the petals out of my curls, so I actually didn't want Amma to throw flowers at me. I'd make faces at Amma and pretend to shoot arrows at her whenever she threw flowers at me. This made Amma throw *more* flowers.

Looking at the video of this makes me very happy. I think, "That's a very cute kid!" I don't feel awkward saying that because it was so long ago. I see the kid and recognize that it was me, but I hardly remember playing with Amma and having trouble getting flower petals out of my hair. Today I think to myself, "I'm Lakshman." I felt that way as a kid, but we are hardly the same person anymore. Only one thing has not changed in me. The Awareness that observes all the changes.

My name is still 'Lakshman' but who *is* Lakshman? I'm not as innocent as the three-year-old Lakshman was. I don't identify with the 15-year-old Lakshman or 20- or 25-year-old either. 'Lakshman' is a changing entity (*mithya*) that borrows its reality from the Self (ātmā). Amma and the scriptures proclaim, "*Tat tvam asi*" (You are that). You are not the decaying body or the restless mind. You are the perfect, blissful, beginningless and endless Self.

It's so hard for us to realize this. Amma once said,

> Even though the scriptures say, 'That Thou art,' and 'I am Brahman,' our ignorance has to be dispelled before knowledge of Reality can shine. If you write the word 'honey' on a piece of paper and lick it, you won't taste any sweetness. Children, it isn't enough to talk about Brahman. We have to make it our own experience, not just repeat the words of the ṛṣis like a parrot.

We are so lucky to have Amma to teach us and guide us along the spiritual path.

We've all experienced that Amma prefers real life lessons. She puts us in situations that stretch and push us further than we think we can tolerate. This is how she teaches us that we aren't this small individual. We are complete and full. But we have to develop love and surrender to Amma as our *Guru*. This is supported by the *Upaniṣads.*

Śvētāśvatara Upaniṣad 6:23 says, "These truths shine forth only in that high-souled one who has supreme devotion to God and Guru." And what are the truths taught in this *Upaniṣad*? The same truths Amma teaches us: You are Brahman. We are not two but one. They tell us to focus our mind and overcome our likes and dislikes so we can see the universe as Amma sees it—as our own Self.

But Amma doesn't just tell us this. She creates situations where we see our lack of śraddhā and our *vāsanas*, and then she pushes us to do better. Amma's lessons sometimes hurt. But, Amma says that a good doctor will perform the surgery, even if the patient feels pain, because, without the operation, the patient may even die. Our love for Amma is like an anesthetic. Even if we feel hurt, her love can heal our pain.

Every fall on the path is a learning experience. It's also embarrassing, but Amma is there to pick us up and console us. She gives us the strength to move forward. For this to happen we must love and surrender to Amma as our *Guru*. We have to put ourselves in her hands and have the faith.

My first lesson in surrender to my *Guru* came when I was 16 years old. I graduated high school early so I could come to Amṛtapuri. I didn't think of Amma as my *Guru* then. I wasn't even interested in spiritual upliftment. I came because I loved Amma, but also, honestly, so I could travel! I thought I'd see the world, get some hugs from Amma, and return to my normal life in America.

When I first arrived here, I didn't feel much connection to the āśram. My first day here I just wanted to go back home. I know some people watching [online] have never been to India, so allow me to explain. India is really hot. Slap you in the face hot. I had grown up with air-conditioning, and I wasn't ready for the heat. Then there was the laundry. In the āśram we do laundry in a bucket with a scrubber. My mom always did my laundry, so I had never even used a washing machine. Now I had to scrub my underwear!

And, of course, there were the toilets... In America, at the beginning of the pandemic, there was a toilet paper crisis. People were so scared they would run out of toilet paper that they bought stacks of it higher than their heads! A lot of āśram residents were confused by America's crisis because the plumbing system here doesn't work with toilet paper. But I understood, because fifteen years ago I was having the same crisis going to the bathroom without toilet paper! I also didn't have a seat on my toilet. I had to climb up, squat, keep my balance, but stay relaxed. It was like an advanced yōga pose!

Another thing—I generally don't like music, so I never really liked *bhajans*. Meditating more than 10 minutes was torture. Here we chant *arcana* at 5am in the morning. Imagine being 16 and trying to get up at 4:30am to chant 1000 names?!? That's *a lot* of names! And it was 1000 names that I couldn't pronounce!

What made everything bearable, in the beginning, was *darśan* and *sēvā*. The more *sēvā* I did, the more my mind calmed down. I learned to lose myself in work. During the next two months, I got used to life here, and I started to love it. I adjusted to the heat. I got pretty efficient at bucket laundry. And I actually grew to prefer the bathrooms in India to the ones in the west! I started going for *bhajans*, and I would be mesmerized watching Amma's complete focus and love as she sang to God. And to this day, meditation and *arcana* are the most precious parts of my *sādhana*.

I was particularly moved by how fun and devotional the holidays were. On Kṛṣṇa's birthday, late at night, Amma sang special *bhajans* and danced with joy. I remember going to my room around 2am and thinking, "I could live like this forever!" I'd go through anything to be with Amma. I loved Amma as my mother, but that was the time I accepted her as my *Guru* (as much as a 16-year-old boy could). That was 15 years ago. What I thought would be a four-month detour has become my life. In those early days, I learned how Amma, as my *Guru*, even from afar, could create lessons to show me where my ego was hiding.

A few years later, I went with Amma on the Europe tour for the first time. The *sēvā* coordinator asked if I wanted to join the pot-washing team. At first, the idea of pot-washing scared me. My mother never let me wash the dishes when I was a kid, so

I had a lot of self-doubt, but I also thought it would be good to do something new.

Then, for some reason, everyone dropped out at the last minute. When the coordinator offered to give me new team members, I was a little scared, but I decided I wanted to do it alone. I started to feel pretty good about myself. "I'm only 16 and I'm in charge of a whole department!" I thought.

Then I saw where I was to do my work. It was October in Switzerland, so it was cold. We walked to this big tent filled with burners and large pots. It was nice and warm, and everyone was working together, laughing and smiling. Then they took me outside to the back of the tent and showed me an empty field with a few wooden pallets, some sponges, and a hose with ice cold water. Then I realized, *this* is my life for the next six weeks.

There were already dirty pots there, so I started working. Eight hours later, a wild man came over. He had coke-bottle glasses, long unkempt hair and dirty clothes. He said, "Jai Ma! I'm here to help!" and he started washing pots. The first pot he put away still had food stuck to it, so I told him that he needed to make sure he cleaned it properly.

He got angry and said, "Oh! Are you the chief here then? Are you in charge? Are you going to be telling me how to do every little thing?" Then, *I* got angry and pretty egotistical. I thought, "He can't talk to me like this! I'm the head of a department." (This after only eight hours.) I said, "Yeah, I am the chief. It's my job to make sure you do your job properly!" He blew up. "With you it's all me me me and my my my. You're so egotistical!" and he kept on shouting.

I got completely tangled in my ego and said, "Listen, if you're not going to respect me or the pots, you gotta go!" *Then* I saw how quickly I could get proud and arrogant when I'm in charge of something. At the end of that first day, after arguing with a crazy person and 14 hours of being cold and wet, I was exhausted. I took a quick shower, walked straight past the hall without looking in, and collapsed in bed. I was tired and unhappy and felt completely alone. All I could do was pray: "Amma, I give up. I can't do this. It's too much. You're going to have to help me if you want this to work."

I had slept for maybe 20 minutes when someone woke me up saying, "Lakshman, get up! Amma's calling you. Hurry! Darśan will be over soon." Shocked, I jumped up and threw on some clothes. My hair was uncombed, and my face was puffy. I just stumbled into the Hall.

Amma looked at me and started laughing. She called me, gave me a sweet smile, grabbed me and hugged me, saying how happy she was to have me on tour. Then she looked at me with a knowing smile and said, "I heard you were fighting." I nodded sheepishly. She laughed and someone translated to me that the man had already told Amma all about it. Amma explained that he was a little weird, but he loved Amma very much; and, Amma had told him it would be good for him to do a few hours of *sēvā* in the kitchen every day.

I cherish that experience. I felt Amma's love so much, and like a weight had been lifted from my shoulders. I knew I could lean on Amma, and she would pick me up when I fell. This is what a real *Guru* does.

Amma creates situations so we can learn. Sometimes, I think of Amma as a great *haṭha yōga* teacher. She is a master at putting us in uncomfortable positions so that we see and feel where our resistance is, and where we have to focus to progress. And, like a great *yōga* teacher, she stretches us farther than we want, but always releases the pressure at the perfect time. She knows how not to injure us or make us want to quit.

When I first came to Amṛtapuri, the adjustment to āśram life was a big, painful stretch for me. But *sēvā* and being with Amma gave relief. Then I went on a Europe tour. Just being on tour was hard. But Amma called me and hugged me and reduced my tension enough so that I could keep going. Now, living in the āśram and going on tour are my normal life. Sometimes it's hard, but it's easier than before, because of Amma.

After about three years of living with Amma, I had become quite comfortable. Then she started pushing me to get my college degree. I didn't want to leave Amma, so she told me to study at Amrita University. It was extremely difficult. I was the only westerner in my class, and one of only two westerners in the whole campus. The first few weeks, all the students just stared at me.

Everyone was super nice, but I felt completely alone. I've known Indians my whole life, and I had lived in India for three years. Still, I had *no* idea how little I understood Indian culture. Exams were different. Studying was different. Socializing was different. I felt like an alien from another planet. In the first semester, Amma went on Europe tour, but I had to stay back to attend classes. I felt abandoned. The whole time Amma was gone, I was angry at her for making me stay back, and in such a hard situation.

When Amma returned, she quickly started recording new *bhajans* on the stage late at night. I thought this was my chance. I'd be near Amma with very few other people. It would make up for being away from Amma. But, when I tried to get in, they told me, "You're not allowed to come in." I saw other people that didn't sing or play instruments, so I couldn't understand why I wasn't allowed in. I was angry at Amma and felt betrayed.

Two other people came to the door, and we stood there listening to the music. I decided to walk off some steam. After getting some water, I figured, before going to sleep, I'd look in again. When I got there, no one was standing outside the door. Through a small glass window, I could see the two who had been outside with me were inside.

I was furious. I thought, "I do what Amma tells me, even when I don't want to. Now, she leaves me out here. She's forgotten about me. She doesn't care. Well, you know what? I don't need her. I have Rama. I don't need a personal relationship with Amma. I can live here and have devotion to Rama and do my practices. If she doesn't love me, I don't have to love her." I left to go to sleep.

When I reached the *bhajan* hall, everyone was lining up as Amma was walking down from the stage. I decided to join just so Amma could ignore me and prove her lack of interest. I stood there with my arms crossed, waiting for her to walk by me without looking. As she came near, she started to look away. I thought, "I *knew* it." Immediately her head shot in my direction. She gave me a bewildered look and called out "Lakshmana!" I was shocked, and my feelings were so strong that all I could do was bring my hands together in *pranāms* and feebly say, "*namaḥ śivāya.*"

She did the same, loudly. "*ōm namaḥ* śivāya," she said, and gave me her 'What's wrong?' look. I shook my head and shrugged, fighting back tears. She beckoned me to come to her. I shuffled up to her, crying. She grabbed me and brought my head to her shoulder. I started crying harder and harder. She put her hand on my heart and rubbed my chest. As I was crying uncontrollably, with my head on her shoulder, we walked the rest of the way back to her room. Before she went up to her room, she said, "Don't worry. Amma understands why you're upset. Everything will be ok. Skip a few days of school and come with Amma on the South India tour."

I never told her my problem. I couldn't say anything but "*namaḥ* śivāya." But she *knew*. She always knows. And she knew exactly what to say to comfort me. Amma pushed and stretched me hard by putting me in a university where I didn't feel comfortable. I felt she had abandoned me. I felt angry towards her; and, because I was angry at her, I thought about her all the time. It was a blessing. Every time there was a problem, I'd think of her. She pushed me so hard that I thought, seriously, about running away. So hard that I really thought I couldn't survive another minute. So hard that I wanted to give up on her. But then she picked me up and relieved my stress. She dragged me forward with her love and kept me going.

Amma does this for all of us. She walks with us. She pushes and pulls us along the path. When I'm away from Amma physically, it really helps me to remember—Amma knows. Amma is with me even if I don't feel it. Everything will be okay.

Amma says, "The *Guru* will test the disciple in different ways. Only one with strong determination can withstand the tests and proceed on the spiritual path. But, once those tests are passed, the infinite grace of the *Guru* will flow towards the disciple unimpeded." We need *both* self-effort and grace. The biggest part of our effort is to grab the *Guru's* feet and hold on as she drags us forward. It is my sincere prayer that we all hold onto Amma's feet as she takes us along the path.

20

Leading Us Back to Wholeness

Aparna Kreitzer (Germany)

A good talk and meditation have more in common than most of us realize. Not long ago, I was flipping through YouTube looking for good, spiritual talks. Videos from "*Amrit Ganga*" and "From Amma's Heart" series scrolled by; then, at random, a short TEDtalk on "Speaking with Confidence." (This was *before* I was asked to prepare a *satsaṅg*.) Still, it sounded interesting. The coach stressed finding confidence *within* and suggested three exercises.

First, practice speaking. This can also be done by singing, which we do every day during *bhajans*. Second, relax your breath. Amma trains us in this during meditation. And third, when breathing in, think of love, so that, when you breathe out, what you say carries love. We practice this daily during *Mā ōm* meditation. Amma's holistic way prepares us for all challenges in life. This is only one example. Amma is our coach for everything. The invocation verse of the *Īśa Upaniṣad* says:

ōm pūrṇamadaḥ pūrṇam idam
pūrṇāt pūrṇam udacyatē
pūrṇasya pūrṇamādāya
pūrṇam ēvāvaśiṣyatē
om śāntiḥ śāntiḥ śāntiḥ

That is the whole, this is the whole.
From the whole, the whole becomes manifest.
Take away from the whole, the whole remains.
Om peace, peace, peace

Over the years, I have understood that *Sanātana Dharma* is the science for human living in the highest, truest and fullest sense. It can lead us to the state of absolute Oneness with all of existence, to wholeness (*Pūrṇatvam*). This universal approach includes perspectives of all different faiths. *Sanātana Dharma* can also be practiced by those who do not believe in any God at all, by reflecting on Consciousness as universal, the inherent principle and indweller of all that is. It gives right place to everything and everyone in the whole of creation.

This vision is dear to my heart as it includes everybody. A loving mother will only walk at the speed of her slowest child. The older children may wander ahead, as they have developed confidence in themselves, but will return to their mother to seek solace, rest and nourishment. Amma is the perfect embodiment of this. Her every thought, word and action is for the good of creation. By this, she ever assures us of our unity with her.

Even before meeting Amma, I got the chance to experience her birth country, India. In 1984, I was not yet two-years-old, so air travel was free for me. My mother and friends were visiting Sathya Sai Baba in Puttaparthi, in Andhra Pradesh, and brought me along. Even at my tender age, India's spiritual heritage made a deep impression, and I expressed it soon after returning to Germany. To the surprise of the rest of my family, I would stand up on my chair during dinner and sing with all my might, "Hare Kṛṣṇa, Hare Rāma, Kṛṣṇa, Kṛṣṇa, Rāma, Rāma." Later, exhausted from my performance, I would fall asleep on the same table with half-chewed food still in my mouth.

When Amma visited Europe the first time in 1987, I was four years old. My mother took me and my sister to meet Amma on her last stop in Austria, only a five-hour car ride away. Meeting Amma was like seeing light after a long period of darkness. Spring had finally arrived with birds chirping and flowers blossoming all around. It was so joyful, gentle and sweet. I was too young to remember the physical encounter, though the impression was very deep, and my inner world started to light up. I would say it was then that my life began.

At the time, my mother spontaneously asked Amma if she would hold a program in Munich on her next world tour, and Amma said, "Yes." In this way, Amma moved into our everyday life. My mother started organizing her programs, holding regular *satsaṅgs* and other activities inspired by Amma. In the early years, Amma's Europe tour was during our summer vacation, which made it easy to follow along and camp. Our favorite tour stops were the Schweibenalp in the Swiss mountains, and in the hills of Assisi in Italy.

I first visited Amṛtapuri in 1992. I was nine years old, and I instantly felt this was where I wanted to live. It truly felt like home. I had a great time. I got to go to Amma's room with the other kids. Amma fed us by her hand straight into our mouth. I received my name and was initiated into my *mantra*. Convinced that I could stay right away, whether or not it was practical, I asked Amma. To my surprise, she said, "First finish school in Germany, and come after."

I was dumbstruck, literally. I pretty much stopped speaking for the remaining few days as the lump in my throat made it hard even to breathe. On my last visit to Amma's room, the other kids thought I was behaving very oddly. Amma told them, "She is very, very sad." They translated to me what Amma had said, but I was unable to reply, because I used all my strength not to burst out crying in front of Amma. I felt it would be rude to cry, and it would show that I was not able to accept her guidance.

She tested my ability to choose between what would please me in that passing moment, and what was right or good for me in a more permanent sense. Similarly, in the beginning of the *Bhagavad Gītā*, Kṛṣṇa had to school Arjuna in decision-making for a higher purpose and overcoming his likes and dislikes.

As a child, I couldn't understand about being tested. I was confused by my feelings of sadness and rejection, as other kids were allowed to stay in the āśram, but I was not. This made me feel jealous. Nevertheless, Amma remained my dearest companion and refuge. She is like a magical mirror. When we feel anger, disappointment or other negativities, she only reflects divine love and compassion back to us. Amma interrupts our negativities and replaces them with by pure qualities. This is the greatness of our *Sadguru*. She assumes the burden of our self-created sufferings; and, by this, she frees us from worldly bondage and enables us to turn inward to discover our true identity.

Amma tells us she is present within us in the way Creator and Creation are one.

Srīṣṭiyum Niyē Sriṣṭāvum Niyē
Śaktiyum Niyē Satyavum Niyē
Dēvī... Dēvī... Dēvī...

Creation and Creator art Thou,
Thou art Energy and Truth,
Oh Goddess... Goddess... Goddess...

No matter where Amma is in the world, when she sings this song, the Truth proclaimed of the all-pervading divine Infinity makes every seeker's heart beat faster. For a moment, they dive into her experience of Oneness. In *Bhagavad Gītā* 10:19, Śrī Kṛṣṇa says: "... there is no limit to the magnitude of my manifestation." *Aṣṭāvakra Gītā* declares: "The Self is in all beings, and all beings are in the Self."

Diversity is a fact of our daily experience, but rather than being trapped in differences, we can allow our limited mind and intellect to seek, or at least imagine, the Oneness of all that is. In verse 20, Śrī Kṛṣṇa reveals his identity with the Self as "seated in the hearts of all beings." Amma often reminds us that she "dwells in our hearts" just as Kṛṣṇa tells Arjuna in the *Gītā*.

Sometimes, it is enough just to remember this and seek her within and around us. This great spiritual practice creates a feeling of closeness to Amma in the moment. Nature reflects the divine beauty. At other times, a smile or act of compassion reveals Amma's omniscience. During the 14 years of waiting to finally move to Amṛtapuri, I liked to look out for car license plates that included letter combinations such as MA, OM, AUM; or numeric combinations like 108, 54 and 9. They would often surprise me and reassure me of Amma's presence.

At other times I would stare at Amma's photo hanging in my room (the beautiful black and white picture of Amma meditating). I hoped she would open her eyes and look at me. Sometimes, I would think she actually did open them for a split second, but it was only my own eyes blinking that made me think her eyes were moving. The eyes on the picture never really opened, but Amma sees everything *within* herself. She doesn't need to use tricks like opening her eyes on a photo.

The purification of our mind that comes from one-pointed, devotional longing is precious. To hold on to Amma, to endure and to focus, to be enthusiastic and caring for others, is even more important than intelligence.

Once, Amma enacted a play with me to reveal exactly this. The situation was very important as it was about my high school exams. Since I was in a private school, our graduation exams had to be approved by a government school to ensure we were taught up to the government standard. It was always very stressful for both the teachers and the students because, if a certain quotient failed, the school would lose its permits and financial support to prepare for the graduation. To be safe, the school would identify the weaker students beforehand. Each student received a strong recommendation whether or not to continue the year of exams.

Our teacher in-charge was new, and she recommended I not attend the exam year. She kindly explained that I had a strong EQ (Emotional Quotient) but not so much IQ (Intelligence Quotient). I didn't know what EQ meant, but I knew about IQ. The truth is, I had not studied well the last two years. But I really wanted to finish high school exams so I could continue higher studies. My astrology showed I was in a difficult period, but would transit into Jupiter the following year, which would ensure success in studies. I didn't want to accept her recommendation. Instead, I booked a ticket to India to ask Amma for advice.

I had written my question as briefly as possible for my last *darśan*. When nearing Amma's chair, I started to feel sick; but I didn't want to miss my chance to ask Amma, so I stayed in line. While in Amma's arms, I felt even worse, and I totally forgot to ask my question. As I stood up, she gestured for me to sit near her, but she didn't reply to what was translated.

Even though I felt really sick, I made myself sit near Amma. Not long after, I heard a clear voice within saying, "We will do this together, and we will shake them up a little!" The voice was so clear and from so deep inside that I knew it was not just my mind. It was Amma's voice and her reply to my question. I could experience her presence within and put full trust that everything would go well.

The coming months were not easy, but with prayers and the conviction that Amma was with me, I managed to graduate with a little over the average marks. Amma had promised that we would do it together, and she had also promised to "shake them up a little." The one student, who, over the years, had always thrilled himself by scoring highest, had failed. He had a very high IQ, but his EQ was not up to the pressure of the examinations, and he started having blackouts from the stress.

Western psychology only started to acknowledge the value of EQ in 1995 but gave IQ a higher value when predicting success in life. Nowadays, they say EQ should be twice as high as IQ when pursuing a career. Skillful emotional management has to support intellectual achievements. EQ is the ability to be aware of ourselves, to control negative emotions, to be enthusiastic and empathic, and to have social skills, especially when problems arise and when facing deadline pressure.

I felt sorry for the student who had failed, so I kept in touch to see how he would continue his life. Failing made such an impact on him that he totally changed. He left his family and moved to another city. The experience of failing, despite his hard work, enabled him to be himself as he was. Life did him a favor. Most of us have probably experienced some failures that gave us an opportunity for a new start. I have a long list of my own.

In *Bhagavad Gītā* 2:62-63, Śrī Kṛṣṇa says that focus on the divine is needed for a strong intellect and a controlled mind to develop. He also explains that, without a strong mind one cannot succeed. Amma's grace and presence is most important. I would be lost and confused without her guidance and the blessing of my bond with her.

The *Taittirīya Upaniṣad* describes the *pañca kōṣas* (five sheaths): the physical body, the breath or energy body, the mental body with the senses of perception, the intellect for gaining knowledge, and the causal body). Those layers are *not* our true identity. We are the supreme Self, divine consciousness. The Self pervades the *kōṣas.*

Amma says, "Spiritual bliss cannot be experienced by the intellect. The heart is needed. The intellect cuts things apart like a pair of scissors, but the heart sews things together. Amma isn't saying we don't need the intellect; both the heart and the intellect are needed. Like the two wings of bird, each has its place."

During Amma's 50th birthday celebration, artists created an exhibition of paintings inspired by incidents in Amma's life. One of them depicts the divine Mother, our Amma, sewing the world together. From a young age, I loved to sew. I probably started around the same time I met Amma, because I still remember my first sewing projects were patching dresses for my Amma doll, even before I started going to school. Now I know it was a boon from Amma.

During my first visit to the āśram, I got to help with a sewing project, and was praised for my patience. All the other kids preferred to play. Amma often says, "We need the same level of awareness, in every moment of life, that we have when threading a needle." For sure, I would instantly feel the prick of the needle when I was careless, or my mind was distracted and far away.

On weekends and in my spare time, I spent entire nights experimenting how to sew sweaters, skirts and pants. I cut up old clothes or new fabric and sewed it together. Measuring, drafting, cutting, sewing, fitting and finding mistakes. Opening seams, resewing, refitting, recutting, resewing was a tedious process. Then sometimes discovering it was impossible to fix. How many hours and materials were wasted. But my enthusiasm held, and some successes would surprise me. In my youth, it was a great lesson in how to see failures as steppingstones to success.

I was delighted to learn that Amma, herself, studied tailoring with the intention to make money to serve the poor. Picturing Amma, who is Saraswati Dēvī herself, the divine Goddess of knowledge and the source of all skills, humbly learning tailoring still touches me deeply.

After high school, I studied fashion design and dressmaking at a school in Vienna, Austria. To receive Amma's blessing for this, I joined Amma's US tour in Boston. I cried intensely when I asked whether to join the school before moving to the āśram. Amma gave me a beaming smile and said, "It is always good to study." I was thinking, "I will only learn sewing." I never dreamed I was preparing for āśram life.

Eight months before I finally joined the āśram, in August 2006, Amma already had my *sēvā* in place — half-time in the western kitchen and half-time in the cloth department sewing for Amma's foreign tours. Eventually the cloth department *sēvā* became full-time, and a western tailoring team started forming. I also helped with the production of a six-month computerized tailoring course with Ammachi Labs; and with the development and design of the reusable sanitary pad, *saukhyam*, for the 101-village project.

When the pandemic started, Amma asked us to make PPEs (personal protective equipment) for the medical staff at AIMS. The girls' hostel study-hall and adjoining rooms were converted into a manufacturing unit, and many āśram residents, both Western and Indian, came to help. About 50% of them had never sewn before. It has been a heartfelt collaboration of all tailoring departments within the āśram, as well as many departments and individuals with their own sewing machines in their own rooms.

Our one common goal, as Amma says so beautifully, is "to serve the servants." Doctors and nurses are truly the heroes of this time. They put themselves at risk to save other people's lives and willingly endure sacrifices. Even here at the āśram, when everyone was strictly "locked down" in their rooms because several people had the covid, the various teams providing food and other essential services to our rooms wore our PPE suits for protection.

When you get a chance to do the right thing, take it. Do it diligently, without letting anything distract you. Humbly offering the effort as service brings grace that uplifts us and removes the impurities of our mind. This is the fruit of sincere *sēvā* on the path of *karma yōga.*

Now and then, Amma has sent us little encouragements. The area behind the girls' hostel had been a garbage dump for many years, as the students rained down their plastic snack wrappers from their rooms. I always dreamt of converting this area into a garden. Halfway through the lockdown, a team led by French Raksha cleaned the area, put new soil and planted edible plants, flowers and creepers that grow up on pipes and walls. They also placed plants in hanging pots and created a meditation corner. Inside, we work solely with synthetic materials; but just outside our window, we can now see beautiful Nature. This is such a sweet gift from Amma.

At critical times, now and then, our dear Swāminī Kṛṣṇamrita Prāṇa boosted our enthusiasm by saying, "We are doing a war effort," and "What we do is helping to save lives," and "This is the most righteous thing to do right now." One time, Amma asked for a sewing machine to be brought to her room. Later, we got to see a video of her, skillfully and elegantly, sewing one of her own dresses. Indeed, Amma is sewing the world together again, leading us back to wholeness (*pūrṇatvam*).

I want to end with this poem during this confinement...

> Only You (Amma)
> In this most attractive form,
> The form of my Mother and my Guru,
> You share your gentle touch in an embrace,
> And spread the fragrance of 1000 roses.

Giving the most favored taste, a sweet for the tongue
And with a voice from eternity calling us Her children
In the painting imbibed through our experiences.

The Amma of our memories belongs to us alone
Overwhelmed with gratitude
For how You continue to share
And give Yourself.

Trusting that we may honor and carry
This gift in Love and Reverence.
You alone exist
In this ever-changing reality we live in.

You alone,
The indestructible core in every being,
May we grow in humility
To gain the space within, to receive You fully.

May there be only one thought
Our dearest Mother – Amma
Eternal in our memory.
You alone exist
Only You.

21

Motherhood, a Spiritual Path.

Treya Triay (Spain)

I pray to Amma to calm me down and to speak through my heart. I humbly bow down and offer my mind at Amma's Lotus Feet. My *pranāms* to all of Amma's children gathered here today. I would like to express my gratitude to each one of you because of the spiritual company and inspiration that we offer one another. Also, because of the opportunity that we have to work together in service, becoming an instrument in Amma's hands. And also, because, when our interaction seems difficult, it is a great opportunity to introspect and to work on ourselves. For all these, I thank you.

In my mother tongue, Spanish, the word for 'thank you' is '*gracias*,' and the word for 'grace' is '*gracia*'. It is the same word. Adding an 's' at the end of '*gracia*' makes '*gracias*'. It is beautiful to see how our language expressions are made. What I understand is that, when something beyond our control brings goodness to us, we express gratitude for the factor of grace that unfolds. Since I met Amma, every time that I say '*gracias*' I know that I am bowing down to the all-pervasive mother of grace, Amma.

Who is Amma? What is Amma? Even the purest expression cannot define the depth of Amma's existence and grace. Amma is the divine mystery, beyond words. So, the only thing that is possible for me here, is to try to share my humble inner understanding about Amma, and how Amma has changed and is constantly changing my life and my mind. This is just one more testament of Amma's divinity.

Even though Amma has taken such a beautiful human form, we cannot say that Amma is a person. Neither can we say that Amma is an objective experience since Amma cannot be measured in any way. To me, and I believe to all Amma's children, Amma is one with the supreme Self. From the supreme Self, Amma manifests herself, and this Creation appears. Amma simply *is*. And in her solitude, she is both Creator and Creation.

Everything is born from Amma. Everything exists in Amma. Everything dissolves in Amma. Being the essence of all that exists, Amma is present everywhere. That is why Amma can reach us wherever we are to help us. Also, Amma works on us in ways that we cannot comprehend or predict. Amma works on us from inside, from outside from anywhere, to dissolve all that separates us from her. She has taken a body only to save her children. Amma is God, supreme *Guru* and Mother. I understand that Amma has taken the form of a Mother, not only because we exist in her, and not only because she is taking care of each one of us. But also, for us to be inspired, to learn and to develop the qualities of the mother which are needed for our spiritual growth and for the world. To awaken the inner motherhood, some of us need to experience being a biological father or mother. But Amma says motherhood is not limited to a woman or parents. Motherhood is a divine quality, a gift from

God. Or, we can also say it is a direct manifestation of the Divine. Everyone, including the small kids around Amma, awaken their inner motherhood. As Amma told my daughter, Tapasya, when she was a little girl during an Indian tour: "You are the I in Me, as I am the You in you."

This is the breath and the state of our Divine Mother. Amma tells us:

> I am here to remind you and to take you back to your real source, your real nature. Like the waves that exist in the water, and the water that exists in the waves, I exist in you, like you exist in me. Come to my arms, and I will show you.

From this supreme state in which Amma is established, compassion, sacrifice, acceptance, forgiveness, patience and perseverance flow naturally. These are all qualities of motherhood that Amma inspires us all to awaken within.

In my case, I could only reach Amma after becoming a mother. I was blessed to become a mother, not long after my own mother passed away. I was holding her in my arms when she left her body. It was after a short period of nine months of cancer. She was 51 and I was 24 years old. Being completely aware and embracing her death, she prepared everything for us. She also left a poem from a famous Spanish poet (Francisco de Quevedo 16-17th century) for us to read during the funeral. The title of that poem in Spanish is:

> *Amor constante más allá de la muerte.*
>
> Constant love beyond death.

Through this poem my mother was telling us that she was ready to embrace death but not stop loving. Only to melt in love. And to love forever. When your own mother dies with so much surrender and dignity, only Grace can unfold. And today I can say that, in my experience, pure supreme love and death go hand-in-hand. The more we love, the less we can hold onto our expectations or wrong limited beliefs. And when love or devotion reaches the core of our identity, it burns our ego from inside, and leaves us without any external support to hold onto other than the Self or God, other than the *Guru* within.

We, Amma's children, have experienced so many deaths without dying or leaving the body. Amma burns our *karma*. We don't understand what is happening. Inside, a deep operation is going on. Outside, sometimes, situations in life might turn completely upside down.

Saint Teresa (in Spanish, Santa Teresa de Jesus) was a Spanish mystic, also from the 16th century. In her exalted devotion she wrote many poems. In one of them, she proclaimed:

> *Vivo sin vivir en mí, y tan alta vida espero,*
> *que muero porque no muero.*
>
> I live not living in me (in this body), and in my longing for such a high existence, I am dying or desperate because I am still not dying (Meaning because I am still attached to this body).

This verse describes how I used to feel before meeting Amma. During my whole life, I had never really wanted to be in that society where I grew up. I knew it was not my home. I remember riding my bicycle through the city, and pausing to look at the sky, thinking: When will I be able to reach a space pure and vast like the sky above? And today, being in Amma's presence, whenever I look at the same sky, what I see is that the sky, like everything in this universe, is just a son or a daughter of Amma. One more aspect of her Creation.

Amṛtapuri exists on planet earth but is not *of* planet earth. Beyond space and time, this āśram, or what we call Amma's presence, is the heart of the heart of God. I searched for our Amma since very young, everywhere I could—climbing high mountains and swimming all alone deep in the ocean. I did lots of physical exercise in solitude, out of my desperation.

And when I gained permission from my parents, I travelled to South America many times to do selfless service. Also, to study and practice Natural Medicine directly from excellent doctors there. I also graduated in Philosophy, in Spain. But nothing, *nothing* was sufficient. Why? Because everywhere I went, everything I learned, was still in the name of the ego. It doesn't matter if it is natural medicine, philosophy, even selfless service. If your *Guru* is not there, if God is not seen, it is a path for the ego but not for liberation.

After my mother passed away, I went to a Tibetan Buddhist center and received teachings from the master there. I practiced and dedicated myself to that *sādhana* for some time. In the Buddhist Centre, I met a very devoted man who was destined to become Tapasya's father. For several reasons, after I got pregnant, he made the decision to continue to follow his Buddhist Master. And he left. I understood that I would raise the child alone. With this understanding, a clear image came into my mind and heart—the image of a tree, strong and rooted in faith. I also understood the gift and teaching of motherhood:

Surrender. I deeply felt that God was transforming a whole situation into a blessing.

During the 7th month of my pregnancy, I went all alone to walk the pilgrimage path in the north of Spain called *Camino de Santiago*. There is a belief that this pilgrimage path goes down on earth in the same direction as the Milky Way goes up in the sky. The belief says that the Milky Way is an expression of the nectar of the Mother of God. Also, the path is marked by a series of Madonnas (Mother Mary). We are supposed to walk from one to another. In all the churches and cathedrals along that path, the mother of God is not white, but of the color of the earth, black or brown. While walking, I remember praying to God: *Will you take this baby in your divine lap? Where are You?*

I decided that the name of the girl to come would be of a place from the pilgrimage path: *Irune. Irune* means 'that which is beyond the Trinity'. Tapasya was born at home, in Barcelona, Spain, on a full moon night. Soon after, one lady that I met on the pilgrimage path (Tejomayi, from Czech Republic) told me that a real Divine Mother was coming to Barcelona.

I remember two things from that first time with Amma. One foot inside that noisy, crowded hall was enough for me to know that I was finally at home. A woman came running to give us tokens to go for *darśan*. But having such a strong feeling of Amma inside, I remember telling her: "We already got darśan." But she grabbed us, and in a few seconds, we were in front of Amma. I gave her the baby. I knew that Amma was, that Amma is, her real father and mother. At that time, I didn't know how to speak English, so internally I prayed to Amma: "I got this baby from you. Please, teach me how to be your servant, and to do my part for this little one to reach back to you in this lifetime."

The other thing that I clearly remember from our first time in Amma's program was the Indian snacks, especially the fried onion, the *uḷḷi vaḍa*. In his *satsaṅgs*, our brother Vivekji spoke about the happiness that the Indian snacks bring to Amma's devotees in Europe. I have to confess that I was one of them. I was glued to the Indian snacks, as if a huge rediscovery was happening on my tongue.

Soon after, we came to Amṛtapuri. I remember crying at least three or four hours a day, during the first years, completely shocked to be in Amma's presence. I was crying to God, but with no logic, simply melting inside. And, every time, little Tapasya would ask me: "Again, crying?" And I could only respond: "It is because Amma is God. And we are finally with her!"

When we both asked Amma for a spiritual name, a thought crossed my mind: "Maybe, Amma would give the same name to both of us." Amma gave the name *Treya* to Tapasya. Then Amma smiled and changed it to *Tapasya*. *Treya* would, then, be the name for me.

Treya, like the name I gave to Tapasya (*Irune*), also means 'the one beyond the Trinity'. Also, our last name is *Triay*. So similar to *Treya*. This just shows how much Amma knows everything. And how Amma embraces but also plays with our identity, until we simply let it go.

Some years back, one of the points of Amma's world tour *satsaṅg* was about kids raised by single mothers. Amma explained that both father and mother are very important in the child's education. Since I have always raised Tapasya all alone, I decided to ask Amma for advice and instructions. Amma looked at me as if I were asking the strangest question ever. Very loudly and repeating the same sentence towards the four directions (North,

South, East, West), referring to Tapasya, Amma said, "So many fathers, so many mothers, so many brothers, so many sisters. So many fathers, so many mothers, so many brothers, so many sisters..." Total *four* times.

What I understood from Amma's message in her *satsaṅg* was that everything and everyone (father and mother as well) have an important role to play. But from her answer to me, I understood that, when we surrender our heart to Amma, she will show us that we are not limited to any external situation in life. Everything depends on how we see it and how we understand it inside. And finally, Amma made it very clear that, beyond our personal circumstances, we, Amma's children, are an amazing and real family.

During those days in Amṛtapuri, one lady from another European country approached me and told me how touched she was seeing the relationship between the small Tapasya and me. She drew and gave us a picture of a tree. It was the same image of the holy tree that I saw internally while I was pregnant. The same tree that gave me so much strength and longing for surrender. While receiving the picture, I felt Amma's presence very strongly. The roots, the open heart, the abundant leaves, the three oranges as fruits. The inner silence. Just being and giving without expectations. Without effort. And *Aum* is the signature at the bottom on the right side.

I always kept this picture with us. I used to bring it on all Amma's tours, as a reminder of the attitude that I am seeking in this path. I also made a small copy and gave it to Amma. But then, I forgot about it. A couple of years later, I remember strongly praying to Amma, "Amma, you know that I don't speak Malayalam; and, often, I don't know how to approach you externally. Please, show me that you have taken us forever."

After a few days, a situation unfolded that became the answer to my prayer as well as an opportunity for deep introspection. The āśram kids were called for a project for Amrita TV. I had a question for the main coordinator of that *sēvā*. When I entered his office, I felt Amma's presence strongly. And suddenly, I saw the picture of the tree on his desk (the same small copy that, long back, I had given to Amma but had forgotten about). I didn't know what to say. I didn't want to say anything. But it was as if my soul was laying on his desk. So, pointing to the picture, I asked him, "What is this?" He said, "Amma gave it to me. I never understood why she gave it. Amma only told me that Amma herself drew this picture."

I left his office completely moved by Amma's words. Amma, the supreme artist, who is the essence of our hearts, is drawing our life. But since then, every day, I ponder: Am I allowing Amma to continue drawing my life? Am I surrendering my deepest attachments to her? In one of his *satsaṅgs*, Swāmī Anubhavānandajī asked some devotees: "You have spent 20 or 30 years following your *Guru* everywhere, chanting her names, singing her glories. But have you really changed in your understanding of yourselves, of life and death, of God? What are you ready to offer, after all you have received from your *Guru*?"

Contemplating these questions, I have always understood the experience of becoming a mother as a *prasād* from Amma. But now that my daughter is not a baby anymore, now that she will start moving forward without me, I need to ask myself: "What is the real goal of this motherhood that brought such a rebirth in me, next to Amma? Did I forget the surrender that I felt so deeply during the pregnancy, and that I tried to apply with all my heart while Tapasya was a small girl?"

Recently I was thinking about this; and soon after, just a few Tuesdays ago, Amma spoke about the goal of motherhood. Amma explained that it is normal that, after a certain age, teenagers might not want to listen (like before) to the advice of their moms. (Well, here, just a small clarification from Tapasya. She says that she *listens* to everything I say, basically because I don't give her any other option.) Coming back to the point: Amma said that many mothers might feel sad, might complain, might have expectations of their grown-up children. Amma added, "But the goal of motherhood is to reach the peak of pure unconditional Love. Once the Love reaches its peak, the work is done."

These last words touched me so deeply, like a medicine that opened my heart; and it has been doing so till now. I understood that Amma was not referring to our duty and responsibilities, but to our maturity and spiritual growth. It is for us to contemplate deeply and to decide what we want to do with the gifts we receive from Amma. Let it be a *sēvā*, a position in life, a place, or even our own son or daughter. Everything is Amma's *prasād*.

But do we want to hold onto that *prasād* as the goal? Or do we accept the *prasād*, together with all the love and lessons that we have gained through it, as a means to reach the highest goal of complete surrender? If we sincerely listen to Amma's teachings, we will understand that this changing body, this changing mind and all these changing experiences, *cannot be me*. Also, in our longing, we will have no other option but to pray to Amma. And Amma will come to help us, in whatever way possible, as Amma always does.

Amma knows how to use every situation to make us grow spiritually. Amma can transform any *karma* into *prasād* for us. But I believe that, ultimately, Amma is here to remove our wrong identifications and deepest attachments, which are the *real* cause of all *karmas* and suffering. But for this, our honest surrender is needed. Surrender is easy to say, but so profound to experience. It is the act of letting go of our ideas, our ego, our personal identity, together with the conviction that Amma knows, I don't know.

From the outside, surrender seems like something very hard. But in Amma's presence, surrender is magically happening in our hearts. And if we persevere, Amma will be with us in the transformation from that somebody that we think we are and we are so identified with, to nobody, which in fact we are. When the wave subsides, surrenders and melts in the ocean, there is no more reason to maintain its individuality. It simply is what it is, no more a wave, just water.

Amma is here for us to let go and to melt in her. I pray for all of us to be able to use every gift that we receive from Amma, every experience, to grow in pure love and to let go of our bondage. I pray for all of us to be like that tree: present, sincere, just Amma's instrument, accepting this world as it is, but rooted in faith and in *dharma*.

I pray to always remember that *dharma* is not something that we can choose or manipulate. Our *swadharma* is an opportunity for us to grow spiritually, and to serve Amma. And the supreme *dharma* (the supreme law of this universe) is our path back to God.

I would like to conclude with the last verse of the poem that my mother left for us (which I mentioned before). It refers to death, but I always thought that, in fact, it speaks about letting go of the attachment to the body, and complete surrender:

> *Su cuerpo dejará, no su cuidado.*
> The soul will leave the body but will continue to take care.
>
> *Será ceniza, mas tendrá sentido.*
> The body will become ashes, but it will be full of meaning.
>
> *Polvo será, mas polvo enamorado.*
> The ashes will become dust, but dust that is full of Love.

And I add, dust in pure love and unconditional surrender at Amma's Lotus Feet. May Amma bless us with complete surrender. May we become dust at Amma's Lotus Feet. Gracias Gracias Gracias.

22

Amma is Experience

Jani Macgill (Israel)

Today is Hanukah, the Jewish festival of light. This holy day represents the many miracles of God in our lives, and symbolizes three victories:

- Light over darkness
- Purity over impurity
- Spirituality over materialism.

How special it is to have Amma, the *Guru* — the one who takes us from darkness to light. In Amma's presence, every moment is Hanukkah! Every day is a celebration of divine light! Many people, especially those from Israel, ask me, "Who is Amma?" Even after so many years, it's still hard to express who Amma is, because words cannot describe her. My experience with Amma is the answer that I can give them.

I met Amma on *Guru Pūrṇimā*, in Boston, in 1987. She was sitting on a small, plastic milk crate covered with a little āsana, in a very small living room. Very few people were there, and there was no line. Amma called people one-by-one. When Amma called me, she hugged me for a long time. Then she reached into a big bowl of ash, took a handful, and put it in my hand. Amma was still hugging me, and my hand was full, so I put the ash on my face and on my tongue. Amma said: "She knows what to do with it." I felt that Amma knew me, and I had come home.

At one moment, on that first day, Amma looked straight at all of us, pointed her finger and said:

"AMMA KNOWS ONLY ONE THING: THAT AMMA KNOWS NOTHING." This statement lives in my heart and mind as if I heard it only yesterday. I never analyzed it. I know it is profound and shows who Amma is. The feeling is enough, because, for me, Amma is an experience. When I contemplate it, I realize that Amma was showing us what humility is. She didn't claim anything about herself.

I was born in the year of Israel's Independence. I grew up in Israel, in a kibbutz, which is like an āśram. It is a community based on the principle that everyone should live together, give what they can, and take only what they need. The place was beautiful and surrounded by nature. One of the three rivers that merge to become the Jordan River started in our land at the edge of Israel, near the border of Lebanon and Syria. We were constantly attacked by bombs and always needed to be very alert. We often had to run for our lives to the underground bomb shelter. Loving each other and wanting peace with the neighboring countries helped us to remain positive.

The members of this kibbutz didn't believe in God. They weren't religious, but they were *dharmic*. They had strong values. We didn't know anything about Indian gods. Most of us only learned about Indian culture when we started to travel. I worked as a special education teacher. During vacations, I traveled around the world to many countries. In 1982, I traveled to India. During my visit, I had a dream that changed my life's direction. In the dream, a voice said, "You have travelled all around the world. Now, it's time to put down your backpack and travel within."

When I met Amma, I was living in America. A Yōga teacher told me, "There is a very little south Indian woman visiting nearby. You should see her." The house was only a five-minute walk, so I went. When I saw Amma, I felt, "She is the biggest woman in the Universe!" It was totally love at first sight. I felt Amma was "IT." I had no intellectual understanding; my heart just experienced it. Wanting to share this gift with the whole world, I told everybody I met about Amma.

Amma was spending another two weeks in the USA, so, I stopped everything and followed Her. Like a magnet, Amma naturally draws you to follow her. Amma went to a little house in the countryside and gave *darśan* to the small group gathered there. They said that night we would have *Dēvī Bhāva*. I had no idea what that meant. After the morning *darśan*, I stayed on the ground floor by myself.

Suddenly, Amma entered the little eating area, alone. She started moving a table, so I went to help her. When Amma went outside to the yard, I followed her. Amma picked some leaves and gestured that I should follow. She showed me what size leaves to pick and how to pick them. I followed her back into the small room, and she showed me how to put the leaves on the floor. We didn't talk. I had no clue what was going on. Then Amma cut a banana into small rings and showed me how to put them on the leaves. She then gave me an incense stick and showed me how to put it into the banana. Later, I realized that Amma, herself, was setting up the entire *Dēvī Pūjā*.

After we set up the room, people started to arrive. Amma conducted everything. She even sat each person who came next to a leaf. Then she started the *pūjā*. It was my first *Dēvī Pūjā*, my first *Manasa Pūjā*. Soon the *Dēvī Bhāva* started. Everyone received a long darśan and we all sat very close for a long time. It was amazing.

From that moment, I wanted to dedicate my life to the spiritual path with Amma. Amma says, "Every moment is important. If you lose money, you can get it back. But if you lose even a single moment, you can never get it back." After I met Amma I didn't want to waste another moment. Amma gave me real purpose in life.

The next year, 1988, Amma held her program in my house for four days. One night, everyone went to sleep, but I heard Amma awake in her room. I felt that, if you have a guest like Amma, you should not sleep while they are awake. So, I waited alone downstairs. Suddenly, Amma came down, opened the fridge, tasted a little bit of food, and fed me some *prasād*. Amma looked at me and said "Jani, go to sleep!" I said, "I will not go to sleep until Amma sleeps." Amma answered: "You never read the scriptures, but they say the *Guru* should be the last to go to sleep."

Later I learned that the scriptures really say, "The **disciple** should be the last one to go to sleep!" Amma only said that out of compassion, not because she didn't know what the scriptures said. Amma is the embodiment of the ultimate Truth the scriptures describe. Great spiritual masters like Amma are the real authorities on the scriptures. Amma's compassion is limitless. Since that moment, I have seen Amma sacrifice her sleep thousands of times. Even if the crowd is huge, Amma never leaves the stage until every single person has *darśan*.

The next year, Amma asked us to hold a retreat in our home. We lived in a little town called 'Temple.' (Later, that house became Amma's āśram.) It was a big challenge to figure out how to accommodate and cook for everybody. But it was beautiful. Over 350 people registered, and we all stayed together with Amma for three days.

We had many unforgettable, intimate moments with Amma. Once, Amma danced in ecstasy to the *bhajan 'Tanana Tanana.'* Suddenly, she stopped and sat down in *samādhi*. The last night was *Dēvī Bhāva*, which was open to the public. Before *Dēvī Bhāva*, Amma made her own garland. I still see that moment in my mind and heart. She sat on the floor, chose the colors, and strung the flowers herself. Amma is the greatest *Guru* because she teaches through example, showing us her endless humility by doing everything. She never asks others to serve her. She serves us and teaches us to serve each other. The retreat was full of her motherhood.

Now I understand that Amma's religion and her language is love. But then, I longed to understand Amma's words. I started to study Malayalam, but I gave up. I realized I still did not even know English! Amma says I speak 'Jan-ese'. My accent is a big joy for Amma. She loves to laugh at how I talk and hear me say words like 'birthday'.

I learned a big lesson connected to my inability to pronounce anything other than Hebrew. Amma gave me an instruction that I didn't follow. More than 20 years ago, Amma told me to study *pūjā*. She asked Swāminī Karuṇāmṛtajī to teach me. Every day, I studied for hours. I loved all the movements; it was like dance.

But can you imagine me, who can hardly speak English, trying to pronounce and remember all the *mantras*!?

And, physically, I couldn't sit on the floor. So, I never did a *pūjā*. And I never told Amma. (I guess now I just told Amma.) It was a big lesson for my ego. Amma knows who we are more than we know ourselves. If she gives us instructions, we need to have faith that it is for our growth. I didn't follow Amma's instruction and didn't even talk to Amma about it. I lacked surrender, a very important spiritual quality.

Amma said, in her talk at Stanford University: "The main issue is that we believe we are limited. If we believe we are limited, then we can't achieve our goals in life." Amma says, "You are not meek like a lamb, but strong and magnificent as a lion. You are not like a lamp that needs to be lit; you are the self-luminous sun. We are not the limited body, but the unlimited Self, pure undivided consciousness."

After meeting Amma, I immediately started to do all the tours. During one visit to San Ramon, she stayed at Ronji's house, but she said she would also come and visit the main house. We cleaned for many hours. Then, Amma couldn't come! We all felt sad, but it was time to drive to the next program.

During the program, I found a small room behind the stage where I could sit and make an Amma doll. I was still feeling sad that Amma couldn't come to the main house. *Sēvā* is like meditation for me; it quiets my mind and heart. *Bhajans* ended and meditation started. Suddenly Dayāmṛtānanda Swāmī came to the little room and said, "Shut off the light. It can be seen from the stage." I turned off the light and sat alone in the dark room.

Suddenly, I heard footsteps. Someone entered the dark room and turned the light on. It was Amma and her attendant. But how could it be? Amma was meditating in the full hall! But it really *was* Amma. Amma had felt my sorrow and come to me. I was overjoyed. Amma sat next to me and let me put my hand on her knees.

Suddenly Amma asked, "Do you find my talks to be boring?" You know how you become speechless when Amma asks you something? Somehow, I said, "No Amma. Your talks can never be boring, because you speak about the highest Truth, the Truth about life." I have no idea where this sentence came from. Amma said, "Sometimes, Amma has to repeat things over and over because no one listens deeply."

Later, I realized how true this is. How many times has Amma said, 'Amma is always with you'? I've heard this over and over, but, that day I forgot it. Out of her compassion, Amma came and gently showed me that I need to listen and reflect more on Amma's words.

In 1988, I came to Amṛtapuri and became involved in the *sēvā* of organizing the westerners for Amma's Indian tours. Before one tour, a rumor went around that, after Delhi, Amma would travel to the Ganges River. In those days, we used to swim with Amma at almost every stop. But people thought it would be more special to swim in the Ganges with Amma. So, the registration numbers started increasing.

When the Delhi program ended, Amma announced, "We are going to drive back to Amṛtapuri, and stop for a few more programs on the way." Many western children became upset, and some even left the tour. On our first ride, we stopped and Amma came out to make us tea. The group was silent. Suddenly Amma said, "You do not understand who Amma is. You have no idea. If Amma bathed with you in the dirtiest pond or river, it would become pure like the Ganga. Doesn't Amma bathe with you on every trip?"

Complete silence. My eyes filled with tears, and I felt ashamed. Amma also said, "How can Amma go with only this small group for two days when so many of her children everywhere are longing to be with her and have her *darśan*. That is why Amma added more programs." Amma is always thinking about her children. She does not give even a moment to herself.

I love how Amma 'walks her talk'. She does everything she tells us to do. All of us are really good at talking. But in each moment, Amma teaches through her actions. During the Indian tours, I go early to prepare the accommodations for Amma's tour group. One time, when the group had just arrived in Kannur, I got a phone call: "Amma wants to talk to you." My heart sank. Oh no, did I do something wrong? Amma said: "Move all the western women from the school to the āśram, next to Amma's room." The area in Kannur āśram is very small.

I said, "Amma we have 275 women. How can we fit everyone? All the women will first have to go on a diet!" Amma laughed. She said "No, no, Jani. Only you and I need to diet!" We both laughed and laughed. I ran to the Kannur āśram, up to Amma's room. She showed me where the women would sleep, and she moved all the partitions by herself. She rearranged everything to make more space. Can you imagine anyone other than Amma physically arranging their devotees' accommodation, thinking of every little detail? Only Amma really walks her talk.

Visitors often say, "It's too crowded here! How can you take it?" I answered that we are not here because we like or dislike crowds. We come because we love Amma. It becomes a community because we all love Amma, and so we stay together like a big family. At the same time, we learn to adjust to other people, and handle conflict.

When I was a special education teacher, one child couldn't get along with anyone, and I also found it hard to relate to him. One day I thought, "I will be like an actor." An actor rehearses a role many times till it becomes natural. I decided to tell myself, "I love this boy and see only his beauty." It started as an act, but it became real. I learned to love him, and I still think of him. He was a great teacher.

I use this technique in the āśram a lot! Amma says, "Compassion is the most important factor in life. Human calculations may be wrong, but actions born of true compassion can never be wrong because compassion is the law of nature, the power of God, the heart of creation. In truth, the spiritual path begins and ends with compassion."

Amma is the highest example of compassion. When I struggle to love someone, or when I judge someone, I tell myself, "They are showing me how far I am from God." They become my spiritual mirror that shows me the teachings I need to work on.

My birth mother always told me, "You are my favorite child." When I was about 10 years old, I heard my mom telling my older sister, "You are my favorite!" I marched up to my mom and said, "How can it be?" My mom answered, "If a mother has two kids, she doesn't give 50% love to each. She gives 100% love to each. Even if the mother has ten kids, she always gives 100% love to each child. A mother's love is endless. You are my favorite, and your sister is also my favorite." If we could understand this deeply, jealousy among us would disappear. Even though Amma has so many children, she finds ways to make each of us feel close to her.

The *Guru* has infinite love for each disciple. Everything the *Guru* does is only for our growth. Amma has said many times that she is never angry; she only has love for us. But if she sees us moving away from our goal, she will call our attention to that. Even the so-called scolding is *prasād*. She is trying to help us increase our awareness.

Once, I went to Calcutta early to prepare the accommodation for 700 people, including āśram*ites*, drivers, construction workers, electricians, devotees, and more. I tried my best to accommodate everyone and was happy with the results. I often think, "Jani, you are doing a wonderful job."

When Amma arrived, someone complained to her about the accommodation. Amma called me to her room! I expected Amma's 'tuition *prasād*,' and I got it. She was concerned that not everyone had a place to sleep. I was scared to say anything. I just accepted my *prasād* and thought how I could do it better next time. Amma is one with the Supreme Self. *She* is the doer. But I had forgotten this and taken credit for myself. It is only out of her compassion that Amma gives us the opportunity to help even a little.

Two days later, we were sitting with Amma in the airport. I was still feeling sad. Suddenly, she said, "Jani, Ganga Ganga!" I thought, "Uh-oh! What now?" Then the translation came. "Jani, Amma calls you Ganga, because you go ahead of the group and purify the place before we arrive." I realized that, though Amma had scolded me to teach me humility, she knew my heart. It is easy to forget that Amma is all-knowing. We do not need to explain ourselves to her. She sees it all and purifies everything. And she teaches us humility and makes us feel better by giving us a little credit.

Amma's actions teach me more than any scripture. Many times, I have thought, "During *bhajans* Amma calls out, 'Amma!'" If we sang our own name, it would look like we were singing to ourselves out of ego. But Amma, the Divine Mother is singing to the Divine Mother, her own Self.

Amma shows us the same teaching before *Dēvī Bhāva* when she sings '*Ambikē Dēvī*'. She blesses the crown and garland before she wears them. She is the one who prays and the one to whom we pray. Seeing this, I start to understand what Amma means when she says, "Creator and Creation are one." Vēdānta describes this as, "Doing and Being are one and the same. Without Being there is no Doing."

This year on *Ōṇam* and her Birthday, Amma led the *mānasa pūjā* for all of us. It was fascinating to be led by Amma to worship *Dēvī*. Amma shows us that she is both the worshipper and the one whom we worship. We see she is the creation calling out to the Creator; and we feel and know she is both, and beyond both. Amma is beyond words. From Amma's actions, we see Creator and creation are one. We should understand this not only intellectually. The experience of being WITH her teaches us this.

Once, in the airport, Amma called me and said, "You do *sēvā* and you never come close, give *prasād* or do line *sēvā*, etc." Then, Amma told this story: "Once, a disciple told his *Guru*, 'I never come to you. I don't go to the classes. I just do my *sēvā*. Am I still on your list?'" Then Amma paused, looked at me, pointed her finger at me and said: "Maybe you are not on **my** list..." I felt like a knife pierced my heart. Then she continued, "But the most important thing is that I am on **your** list all the time."

God doesn't need us; we need God. Remembering this has helped me all these years to do everything for Amma. The most important thing I have learned from Amma is to serve others. I pray that Amma stays on **my** list. Not just the *first* one on my list, but the *only* one on my list.

23

Amma's Infinite Nature

Nandini Ambrose (United States)

When Brahmacāriṇī Amṛta asked if I would give one of the daily *satsaṅgs*, I shuddered, thinking of this large audience and sitting so close to Amma. Then I recalled giving a *satsaṅg* many years ago and remembered Amma's words: "You are not weak, but a strong lion." So, I accepted the challenge. In the late 1990's, while Amma was away on tour, I gave my first *satsaṅg*. Every evening, after *bhajans*, the *brahmacārīs* and *brahmacāriṇīs* were giving talks. After some time, foreigners were invited to speak. Topic: "Your experiences with Amma."

I chose three stories and went to my Amma doll to ask if the stories were okay. I put two papers: 'yes'/'no'. The one I picked said 'no'. I put three more papers: 'different stories', 'more stories' or 'less stories.' The paper I picked said 'more stories', so I added one more story. Again, the answer came back 'more stories." This went on until there were seven stories. I told Amma, "This is impossible! I only have 15 minutes!" But Amma held firm.

Three days before the *satsaṅg*, I got a serious, extremely painful infection. I could not sit, and we were supposed to sit lotus-style on the floor while giving our *satsaṅg*. The morning of the *satsaṅg*, I decided to keep silence and do *japa* and meditation to prepare myself. Instead, I had non-stop terrible thoughts. I was so upset that I went to the *kaḷari* and stood in front of the big picture of Amma and cried. Finally, I yelled at Amma, "Seven stories! Severe pain! Horrible thoughts! You gave me these experiences, so *you* give the talk!" I walked away crying.

That night, I was last on the list. When I sat down on the floor, suddenly, all the pain was gone. Before I spoke, I left my body and joined the audience. The talk that was to be only 15 minutes lasted 45 minutes. As I was leaving the temple, Swāminī Karunamritaji put her arm around my shoulder and told me what a wonderful talk it was. Just then, I re-entered my body. Amma, herself, actually *did* give the *satsaṅg*. When I went to my room, I couldn't sleep because I was soaked in Amma's *śakti* (energy). I felt like I could have run around the Kali temple 108 times, or even picked it up as Kṛṣṇa picked up the mountain.

I was born into a Catholic family, and from an early age had spiritual tendencies. After my first year of college, in 1961, I joined the Sisters of Charity of the Blessed Virgin Mary. When I was a novice, I wished that I could have lived with Jesus when he was on the earth. I was always looking for a holy soul who could guide me, but I never found her. I didn't know I was wanting a *Guru*. After 18 years, I left the convent and lived a worldly life for many years.

In *Awaken Children 7* p.12 Amma says, "Whenever a disciple falls helplessly in love with the Master, no thinking process is involved. The Master's spiritual attraction is so great that the disciple becomes his." Also, "The power of the Master precludes any choice on your part. The power is the Master's alone. It is the grace for which you cannot take any credit whatsoever." And also,

> You are just a tiny iron filing that is helplessly attracted to the all-powerful magnet of the Master's spiritual glory. An iron filing has no choice. Once it is within the magnetic force of the magnet, it cannot choose whether to come or go. As the magnet draws it, it simply has to move in that direction.

These words describe my meeting with Amma. In 1993, a friend went to see a Holy Mother from Kerala, India who gave hugs and kisses. She bought Amma's biography and gave it to me. When I read it, I thought, "When I retire, maybe I'll go live in Amma's āśram." Six months later, my friend called again and said Amma would be coming for five days (public program and retreat). Did I want to go? I enthusiastically agreed.

During the public programs, nothing special happened. But the very first day of the retreat, I kept thinking, "Quit your job, sell your house, and go live in India with Amma. Now!!!!" I didn't even know who Amma was since I had met her only two days before. The second day, the thought grew even stronger. I got in the question line to ask Amma herself.

After Swāmī Rāmakṛṣṇānanda asked Amma if I should come to her āśram to live, Amma turned to me and just laughed. Swāmī told me, "Amma would be very happy if you came to India." My friend said she was going to get a *mantra*. I had no idea what a *mantra* was, but I also got in line. Swāmī asked me who my *iṣṭa-dēvat*ā was. I didn't understand, but guessed it meant "Who is your God." To my utter surprise and amazement, I pointed to Amma and said, "She is."

I volunteered for *sēvā*. They gave me an apron, a knife and a large plastic bin filled with chili peppers. They told me to cut them lengthwise and take out the seeds. I never ate chilis, so I knew nothing, and chopped them with my bare hands. My hands burned for two weeks. Since I was leaving my old life for this totally new life, I guessed the chilis were burning away any attachment I had to my old life. I think it worked! I've never looked back and never missed anything from that life.

The first morning after the retreat, before leaving for work, I put my television in the car to give away. I had purchased a large photo of Amma and two *bhajan* tapes. Instead of watching TV after work, I played the *bhajan* tapes while looking at Amma's photo and cried because I so wanted to be with her. I also called a real estate person and told her to sell my house. It took a whole year to settle all my affairs.

During the next tour, I was headed for the San Ramon āśram where Amma would serve a meal to all the volunteers. On the way to the āśram, I got into a car accident. A few months earlier, a Vedic astrologer had warned me that I would be in a serious car accident, and I should be careful. The accident happened, but it *wasn't* serious. Amma was present. To make sure that I knew Amma was taking care of me, the insurance company of the man who hit my car was just across the street from the accident. I had no problem getting the car repaired quickly, at their expense.

After the 1994 tour, I flew to India. When I arrived in the āśram Amma was giving *darśan* in the Kali temple. I immediately got in line. When Amma hugged me, she said in English, "Are you happy now?" Amma wasted no time showing me her true nature. In one of Swāmī Amritagitananda's classes, he said, "You know you are with a *Sadguru* or *avatār* because they will show you they are all-knowing, all-powerful and omnipresent."

In the early days, Amma often would say she was a "crazy lady who doesn't know anything...only went to 4th standard." But, later during a question-and-answer session, Amma said, "I know everything." In Amma's 108 names, #93 says that Amma watches all the actions of her disciples. In *Awaken Children 8*, Amma says that "all our thoughts go through Amma's mind first. Amma is aware of everything that is happening to her children."

I was blessed to work with Bri. Nirmalāmṛta. She was humble and had deep devotion and love for Amma. Together we chopped veggies; and, while she cooked the meals, I did the dishes, cleaned the small canteen, and served all three meals. One day, a visitor came to help with veggie chopping. Amma always says to chant your *mantra* and have good positive thoughts while preparing food because your energy goes into the food, and then into those who eat it.

This new helper was extremely annoying. She didn't do one single thing the way she was instructed. I became angry. I knew this was not what Amma wanted, and I felt badly. That night, at supper, after everyone had taken their food, Amma came in. Instantly, I was afraid. I *knew* she had come to "get" me.

Only soup was left, so I quickly put some in a cup and handed it to Amma. She looked at me so fiercely that I was sure the Kali temple behind us would collapse. Amma put the cup down and looked sweetly at everyone and smiled at them. Then she turned back and gave me her fierce look again and left.

She never said a word, but I was devastated. I ran from the canteen to my bed and began to sob. I cried all night and through 4:30am *arcana*. After *arcana*, I sat in front of Amma's picture in the Kali temple. I prayed: "Amma, I know I cannot stay here in your home and think badly about others; but what do I *do*? I don't *like* this woman." Amma replied, "The woman is innocent. I used her to show you that you need purifying." Then I felt gratitude for the woman.

Amma's fierce look had shattered me. Soon, Amma left on tour to Australia, Singapore, Mauritius and Reunion Island. I couldn't afford Australia, but I booked the rest of the tour. While Amma was in Australia, I cried every day. I thought I would have to go back to the US because I was not good enough to live with Amma. I so wanted to be near Amma and be her darling daughter. Instead, I would have to leave it all. I cried and cried over this.

In Singapore, Amma called all tour people for *darśan*. My last encounter with Amma had been her extraordinary fierce look and I was afraid; but I gathered courage and got in line. First, Amma held me in front of her and said clearly and slowly, "You are my darling daughter." Then she gave me a loving hug. Since then, I have never again doubted that I belonged in Amma's home. It was clear she knew my thoughts during veggie chopping, and she knew I was crying all the time she was in Australia.

After the Singapore program, we flew to Mauritius Island. On arriving, we learned that a hurricane was headed for the island, but as it neared the shoreline, it suddenly turned and headed back out to sea. Late that afternoon, everyone was saying that Amma had turned the hurricane. I was very new to Amma, so I wasn't sure.

Our last stop was Reunion Island. Our accommodation was in the āśram. On one side were some houses but, on the other side and behind the āśram, there was a huge open field. One morning, we awoke to see the field on fire with flames four to five meters high, and dark clouds of smoke. Everyone was alarmed, but Amma told everyone not to worry. When the program started, I sat near the large windows keeping one eye on Amma giving *darśan*, and one eye on the fire. Every so often, Amma would gaze out at the fire, and then the wind would shift directions.

Near the end of *darśan*, a woman arrived with her very elderly, frail mother. She died on Amma's lap. Her daughter informed us that her mother had had a few heart attacks in the last two weeks and had told her daughter that she wouldn't die until she got a hug from Kṛṣṇa.

After the fire burned itself out, I went to look around. In a big fire, usually, there is a line where the fire stops. Beyond that line will be a few meters of dead grass or ground cover due to the intense heat from the fire. I found the line where the fire stopped; but, beyond that line was green grass and plant life as if an invisible wall protected the āśram. I walked down a small hill to the large canvas tent that was our dining hall. It was in the middle of the fire zone but was untouched by the fire. Then I knew that Amma was all-powerful. She had turned a hurricane, she kept an old woman alive until she got her hug from Kṛṣṇa, and she controlled a raging fire.

Shortly after returning from that tour, a woman arrived in Amṛtapuri from the US. She had significant gynecological problems which needed surgery, but she refused. She was only in the āśram one day when she began to hemorrhage, and her condition soon became life-threatening. Late that night, a nurse and doctor from the US realized the danger. They wrapped her in a blanket and were carrying her to the backwaters when Amma's youngest brother heard them outside and came out to investigate. Since there was no boat on the āśram side, he swam across to the other side. He woke up a friend with a car and brought back a boat to fetch the other three. They took her to the Catholic hospital in Kollam.

Amma had left on the North India tour. The nurse and I took turns bystanding. One afternoon, the patient was sleeping, and I was sitting in a chair chanting *arcana*. Suddenly, the door slowly opened, and an elderly woman in a traditional white cotton *sāri* entered. She had the most beautiful, disarming smile. Immediately, I thought that if she asked me to jump from a 50-story building, I would. She was the height and size of Amma, and she walked exactly like Amma. She moved to the bedside, and I sat in amazement. She stroked the patient for many minutes. I kept thinking, "She is just like Amma."

Then she came down to the foot of the bed where we had a large photo of Amma. She looked at the photo as both of us were telling her the photo was Amma. She laughed at us. She looked at me with the most powerful, compassionate smile and stroked my face and my head. Then, she returned to the patient and again stroked her. I kept thinking, "She is just like Amma."

Finally, she came back to me, and three times she put her hands on her chest and then raised them up towards the ceiling. She spoke some words I did not understand, then she walked toward the door. I jumped up to follow her. But just before she reached the doorway, she disappeared. I looked in the hall, but she was not there. I ran downstairs to the nursing station, which was next to the stairway, and asked if anyone had gone up or down the stairs. They said no. Walking back to the room, I was given the meaning of the woman's gestures and words: "This is the mother of the whole universe."

When I entered the room, I asked the patient, "Do you know who that was?" She said yes, it was Amma. She was also thinking, "She is just like Amma." No wonder the visitor laughed when we were trying to tell her that it was Amma's photo. For the record, Amma was in Pune that day.

Later that year, when Amma went on the North Indian tour, I went to Pondicherry. Three years before I met Amma, I read the writings of sweet mother of Pondicherry, and I was praying to her. Now, I belonged to Amma. I decided to go to Pondicherry to thank sweet mother for her loving kindness and to put closure on our relationship. When leaving from Pondicherry, I got on a train that would take me back to the main train route from Chennai to Thiruvananthapuram.

The train was nearly empty, but, in the first section, a very old and very small *sādhu* sat lotus-style, in deep meditation. I decided to sit across from him, hoping to soak up some of his intense spiritual energy. When the train started to move, suddenly, five very drunk men boarded. They looked into our section and saw me and the very old, very small *sādhu*. When they started staring at me and laughing in a vile manner, I realized I was in extreme danger.

Then, the men came towards me. At the last second, the holy man opened his eyes and looked at the drunken men. He said something, and they stopped. Their whole energy changed. They turned away and never looked at me again. I knew Amma sent the old *sādhu* to protect me.

Another time, we were meditating on the green roof. Next to Amma was her dish of pebbles. My eyes were closed, and I was deeply praying to Amma to open my heart and fill it with love and devotion. Tears were streaming down my face. Suddenly, something hit me in my chest. I opened my eyes and Amma was looking at me intensely. I looked down and saw the pebble. Her aim was perfect—she hit me right in the center of my heart *cakra*.

In 1994, Amma gave *darśan* to the whole āśram every week. One such day, when I was in line, I was crying because my heart was full of love and devotion. But when there were only four people ahead of me, all the devotion and love disappeared, and my heart felt cold and empty. It was the worst *darśan* of my life. What I realized from this is that every bit of devotion and love we ever feel is a pure gift from Amma. Her grace alone brought us here, and her grace alone gives the precious, priceless gift of love and devotion.

Another day on the green roof, a *brahmacārī* knelt before Amma, crying. He said, "Amma, please come inside my heart." He put his head on Amma's lap and cried. Amma began laughing very energetically. I wondered why Amma was laughing when this *brahmacārī* was so serious. Then Amma lifted the *brahmacārī's* head and said, "Son, I'm home. You are the one who is out." Since then, if I feel a distant from Amma, I don't ask, "Where are you, Amma?" I ask, "Nandini, where are *you*?"

I'm sure, for all of us, our most treasured and sacred moments are in Amma's arms, hearing her say, "Darling daughter," or "Darling son," In those moments, I always pray, "Amma, may I stay here forever."

Amma has shown me that she is always, in every moment, lovingly holding us in her arms. She is always calling out to us, "My darling child. My darling child." The problem is, we think we are separate individuals. We think *we* are in charge of our lives. But if we look even at the gross, physical level, we can see this is not true. Research shows that the adult body has around

37 trillion cells, and each cell does around 30,000 processes every second. Do *we* do any of that? Our nose smells, our ears hear, our tongue tastes, our skin feels sensations, our eyes see—all automatically. Our hearts beat, our lungs take in O_2 and breathe out CO_2, our blood and lymph circulate, and exchange and collect waste *without our awareness.*

All our organs function with precision *without our awareness.* I also read that our liver functions are so extensive, that if we wanted to build a factory to duplicate all these functions, we would need a building at least five square kilometers in size. Our minds are also not in our control. Everyday thousands (maybe millions) of thoughts fly through. In short, an infinitely greater force (śakti) is in charge of everything. Amma is that *śakti* and we and the entire universe are her *saṅkalpa.*

There are now eight billion people in the world. We may imagine that we must be fairly spiritual to be with an *avatār* like Amma; but actually, Amṛtapuri is a spiritual cardiac ICU. Amma is the doctor. She prescribes and administers medicine to heal our damaged hearts, and she removes our blockages. If necessary, she performs bypass surgery. When Amma's treatment is working, our actions reveal deep devotion, love, compassion, respect and reverence for all that is. When we are aware and quiet, we can feel and hear her loving presence in each moment.

Amṛtapuri is also a spiritual medical and surgical ICU. We all suffer from stage three or stage four cancers of ego-mind, attachments, likes and dislikes, and the illusion of doership. Dr. Amma's surgical, radiation, and chemotherapy interventions are specialized and unique. We know Amma's treatment is working when we become peaceful, empty and silent. Thank you, thank you, thank you, Amma.

24

The Perfect Answer

Kripa Gressel (United States)

I'd like to begin with a story. This is one of the most beautiful stories I have ever heard, and I think about it frequently. It is a story of Śrī Adi Shankaracharya. It is said, at one point on his spiritual path, he believed only in *Advaita Vēdānta*. In fact, his faith in *Advaita Vēdānta* was so firm that he denied any other path was a viable way to attain Realization.

During this phase of his life, he was once meditating on oneness with the universe. Suddenly, Shankaracharya had the thought, "I am thirsty." A little while later, he opened his eyes, still thirsty, and saw a gold cup with milk in it. Pleased with himself, he thought, "See, I am so at one with creation that I have a thought and the thought manifests." He then reached up to grasp the cup of milk. Except - he could not move. He could not blink, could not even form another thought. Then, *Dēvī* appeared before him in all of her glory and splendor, and she began to laugh.

Now, when I hear this story, I always imagine the incomparable form of our beloved Amma in *Dēvī Bhāva*, wearing a gorgeous cream-colored blouse with a dark red sari covered in gold embroidery, and with a thick, elaborate border. I imagine her laughing face with its sparkling nose ring and her dangling, shining *jimmikki* earrings, and wearing the cutest, most delicate gold anklets on her ankles, and jingling bangles on her wrists. I imagine her beautiful belt, and, of course, her crown, shining in the light, illuminating everything around her.

I can't begin to imagine what form of *Dēvī* Śaṅkarācārya saw. I also, personally, can't believe that she could have been more beautiful than our beloved Amma. However, according to this story, he was so overcome by *Dēvī's* beauty that he tried to prostrate in front of her, but even that was not possible. Only when he completely surrendered his own ego at the feet of *Dēvī* did she permit him to fall at her feet, showing Śaṅkarācārya that *nothing* is possible without her will – her grace.

I absolutely love this story. First, because every time I think about it, I get to imagine Amma in *Dēvī Bhāva*, which turns my heart to mush. Second, because it is an important reminder to me that nothing in this world is possible without God's will and grace, and that the only way forward is to surrender to that fact.

My family met Amma in 1989, when I was three years old, and my younger brother was three months old. Amma and my parents have both told me their memories of it, but I have absolutely zero memory of it myself.

It has come up in many discussions over the last several months, how, as we listen to the *satsaṅgs* that people have shared, it is deeply inspiring to hear of the struggles people went through to come to stay in the āśram. To my great fortune, I don't have a story like that, per se. Although I've had my fair share of struggles, Amma has been the central facet of my life since I can remember. She has always been by my side, guiding my life and correcting my path whenever I have wavered. My family are all devotees, and I am even fortunate enough to be married by Amma to a devotee who also wants to stay in the āśram. I try to stay grateful for this fact at all times. But the truth is that I often forget and begin to take Amma for granted – quite often, even on a daily basis.

Amma talks frequently about how people come here because of their love for Amma rather than their burning desire for God Realization. I am the first person to agree whole-heartedly with this. To be perfectly frank, I do not consider myself a spiritual person; therefore, I don't think this can actually be called a *satsaṅg*. Rather, I am just sharing my experiences with Amma, and some of the things that inspire me to continue at least to *try* to understand the spiritual path.

I actually expressed this feeling to Amma when I was 18 years old. I was on my first foreign tour with her in Europe. During that tour I had reconnected with a childhood friend from my hometown. As we got reacquainted, I noticed how focused she was. She would stare at Amma for hours, crying, meditating, chanting *arcana*, and generally behaving as a true spiritual aspirant should – at least, according to my understanding at the time.

I asked her why she did this, and she said she wanted to attain realization. At that point in time, my biggest concern was whether there was somewhere fun to go sightseeing during my break. So, when I heard her answer, I started to feel depressed, comparing myself to her. I spent several cities wallowing in the fact that I didn't have any desire for God or God realization. I kept wondering how I could want something when I didn't understand what it even meant?

One night as I was sitting near Amma, she saw me and called me around to the other side of her chair. I walked around and stood there with my arms crossed over my chest and my feet planted wide. Amma looked at me and started laughing. "You're standing there like an army general! Why so stern?"

I turned bright red and told Amma, "Actually, I am terrified, I'm just trying to cover it up." She smiled and said "You aren't a little lamb anymore. You are a lion cub!" That gave me the courage to tell Amma what had been eating at me for weeks. I said, "Amma, I don't have any desire for God Realization." Amma turned to me and said, "That isn't a problem. Learn to have compassion for the world, and the door will open, and God will flow into your heart."

The beauty of Amma's answer is manifold: first, it comforted me, reassuring me that I was not a bad person. Second, it indicated that she understood my heart in that moment and answered in such a way that I would not become discouraged. And most importantly, she gave me a way forward. Learning to be more compassionate than I am is something I can at least understand, even if I fail at it consistently. It is, in reality, a much larger request than I initially understood. Ultimately, having compassion for the world equates to experiencing the entire world as an extension of yourself...but I didn't understand that at the time.

I was raised in a community of people who regularly practiced meditation. My parents met through that community, and shortly before I was born, they moved to a small town so that my brother and I could attend a school where we would meditate daily, learn Sanskrit and *shastra*, do *yōga* āsana and follow an ayurvedic lifestyle.

I look back at this experience with mixed feelings: on the one hand, it was a beautiful environment to grow up in. On the other hand, the way that I was taught about spirituality there was very theoretical. The focus on the benefits of meditation in worldly life did not make any sense to me at all. It was only Amma's consistent presence in my life as a child that kept my focus on God in any meaningful way. So, when Amma told me to learn to have compassion for the world, it was the first time I was able to make sense of anything related to spirituality. And learning to have compassion became the underlying lodestone for my path forward. I still struggle in many situations to be compassionate, but every day is another opportunity to improve.

As I grew older and more attached to Amma and more attracted to trying to live a spiritual life, I spent a great deal of time trying to understand spirituality. I am still trying. But honestly, I like shopping, and reading, and cooking, and traveling, and many other very normal things, and one thing that I can't stomach is trying to be someone that I'm not. At the same time, I know that my life is miserable when I am not with Amma, and that trying to follow Amma's example is the only thing that brings me "a feeling of a clean heart" – a phrase a dear friend expressed to me when I was a teenager. So, I have had to find ways to balance my desire to be with Amma and my more mundane interests.

Several years ago, I was working in the café here (Amṛtapuri) in the mornings, and I would listen to chants in the early morning hours to keep my mind focused. I came across the *Bhavānī Aṣṭakam*, written by Śrī Ādi Śaṅkarācārya. The entire chant is beautiful, but there are two verses in particular that I identify with more than the others:

I do not know how to give,
Nor do I know how to meditate.
I do not know *tantra*,
Nor do I know stanzas of prayer.
I do not know how to worship,
Nor do I know the art of *yōga*,
So you are my refuge and my only refuge, *Bhavānī*.

I know not how to be righteous.
I know not the way to the sacred places.
I know not methods of salvation.
I know not how to merge my mind with God.
I know not the art of devotion.
I know not how to practice austerities, O mother,
So you are my refuge and my only refuge, *Bhavānī*.

Aside from how beautiful these verses are, I honestly feel that this type of prayer is my only hope. I don't understand any of the formalities of spiritual life. I am supremely human. I get jealous very easily, and don't know how to control my mind very well. I feel very strongly that any understanding I have of spirituality is simply due to Amma's infinite compassion for me and her ever-flowing grace.

I will share an experience that demonstrates this. I started university after spending a year and half with Amma on tours and in India, and then moved to Amma's California āśram to begin school nearby. The first US tour I went on, after I started school, began with one big expectation:

That Amma would shower me with attention and questions about school, life in San Ramon, and if I were okay living away from India. I really thought Amma would tell me she was so sad that I was far away from her!

However, my brother had caught the measles on the Australian tour just a few months before, and all Amma would talk to me about was him. Every time I went near her, she would ask about him, talk about him, or tell me about how sad he was when he had to leave the tour. I was so angry and so hurt. I spent the entire six weeks trying to create situations in which Amma would talk to me about *me*. I asked questions about what to study. I tried to talk to her about the San Ramon āśram and spent many hours crying about Amma "ignoring me".

One time, when Amma asked me about him, I was so fed up that I blurted out "Amma, he's upset that I'm upset that you keep talking to me about him!" Both Amma and the woman translating for me were a little stunned that I so openly said that. But I was pretty desperate. By the time the tour ended in Toronto, I was exhausted from my emotional turmoil.

It was the last night of tour, and I was taking my turn doing a shift next to Amma when my parents and brother came for darśan. I started crying the moment I saw Amma even SMILING at my brother. He was upset that I was so sad, and so he tried to tell Amma to stop talking to me about him. Amma told him, "No. It's not about you. She is sad because she can't be in India with Amma." Then she turned to me, smiled so sweetly, and said, "When you finish college you can come and live in India, don't worry." Immediately, my heart melted, and all the jealousy, anger, and frustration I had felt over the previous six weeks evaporated. Amma understood the true underlying reason I was upset, even when I didn't.

This illustrates one of the points that Amma has discussed before: how our minds can block the experience of grace that is ever flowing. Even when we are in ideal situations, if the mind is churning with emotions, judgments, anxieties, or simply jumping around from thought to thought with no concentration, we cannot experience that perfection.

When I contemplated on that summer's events, I felt foolish for resenting the attention my brother had been getting, and even more foolish for resenting that Amma spent the summer talking to me about him. If only I had had the kind of mental grace that would have allowed me to be grateful that Amma was talking to me at all! Who cares about what topic! My own selfish desires had blocked that flow of grace. I was not able to receive the grace that Amma was showering on me because I did not have the grace of my own mind.

Amma gives a beautiful example of this. She says, "Even if a person sits right below a radio station, they will not be able to listen to music unless they tune their radio to the right channel." Through this example, Amma tries to teach us that even if we sit in God's lap, we will not be able to perceive God's grace without our own grace.

But that kind of correct tuning can be difficult to achieve. In fact, I frequently let my mind run wild with anxieties about just the most ridiculous things. My husband says that I am consistently able to find the worst-case scenario for anything. The only thing that has ever truly helped me to calm my mind of this kind of chaos is remembering that Amma is the one taking care. This is a very profound relief, but if my mind is not attuned to Amma, it is not possible to experience.

This also points out the relationship between anxiety and lack of faith. If one understands that Amma – *Dēvī*, she who creates and sustains this creation – is actively involved in one's life, where is there room for anxiety? It reflects upon the fickleness of the mind and the lack of faith we can have on subtle levels. Fortunately for us, we have Amma's physical presence to right that ship, and give us the tools we need to re-focus and deepen the wells of our faith.

As I mentioned before, I love shopping. A few years ago, my husband and I were staying with his parents in California for a few months while he worked, and I finished my masters' thesis. I was at the library one day when he sent me a message: "The house has been robbed. You should come back." I rushed back to the house to find that the robbers had destroyed the house and stolen so many things – many that I had just recently purchased in a shopping spree. In the grand scheme of things, it could have been so much worse than it was, as insurance covered all of the losses, and somehow the thieves had missed my wedding jewelry. I was surprised to realize how few of the objects I was actually upset about having been stolen. In fact, there was only one thing that I was truly upset about – my *arcana* book bag that had my newly made *arcana* book, and, more importantly, a photo of Amma kissing my cheek when I was a little girl. I was heartbroken about this photo, as it was the only one in existence. It had been with me through all of the difficult years of college as a reminder that Amma was with me.

My relative detachment to the things that were stolen was pretty shocking to me. I had spent so much time researching and purchasing the right things, but in the end, they were just things. Plus, I got to go through the process of buying new things. (I am not much better now than I was then. I still love shopping.)

However, something even more important came out of this experience: in the aftermath of the robbery, my already anxiety-ridden self became so stressed that I could barely sleep. I tend towards stress and anxiety anyway, and this pushed me over the edge. Whereas before, I had been afraid to cross the street alone, then I was afraid to even go out of the house alone.

By the time that summer tour began, all I could think about was telling Amma. The first moment I was next to Amma, I couldn't keep my mouth shut. "My in-laws house got robbed, Amma," I said. She was concerned, so I went on to tell her about all of the stress and fear I was experiencing. I really expected her to console me lovingly.

Instead, she looked at me almost in disbelief, and gave a bit of a laugh. "Who do you think it is that crosses the street? Who do you think it is that is wearing that dress right now?" was all she said.

What relief this provided – so much more than simple consolation! I immediately recognized that she had acknowledged that she is still always with me, whether I have a photo of her kissing my cheek or not.

I think about this interaction almost every day. It has provided me with countless moments of stress relief throughout the years and has inspired me to pray for more surrender and understanding that I am *not* the doer. To try to remember that, if it is Amma that wears this dress, it is also Amma who studies complex and slightly depressing gender issues. It is Amma who writes papers. It is Amma who will get me through my PhD course. It is Amma who carries my burdens.

And this is just a spectacular example of how Amma will take us from wherever we are just one step further upon the path. Amma gives us such support, and only requests that we step aside and let her do it all.

Amma encourages us to recognize that she is the ultimate force. Just as *Dēvī's* appearance in front of Śaṅkarācārya taught him that he is nothing without her grace, we too, are nothing without her grace. But even beyond that, she asks us to find her *inside*. Amma repeats over and over and over again that we are not different from her. We have everything within us. We just have to realize it.

Dēvī came to Śaṅkarācārya at exactly the right moment to reveal to him the truth that all is sustained by her alone. Our Beloved Amma comes into our lives and our hearts at all of the right moments to lead us along the path with the ultimate compassion – that compassion that will remove our egos and bring us closer to her.

I would like to close by reciting the 27th verse of the *Saundaryalahari*, also by Śrī Ādi Śaṅkarācārya:

> Oh Mother, let my every word be a prayer to you,
> Every movement of my hands a ritual gesture to you,
> Every step I take be a circumambulation of your image,
> Every morsel I eat a rite of sacrifice to you.
> Every time I lay down a prostration at your feet,
> Every act of personal pleasure and all else that I do,
> Let it all be a form of worshipping you.

I pray that we all strive to embody this verse, and I offer my words at the lotus feet of our Beloved Amma.

25

From Unawareness to Light and Love

Sunanda Rappaport (Switzerland)

Construction work is always going on in Amṛtapuri. The constant noise reminds me that Amma is working on each of us. Her true miracle is that she transforms our rusty minds into pure, fragrant gold. We have to cling to her feet and *never give up!* Amma loves to move at high speed. It's not light-speed. It's *mind*-speed, which is much faster! Nothing stops Amma. Even if she has to wait for ages for her ignorant ones, Amma is willing to take any number of births to lead us to the supreme goal!

Through her own life, Amma shows us how to overcome all obstacles. She makes us strong and detached so she can lift the burden of our sorrows. Amma is the universal Divine Mother of Compassion, and her omniscient presence and guidance are the answer to the prayers of all her children in the world. Swāmī Paramātmānanda says, "The real *Guru* is God. He is always within us and manifests as the Teacher when we are ready to return to our Source."

In kindergarten, I met my best childhood friend. She opened many doors for my spiritual path with Amma. From childhood onwards, I was considered a foreigner wherever I went. Now I understand this was a blessing, as we all are only temporary guests on this planet, coming and going. Only *mahātmās* like Amma bring us to our true home, our True Self.

My parents are from different countries and finally settled in Switzerland. We spoke three languages at our dining table: French, Finnish and Swiss German. Because we were foreigners, my mother wanted her children to learn music, a universal language understood by all. Early on, I learned the silver flute and discovered the healing power of music that brings harmony into life. Amma's music is the true source and ultimate divine glory.

When I was young, I felt the contradiction in society. How can an outer world function in harmony when the inner world is in disorder? Amma says, *"The teaching of universal spiritual principles and human values should be a standard part of general education."* Only incarnations like Amma can make this be true for the whole world. She embodies the language of love and unites all hearts! All significant contributions for dharma in society have always come from *mahātmās* (great souls) out of their selfless compassion towards humanity.

Around age 12, I read the *Children's Bible*. The teachings of Jesus inspired me to do good to others impartially. When Jesus asked Peter to follow him, he left everything for Christ. I had this desire to do the same and was convinced that Jesus would come to earth again very soon. Seven years later, at the age of 19, I met Amma, my Divine Mother!

In 1993, Amma came to Zurich, Switzerland, near our place. My childhood friend and I were very excited to meet a saint for the first time in our life! Morning meditation started with the primordial sound *OM*. Swāmijī's powerful inward-going voice still resonates in my memory. Afterwards, we joined the *darśan* queue. There were, maybe, 200 people present. After *darśan*, I cried and cried...non-stop...as if my tears would purge eons of pain and longing...a coming home to my real Mother. My yearning for a purpose in life was fulfilled.

My focus in life shifted. People and things just dropped away, making room for spirituality, and I began a daily meditation practice. I started professional flute studies in western classical music. In 1994, Amma gave me a *mantra.*

My childhood friend and I attended Amma's *satsaṅg* and *bhajan* groups. Amma graced us to sing and play the flute during her programs. We sang in the huge, empty churches of Zurich with their wonderful echoes; and on the streets, including various programs for charity. Since 1995, I've followed Amma, every year, on her European tours. Forgetting about food and sleep, I did lots of physical *sēvā*. All this increased my faith and strengthened my bond with Amma. Amma's energy gives us the strength for *sēvā* and reduces our need to sleep!

Shortly after meeting Amma, a deep thirst to know pure love arose in me and, when Amma passed, I spontaneously asked her, "What is Love? I want Love." Amma looked at me compassionately. Her answer was not verbal. Soon after, I sensed a warm feeling of love in my heart like I had never felt before. Amma opens our hearts.

Upon arriving in Amṛtapuri, in October 1995, I understood that I'd reached Amma's abode when the Kali Temple appeared before my eyes – the heart of Amma's āśram! Full of gratitude, and exhausted from the long travel, with tears, I prostrated to this sacred land. Suddenly I heard Prabha's voice in Swiss

German: "Was tuesch grännä?" (Why are you crying?) Amma's light was welcoming me, in a familiar language, to her world family!

The pink Kālī Temple looks like a huge, colorful, scrumptious cake and invites our celebration! Its artwork reveals, to the seeker of Truth, the way to reach to the Cream of the cream! The āśram symbols, Śrī Kṛṣṇa and the various manifestations of *Śakti* and Śiva, lead to the inner cave of the heart, where Kālī stands still on Śiva. That is Supreme Consciousness!

> *Tyāgēnaike amṛtatvamānaśuḥ*
> By renunciation alone immortality is attained.
>
> *nin prēmam koṇḍenne unmattan ākkuk-endamme avīṭunnu snēha pūrvam*
> *gaurāṅgan śrī buddhan yeśu mosas ivar nin premonmattarām puṇyātmakkaḷ*
>
> O Mother, make me mad with thy Love!
> Gauranga, Buddha, Jesus and Moses,
> are all drunk with the wine of thy Love.

Mahātmās like Amma abide always in a natural state of blissful, immortal intoxication!

During my first three-week visit, Amma gave me an unforgettable experience of her love and light. The entire āśram is soaked in Amma's love, and I guess I got drunk from an overdose of ambrosia!

One night, we all did sand *sēvā* to prepare the venue for Amma's birthday celebration. 20,000 guests were coming. The rain puddles at the birthday site needed to be filled with the sand that we brought from the seashore. At the āśram, Amma stood about seven meters away from me, holding a torch in the dark. When I asked Amma *internally* (not verbally) where to put the sand, immediately she pointed her torch at the exact spot! Just ask: Amma will shine her light on us!

Going back and forth to the beach, I walked very fast, imagining this was my spiritual path to Amma. I felt so blessed to be here in her birthplace and stood near the ocean enjoying this blessedness. Full of love and gratitude to Amma, I prostrated. My forehead touched the sacred sand. After the *sēvā*, we walked to the drinking water station to drink water and refill our bottles, and we were laughing. I had my water bottle in my hand when Amma suddenly appeared with a small group and headed straight towards us. In a strict tone, Amma asked me, "Did you drink?"

In the West where I grew up, when this question is asked with such strictness it means: "Did you drink *alcohol*?" When Amma asked this question, a yellow bottle labeled "Whisky" appeared in my mind, but I don't drink alcohol and don't even know the taste. My conviction was that Amma knows everything. So Amma's question puzzled me. I wondered what she meant. I couldn't answer even after Amma repeated her question several times. Also, there was all this love. I found myself in an inner state where I was observing the happenings from above my head, witnessing, like from a bird's perspective. I felt totally detached.

When Amma turned towards my friend and asked her (with that finger turning), if I was crazy, it didn't affect me at all! My friend, who was working with really severe cases in psychiatry, answered, "NO!" Then Amma turned to me again and asked, "Did you drink?" A *brahmacārī*, (now Swāmī Avyāyāmṛtānandajī) said, "Answer now!" My answer finally poured out, "Water and love!"

Amma smiled, and tenderly, with her own hand, wiped away the sand that was still sticking on my forehead, responding to the love I felt when prostrating at the seashore. Then Amma embraced me and whispered in my ear, "No." That was the answer I *should* have given. Amma clarified that she knew I don`t drink alcohol. Then she sent me to my room. I obeyed. Without even prostrating, I ran away like a rabbit. Actually, we were staying in the huts, but I stopped in front of the Kali Temple and said, "This is my room."

My friend found me there after Amma had asked her to bring me to the room. She had also run away, like me, and felt ashamed; but I felt blissfully graced. I really was drunk with that love, and also excessively *vata*! Amma was shaking me from my drowsy state. I had to learn to stay grounded in Amma's powerful presence. But tonight, let's all get drunk with Amma's supreme love and glorious light, as she showers her grace all over the world! Our precious experiences with Amma are timeless and ever fresh in us! This is due to Amma's exalted state of enlightenment in pure Existence, Consciousness and Bliss (*sacchidānanda*)!

Lalitā Sahasranāma #6:
ōm udyad bhānu sahasrābhāyai namaḥ

I bow to her who has the radiance of a thousand suns.

The scriptures in many religions describe that supreme state as having the brilliance of a thousand suns. Amma sees all her children as embodiments of the light of Consciousness and unconditional Love. *Śiva-Śakti* and the sacred syllables *Mā* and Ōm convey the same principle.

Once Amma said to me, "Although some people had memory loss, due to their constant *mantra* practice, they remembered the *mantra* "*Mā*" in their last breath." If we want to remember our *mantra* when we die, we need to chant it constantly, with intensity. Only then will the *mantra* penetrate deeply into us and vibrate in all our cells as our entire body chants!

Spandanam is the energy of pure love pulsating in everything. *Sphuraḥ* is the light of the true Self shining in everything. It is also true that love and light are the last form before the formless. The all-pervading consciousness illumines everything. Yet supreme Consciousness is devoid of any form, of any attributes. The *Kaṭhōpaniṣad* states:

> *Na tatra sūryō bhāti na candratārakaṁ nēmā vidyutō bhānti kutō'yamagniḥ |*
> *tamēva bhāntam anubhāti sarvaṁ tasyabhāsā sarvam idaṁ vibhāti ||*

> There, within the innermost Consciousness of every living being, the sun shines not, nor moon, nor stars, nor fire, nor lightning, much less this tiny mortal flame. That One light shining, all else shines. By Its light, all is made radiant. May the hearts and minds of all beings perceive this Light. May all beings be illumined.

Amma says, "Love is shining in each and every one of us. There cannot be any manifestation of any kind without this power of Love behind it." Love and light increase and decrease simultaneously. More Selflessness, more light; more selfishness, more darkness."

Amma explains that "The qualities of love and compassion will be present even in the most hardened criminal when he sees his own child." We understand from this that, even in hatred, a spark of love is present. By igniting it, a murderer's dark path can open up to the light. This means that no one is an eternal sinner!

Lalitā Sahasranāma #860:
ōm akantāyai namaḥ

Adorations to Dēvī who ends all sins and sorrows.

From 1995 onwards, I repeatedly asked Amma for permission to join the āśram. Amma told me to continue my flute study, and come, at first, for three months, to see if this path was for me. Later Amma said: "Think very clearly!" I struggled for nine years, until Amma's grace cleared my path to move to India. Every day, with tears, I questioned about my flute study. What is this for? I had no interest in worldly pursuits. I only wanted Amma and *bhajans.*

Once, in 2001, I mentioned to Amma that I was always thinking about her, and I wanted to know if Amma heard me. Amma's simple yet profound reply was: *"Sometimes."* At first, I was stunned. Then I reflected. Amma showed me how shallow my remembrance of the Divine was, and that much more intensity was needed! I then realized that Amma is my only true friend, no one else.

Only when nothing was left but longing to live in Amma's physical presence could I finally join Amma in India. I joined the āśram in February 2004 during *Śivarātri*, intending to lead a life of *brahmacarya.*

Once, long ago, when I was alone in my room in Switzerland, I heard very clearly a voice saying in German, *"Lass los Kind!*

Lass los von all deinen Vorstellungen." (Let go child, let go of your notions and concepts.) This affected me deeply. To give up my jobs and material belongings took me nine months. But, only Amma can remove, for good, all the mind-stuff I've carried for countless births.

Once a journalist asked what Amma would be if she could rule the world. Amma said, "I would be a sweeper. I would sweep everyone's mind clean!" Amma uses every opportunity to clean our hearts. Amma prefers to describe herself as a humble sweeper of human minds. She hides her divine glory!

Once, I was going through a turbulent period, and my mind was disturbed. During *bhajans* I sat in front of Amma, near the stage. Heavy thoughts kept turning around the same topic. Suddenly I noticed my thoughts had disappeared! I asked within, "Who took my thoughts? Amma...did You?" When I looked up, Amma already gestured to me in affirmation with a mischievous look! My eyesight is not so good, but because I sat so near, I had no doubt. Amma cleaned up my mind! Amma pulls us out of the dark pit of our ignorance and uplifts us to our true purpose in life.

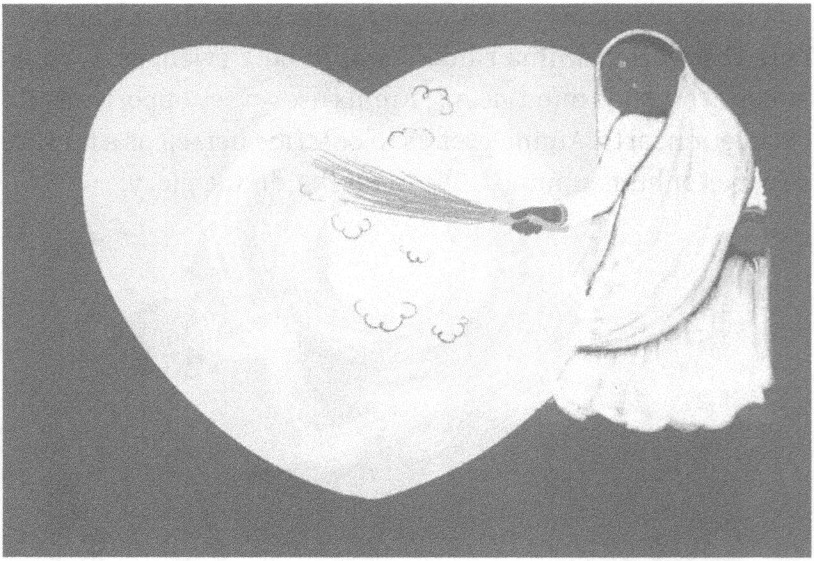

About this dark age of materialism, Amma says,

> Since people's minds are very gross, practicing self-control through singing and doing worship is much easier than through meditation, which is subtle. Likewise, to overcome the negative sound vibrations, we need another sound. That sound is the Divine Name.

Sound has a unique capacity to transform. Amma is a living example! When Amma sings or speaks, it becomes the Truth; it becomes the Scripture! Her divine life-force reaches us in the form of powerful sound waves that destroy the noise within, giving space for inner silence! Most of the spiritual practices at our āśram are related to sound.

Here are a few of my experiences:

1. Long ago, when learning to chant *arcana*, I tried to pronounce the Sanskrit correctly. I could feel my brain becoming structured and my mind awakening from dullness.
2. During a restless period, I chanted *arcana* three times daily. It felt like sitting in a plane flying above the clouds where the sun always shines. Below, there might be a storm, but you remain unaffected, flying above it at a high speed.
3. In 2017, when the security forces started their services here, Amma had the *brahmacāriṇīs* learn *Vedic* chanting. It felt like a wall of pure, white-light protection. The divine chants enliven every cell and leave me sitting in a vibrant silence.

In spite of following the spiritual disciplines, sometimes, I feel far away from Amma. Recently I was feeling this pain of separation. Amma showed me that she is ALWAYS NEAR when we tune to her divine presence within! During *bhajans*, Amma said, "In silence, we can hear God`s voice in the *sanctum sanctorum* (inner temple) of our heart. When your mind is still, you will see God."

During one Europe tour, Amma sang *Īśvarī Jagadīśvarī* in German with me in backup. That night she pointed for me to sit at her feet where she kept my heart open for surrender. The next night, Amma told me with a smile: "Practice silence." Later, I asked, "How?" Amma scoldingly said, "Just keep quiet! *Vairāgya* (dispassion)! Mother no English!" The point I got first was to keep quiet when facing insults. I often get scolded, even for no obvious reason. May this *karma*-chain break! May we not harm anyone by thought, look, word or deed.

Amma mentioned three points which compel me to deeper reflection until this day. Meanwhile, Amma instructed me to take a vow of silence when she was not here in the āśram. I followed this strictly for about two months, at the time. Initially, my mind was very extroverted. Just to keep my mouth shut already gave great results! But soon, I became more introverted and started to observe the inner movements of my mind. That's when my *sēvā* changed to laundry service. Amma also put me into *Amritayōga*, and my body structure changed. Soon, I could sit upright with increased focus! As awareness dawns, meditation practice becomes more silent in that Presence.

Amma says, "Focus on the center of love and not on the outer drainage of the world." We can see this principle very clearly in the spinning machine that drains the wet clothes. When the spinner spins at high speed, the center remains still. We can even touch it with our finger, because it is still. Just don't go too far, because the world is full of turbulence! We can observe our thoughts go round and round!

It is the same in nature. Creation is full of circles where you get spun and spun around. There is an inevitable pull from creation that spins us back to the very center of our existence. That pure energy of Love and light of Truth culminate in that center of the Ocean of Nectar, *Sacchidānanda*.

> Feel the flutes' sound vibration silencing
> Creation and Creator art Thou
> Thou art Energy and Truth
> Dēvī.... Dēvī... Dēvī...

Amma, you are that fully open, expansive Heart! May we all surrender at your holy feet and merge with You.

Pronunciation Guide

Vowels can be short or long:
a – as 'u' in but; ā – as 'a' in far
e – as 'a' in may; ē – as 'a' in name
i – as 'i' in pin; ī – as 'ee' in meet
o – as in oh; ō – as 'o' in mole
u – as 'u' in push; ū – as 'oo' in hoot

ṛ – as ri in crisp
ḥ – pronounce 'aḥ' like 'aha,' 'iḥ' like 'ihi,' and 'uḥ' like 'uhu.'

Some consonants are aspirated (e.g. kh); others are not (e.g. k). The examples given below are only approximate:
k – as 'k' in 'kite;' kh – as 'ckh' in 'Eckhart'
g – as 'g' in 'give;' gh – as 'g-h' in 'dig-hard'
c – as 'c' in 'cello;' ch – as 'ch-h' in 'staunch-heart'
j – as 'j' in 'joy;' jh – as 'dgeh' in 'hedgehog'
p – as 'p' in 'pine;' ph – as 'ph' in 'up-hill'
b – as 'b' in 'bird;' bh – as 'bh' in 'rub-hard'

r – as 'r' in ride
ñ – as 'ny' in 'canyon;' ṅ – as 'ng' in 'sing'

The letters ḍ, ṭ, ṇ are pronounced with the tip of the tongue against the hard palate, the others with the tip against the teeth.
ṭ – as 't' in 'tub;' ṭh – as 'th' in 'lighthouse'
ḍ – as 'd' in 'dove;' ḍh – as 'dh' in 'red-hot'
ṇ – as 'n' in 'naught'
ḷ – as 'l' in 'revelry'
ṣ – as 'sh' in 'shine;' ś – as 's' in German 'sprechen'

With double consonants the sound is pronounced twice:
cc – as 'tc' in 'hot chip'
jj – as 'dj' in 'red jet'

www.ingramcontent.com/pod-product-compliance
Lightning Source LLC
Chambersburg PA
CBHW071206090426
42736CB00014B/2727